Anthropology and the Individual

MATERIALIZING CULTURE
. . . .
Series Editors: Paul Gilroy and Daniel Miller

Anthropology and the Individual

A Material Culture Perspective

Edited by
Daniel Miller

LONDON AND NEW YORK

First published 2009 by Berg Publishers

Published 2020 by Routledge
2 Park Square, Milton Park, Abingdon, Oxon OX14 4RN
605 Third Avenue, New York, NY 10017

Routledge is an imprint of the Taylor & Francis Group, an informa business

© Daniel Miller 2009

All rights reserved. No part of this publication may be reproduced or transmitted in any form or by any means, electronic or mechanical, including photocopying, recording, or any information storage or retrieval system, without prior permission in writing from the publishers.

Notice:
Product or corporate names may be trademarks or registered trademarks, and are used only for identification and explanation without intent to infringe.

Library of Congress Cataloging-in-Publication Data

A catalogue record for this book is available from the Library of Congress.

British Library Cataloguing-in-Publication Data

A catalogue record for this book is available from the British Library.

Typeset by Apex CoVantage, LLC, Madison, WI, USA

ISBN13: 978-1-847-88495-4 (hbk)
ISBN13: 978-1-847-88494-7 (pbk)

Contents

List of Illustrations   vii

Notes on Contributors   ix

Introduction   1

1. Individuals and the Aesthetic of Order   3
   Daniel Miller

2. Trading in Fake Brands, Self-creating as an Individual   25
   Magdalena Crăciun

3. 'Making Things Come Out': Design, Originality and the Individual in a Bògòlan Artisan Community   37
   Bodil Birkebæk Olesen

4. Building and Ordering Transnationalism: The 'Greek House' in Albania as a Material Process   51
   Dimitris Dalakoglou

5. The Christian and the Taxi Driver: Poverty and Aspiration in Rural Jamaica   69
   Daniel Miller

6. How Madrid Creates Individuals   83
   Marjorie Murray

7. Aesthetics of the Self: Digital Mediations   99
   Heather A. Horst

8. Unmaking Family Relationships: Belgrade Mothers and Their Migrant Children   115
   Ivana Bajić-Hajduković

9. Fashioning Individuality and Social Connectivity among Yoruba Women in London   131
   Julie Botticello

| 10 | Creating Order through Struggle in Revolutionary Cuba
Anna Pertierra | 145 |
| 11 | Food, Family, Art and God: Aesthetic Authority in Public Life in Trinidad
Gabrielle Hosein | 159 |

Index 179

List of Illustrations

Figures   **Page**

3.1	A schematic rendition of a piece of cloth and its patterns, consisting of five pieces of strip-cloth.	42
3.2	An example of how stencils circulate between workshops, and kinsmen and neighbours.	43
3.3	Another example of how stencils circulate between workshops, and kinsmen and neighbours.	44
3.4	An example of innovation-through-copying.	45
3.5	Koti's model, made shortly after Hawa finished the model depicted in Figure 3.4.	45
4.1	The coffee-table in the home in Athens.	54
4.2	An identical table as *sofra* in the home in Albania.	54
4.3	The table moved in front of the sofa where we are sitting.	55
4.4	The *'Greek house'* in Albania.	57
4.5	The swimming pool and the vegetable garden.	61
6.1	Madrid's Metro tunnel from the train.	93
6.2	Innocent boy in a bar.	94
7.1	Ann's desk and bulletin board.	102
7.2	Ann's bedroom, one week before leaving for college.	103
7.3	Ann checking her Facebook page.	106
8.1	Kitchen in Vladimir's house.	119
8.2	A detail from Vladimir's room.	119
9.1	An England flag worn as a head scarf during the 2006 World Cup.	137
9.2	Fellow market workers, adorned in red *gele,* assemble their dollars to engage in the spraying.	140
11.1	The line of legitimacy.	163
11.2	One woman, one vote.	165
11.3	Higher authority.	166
11.4	King of the Road.	170

Notes on Contributors

Ivana Bajić-Hajduković is a Postdoctoral Fellow, Max Weber Programme, European University Institute.

Julie Botticello is an Honorary Research Associate, Department of Anthropology, University College London.

Magdalena Crăciun is a PhD student, Department of Anthropology, University College London.

Dimitrios Dalakoglou is a Lecturer in Anthropology, Department of Anthropology, University of Sussex.

Heather A. Horst is Associate Project Scientist, Humanities Research Institute, University of California.

Gabrielle Hosein is a lecturer at The Centre for Gender and Development Studies, The University of the West Indies, St. Augustine.

Daniel Miller is Professor of Material Culture, Department of Anthropology, University College London.

Marjorie Murray is a Lecturer in Anthropology, Department of Sociology, Pontificia Universidad Católica de Chile.

Bodil Birkebæk Olesen is a Postdoctoral Fellow in the Department of Anthropology, Aarhus University, Denmark.

Anna Pertierra is a Research Fellow in The Centre for Critical and Cultural Studies, University of Queensland.

Introduction

Unlike most social science books about the individual, this volume is not concerned with individualism or with the way different societies conceptualize individuals. Because, irrespective of whether people live within a highly individualizing or a highly socialized environment, we still have the task of understanding them as individuals. Furthermore anthropologists, in particular, commonly convey their findings through the presentation of individuals who were encountered during fieldwork.

Using the perspective of material culture, the contributors to this volume create a highly original approach to our understanding of the individual. We start by appropriating anthropological perspectives that were first developed for the study of society and show how these can be adopted for the study of individuals. The intention is to move beyond both an opposition between individual and society, and also beyond the tendency to use the individual as the minimal exemplification of an entity we term 'society'. Instead we recognize how we have to keep focused simultaneously on the larger institutions of kinship, political economy and the state and also on the individual persons that live within and through these.

We achieve this through our analysis of what this volume identifies as an aesthetic of order that may be derived from various relationships. These may be relationships to objects—such as cars, houses and cloth; to places—such as social networking sites on the Internet or a city; to relationships—such as to parents or community, or to larger discourses—such as that of struggle, or fairness. The configuration of such an order may be found both at the level of society but, as this volume shows, also integrated at the level of an individual's sense of himself or herself and his or her world. This approach also makes explicit what is conveyed when we use the lives of individuals to make claims and generalizations about society. The book thereby contributes an original perspective on individuals that is distinctly anthropological rather than psychological. Examples range from Istanbul, London and Madrid to Albania, Cuba, Jamaica, Mali, Serbia and Trinidad.

–1–

Individuals and the Aesthetic of Order

Daniel Miller

A Starting Point

This volume represents the collective construction of a specifically anthropological approach to a question at the heart of all social science. How should we simultaneously account for both society and for individuals? Unlike most social science books about the individual, this volume is not concerned with individualism nor with the way different societies conceptualize individuals. Because, irrespective of whether people live within a highly individualizing or a highly socialized environment, we still have the task of understanding them as individuals. Furthermore anthropologists, in particular, commonly convey their findings through the presentation of individuals who were encountered during fieldwork. So this volume is not especially concerned with the study of individualism, nor with the growth of individualism.[1] The understanding of the individual is something that should be part and parcel of the domain of anthropology even when we are working in a society which seems almost entirely opposed to individualism. We would repudiate an artificial disciplinary history that left social science concerned with that aspect of society that transcended its composition by individuals and ceded to psychology the study of the individual per se. This book creates an approach to people that is no more psychological, and no less anthropological, through a decision to concentrate on the individual as its primary unit of analysis.

The means by which this is accomplished is through a deliberate and systematic appropriation of anthropological models that were originally designed, not for the study of individuals, but as approaches to an encompassing view of society. Traditionally, in social science, these two have been opposed, as a rise of individualism in modern life was seen as the deposition of the larger social order represented by the terms *society* and *culture*. Our discovery was that approaches created by anthropologists for the purpose of contending with society turn out to be singularly and unexpectedly appropriate for the study of the individual. So that instead of abandoning those perspectives, we can appropriate them and apply them to this other terrain. In doing so we employ what has become recently one of the vanguard elements in contemporary anthropology, the study of material culture.

This will by no means be a single or uniform appropriation. In this introduction I will take the most extreme view, suggesting that in a place such as London, the application of this perspective to the individual becomes tantamount to the study of culture as an aggregate of these micro units of society, at least with respect to some forms of behaviour. As befits a situation where all the other contributors have studied with me, the rest of the chapters in this volume all take issue, in some way or other, with my argument and contest it or transform it through its application to quite different circumstances, providing alternatives, and contrasting variants. Either because the situation they are confronted with is very different from that found in London (as I also argue in a further chapter within this volume, set in Jamaica) or because they remain unconvinced by particular aspects of my own argument. So the volume is constructed in dialectical tension between the introduction and the subsequent chapters.

The approach that will be used to illustrate this argument is derived from one of the most established and influential anthropological models of cultural order, that of Pierre Bourdieu and his concept of *habitus*. Students of material culture, which include all the contributors to this volume, are particularly beholden to Bourdieu, because in his book *Outline of a Theory of Practice* (1977), the main process of socialization into becoming a member of any given society was the everyday association with practical taxonomies embodied in the order of material culture. From Bourdieu we learnt how individuals become a typical Kwakiutl, Trobriand Islander or New Yorker through habits and expectations fostered in our everyday object world. Through catching salmon or catching taxis. The best-known example employed by Bourdieu was the organization of space in the houses of the Kabyle, a Berber community. The systematic oppositions found in the internal order of the house were seen as an underlying structure that gave people their unconscious expectations of the order they anticipate in many different aspects of their lives. These underlying structures of order became second nature, that is taken-for-granted habits, that could apply equally to agricultural tasks, meal times, the body or kinship.

This work carried the further implication that although patterns of objects were thereby central to constituting social order, equivalent in many respects to our entire educational system, their contribution was entirely unacknowledged. This corresponded to what I (Miller 1987) elsewhere called 'The Humility of Objects'—the ability of material things to establish the frame for proper behaviour without us noticing that they inhabit this powerful role. I argued that objects performed a task central to what Goffman (1975) and Gombrich (1979) in different ways termed *Framing*—that which orders life and behaviour without our being aware of it.

For Bourdieu this process is effective because in each area of life this underlying structure of order remains homologous to the others. People are socialized into habitus through the habits of everyday life, and reproduce it in their own creations because culture is best understood as practice. So unlike its psychological equivalents, this does not need to be viewed as a cognitive model. It exists tangibly in the order of the material world people inhabit. While anthropologists were most influenced by Bourdieu's application of these ideas to the Kabyle, those in other disciplines were enthralled by his exemplification of these same processes in the book *Distinction* (1979) which examined the order of French society in the 1960s. Bourdieu argued that there was a foundational structural opposition in French society that corresponded to class. At one end of the spectrum were those who preferred the taste of foods that were substantial, the opinions of particular newspapers and saw Holy Communion as the obvious subject for a painting. At the other end were those who had a more minimalist aestheticized approach to food and saw more artistic potential in a car crash. So, amongst both the Kabyle and the French, there were structural oppositions that were productive, in the sense of basic, to the ordering of society.

Distinction neatly demonstrated Bourdieu's insistence upon the virtue of a larger structural understanding of French culture and society in opposition to starting from the perspective of the individual. As he noted, the very term 'taste', was taken colloquially to represent the specifics of an individual's preferences in the world. Yet, in his analysis, he shows how taste actually derives from the highly structured conditions of French class and hierarchy, and is anything but the mere quirky predilection of individuals. Aesthetic preferences thereby exemplify, not individualism, but its opposite, the original holistic tradition of anthropology. People are situated within a general cosmology, as much evident in their kinship and social structure, in the form of exchange and economic orders, as in their beliefs and religion.[2]

Bourdieu was by no means the only exemplar of this holistic tradition. It is implicit in the very notion and structure of the traditional anthropological monograph, and its long commitment to various forms of structural-functionalism. Similarly Clifford Geertz (1973, 1980) could discern a distinctive Balinese aesthetic disposition that could apply as much to statehood as to dance. A typical monograph on an African pastoral society or on Chinese lineage would often link relationships with food to ritual or demonstrate the homology between kinship and village, or indeed urban, planning. Sometimes the academic discerns a pattern that is one of a single and overall consistency within and across domains. At other times, as in the work of Levi-Strauss or Bourdieu's *Distinction,* it is a holism based on systematic opposition, inversion or contrast. Indeed so common is this trope within anthropology that when, in other disciplines, such as where the *Annales* school of French historical analysis treated past societies as quasi ethnographies to examine consistency between cosmology, economy and social order, then the analysis comes to feel anthropological to the degree that it is structurally holistic (e.g. Le Roy Ladurie 1978).

In this context, the study of the individual seems reduced to that of the microcosm that exemplifies the macrocosm, or alternatively the dualism that is society. We see the individual as exemplifying the precise position he or she holds in society and reproducing at this scale the same sense of order and expectation we recognize as that of the society as a whole. A person is his or her place in the overall picture, as is appropriate to his or her categorization, for example by gender or class. Almost as though they each generate and reproduce some larger societal DNA or cultural code. This academic tradition became so established and hegemonic that inevitably it led eventually to an almost violent repudiation. A new post-modernist perspective arose that denounced any implied structural analysis or holism. Post-modernism tried to blow apart this sense of order and refused to see people as any more than the aggregation of fragments. The post-modern assault was generally coincidental with an ever more confident liberalism which saw itself as triumphant over older more holistic political traditions such as socialism. Post-modernism has therefore had a longer lasting impact in the United States which remains far more deeply imbued with a spirit of liberalism and emphasis upon individuals as compared to the more collectively orientated European tradition (Lindholm 1997).

The problem with this history of academic studies is that in many respects it neglects what should have been a core question from the very inception of scholarly interest in society. A question that is sidelined when we start from an opposition between the individual and society, or a subsumption of the individual as mere microcosm to society, or a refusal to accept the existence of either society or individuals as in post-modernism. Instead, we might take as our starting point the coincidence and compatibility of the individual and society, where society is understood as an entity that transcends its aggregate composition by individuals and remains irreducible to them. Individuals still live in society, society always included individuals. The more important question therefore was how these two exist in tandem. If the individual is more than the microcosm of the macrocosm then what is the precise relationship between these two entities? Where do we find evidence for this relationship and how may we reveal it? These are the questions the current volume seeks to investigate.

London

In this section I will represent the most extreme application of our ideas based on the specific conditions of working in London. In the subsequent section I will show how the other contributors contest and expand upon these observations and lead us towards a more generally applicable model for an anthropology of the individual. This initial extreme view corresponds to an appropriation of the word 'aesthetic' to the study of people in households.[3] On three occasions I have carried out studies based on London streets. The second of these was a study of how people use material culture to deal with loss. Since a street is effectively a juxtaposition of unrelated residencies, the unit of analysis has to start from each individual household, quite often simply an individual. While discussing these various cases I found that, in conversation with Fiona Parrott, the co-researcher on this project, I was making increasing use of the word *aesthetic* to describe the underlying order that seemed to pertain to each of the hundred cases that we researched.

Subsequently I wrote *The Comfort of Things* (Miller 2008) which tried to convey, through the portraits of thirty of these individuals and households, what the term 'aesthetic' might mean in this context. One of the reasons for choosing to work on a street was my dissatisfaction with the way social science treated people as tokens of larger social descriptors, which is implied in the model of microcosm and macrocosm. In most urban research undertaken by social science a person is selected for study because he or she is, for example a woman, or working class, or Somali. But a street in South London represented an unprecedented exemplification of an alternative modern condition. Only 23 per cent of the hundred households we worked with were born in London, and in many cases the household itself consisted of people from entirely different backgrounds who had met and become partners in London. Bourdieu wrote books about the Kabyle and different books about the French. But on this street it was entirely possible that one would encounter a Kabyle married to a Parisian.

The temptation would be to regard a Kabyle married to a Parisian as either a hybrid between two holistic forms, or as illustrative of post-modern fragmentation and the end of holistic order. But *The Comfort of Things* shows that these people did not appear as either fragmented or disordered. In many ways they were just as redolent of order and even holism as in previous researches I had been involved in, whether in India, the Solomon Islands or Trinidad. They also clearly lived in society with its cultural orders. Most prior studies of London streets by social scientists had refused to let go of the apparent requirement to see society only in larger entities. The street was judged by its relationship to the neighbourhood or community. But in London it is increasingly clear that this is false, as these households were radically unconnected with either community or neighbourhood. But, apart from some older isolated males, there was no particular sense of alienation or anomie; both presupposed by holistic traditions of social analysis, as conditions which follow in the absence of these wider relationships of belonging. Yet they also didn't particularly identify with London or the United Kingdom, so that the more recent emphasis in social science upon identity seemed equally inappropriate.

The aim of *The Comfort of Things* was therefore not to examine what people no longer were, but to emphasize instead what they had become. These people presented with an internal logic and complex cultural order that still needed to be accounted for. In these studies of individuals and households, just as in traditional studies of societies, I could discern homologies between the underlying order present in different genres. Both material genres such as music, ornaments, clothing, cooking and photography, and also social genres such as parent-child relations, couple formation and break up, individual's relation to work or to pets. The term 'aesthetic' emerged as a shorthand for describing this internal consistency and order. It had no pretension to any art terminology or judgement of beauty per se. But it did imply that there were issues of harmony, balance and contrast in this order.

The argument can be briefly illustrated through a précis of two of the cases that appear in *The Comfort of Things*. Malcolm's work fluctuates between Australia and the United Kingdom, but what he understands as his permanent address is his email, and the nearest thing to home is his laptop. Both his friendships and his work are largely organized by email, a place he constantly orders, returns to, cares for and where in many respects 'his head is'. But to understand the intensity of this relationship to his laptop, we need to read the anthropologist Fred Myers (1986). Myers notes that for many Aboriginal groups there is a tradition of avoiding the physical possessions of the deceased. Malcolm's mother was Australian Aboriginal and most of her possessions were indeed destroyed at her death. But he inherited from her a mission to locate and preserve the history of his family, including those once taken away from their parents. As he sees it, too much Aboriginal history is viewed as lying in police records, he wants a proper archive he will deposit in an Australian state archive.

Malcolm has an antipathy to things. He has given most of his inherited or childhood objects away. In his devotion to immateriality he prefers anything digital. He is getting into digital photographs, he downloads music and immediately throws out the covers. Very unusually for the street, he even gives away his books after he has read them. One could relate this to his mobility, one could relate it to his interest in the potential of new technologies, one could relate it to this Aboriginal inheritance. There is more. His father sold antiques but the result was that as soon as he started becoming attached to things in his childhood, they would be sold, another possible source of his detachment from things. So his personal habitus could be described as overdetermined in the sense of multiple causation. Even he can't decide how much his mobility is cause or effect. But the overall result, as he puts it, is that 'I think I've set myself up to be out of touch with objects and things.' He has a more ambiguous relation to less tangible things like documents, sorting both his mother's and his own things into neat box files. But his real identification is with digital forms. He constantly updates and sorts his emails, which becomes the updating of his social relationships. In going through them he recalls all those friends he owes emails to.

One could try and stretch the Aboriginal inheritance: the laptop as a kind of digital *dreamtime* that connects current relationships with those of the dead, a place he comes in and out of, as more real than merely real life. He retains this intense concern with lineage, devoting much of his time to creating order out of kinship history. He seems obsessed that if he were to die, that thanks to constantly sorting his emails, he would leave a legacy that was archived and up to date, so no one would have to do the work he did recovering and ordering his ancestral lives. But for my purpose what he typifies is first the multiple determination of his cosmology. Father, mother and his work come together as possible explanations. One could not claim to have predicted him, but given what we now know, this relationship to his laptop, that at first seemed so bizarre, can certainly make sense. It is an aesthetic, a material cosmology. We need to understand cosmological issues that pertain to Australian Aboriginal life, but this alone could hardly have given us Malcolm.

The second example, Charlotte, exemplifies the self-construction of the inalienable as a consistent material ontology. She has systematically carried out a very large number of piercings followed by a series of tattoos, and simultaneously developed a clear philosophy of how these acts of self-construction contribute to her understanding of, above all, her control over her own life. She exemplifies both the vertical and horizontal dimensions. The vertical dimension starts once again from her relationship to her mother. This is not a simple repudiation, it was her mother's friend who first introduced her to piercing at the age of eleven. But she then appropriates this as a means of distancing. For example, when her mother said, 'Oh, but you're just trying to be the same as everyone else', she responded by searching out the most extreme and different piercings that for her said (her words), 'I've got a piercing, but not because everyone else has that, but because nobody does, actually.'

From this came her desire to establish complete mastery over memory itself. She established a fictive relationship to her past. Although born in London, she associates herself completely with the country of origin of her lover. She has mastered the accent, had a flat built for her to move to when she has qualified, and was already tattooing designs from that country before ever visiting it. As a lesbian she also feels that her sexuality is something she chooses and controls. Control for her means objectifying memory as a thing one can choose to attach to or detach from the self. Every piercing represents a specific memory. Life consists of accumulating happy memories that are objectified in this way. So even if she is embarrassed by chasing boy bands as a teenager, the memorabilia is retained as something 'happy at the time'. Key piercings and then tattoos represent her best relationships.

With regard to the horizontal, Charlotte carefully considers the precise materiality of each genre within which memory can be objectified. There is clothing she can throw away. Piercings have a potential transience, for example when she moved to another part of London she says 'I took out a lot of my bottom rings, so at that stage, and I think that was probably because I had left a lot of rubbish and a lot of people that were not doing me any good, like old memories behind, so I didn't need it any more.' Abandoned rings from piercings are kept in a box, photographs of piercings and tattoos on her back allow her to recall a memory, but can't be as easily accessed as those she can look at when on the move. The placing matters, as with nipple piercing—viewed as the position closest to her heart. Each material form is used to extend and complement the others.

It is the tattoos that establish the full possibilities of the inalienable. They ensure that memories of the best relationships can never be excised. These include her relationship to the tattooist, a close friend who is practising on Charlotte to obtain her professional qualification; and her relationship to her lover, through their having identical tattoos. The memory is precise. Unlike others she will never have supplementary tattooing, since this blurs the relationship to the particular time the tattoo was created. She thereby works out a material technology of inalienable memory. She can't understand people who tattoo for pattern itself rather than to establish the inalienable. She starts from an awareness of people such as her grandfather who lived to regret the tattoos of their youth, yet now has complete confidence in her current total leg tattooing. She does understand the logic of those who tattoo a cross for a deceased love one, but remains consistent to her own systematic accretion of happy memories and relationships.

Charlotte is not then just another person who does piercings and tattoos. In her early twenties she has a systematic cosmology of memory and objectification. This allows us to see the analogy between the study of the individual and society. I have used the term 'inalienable' in my description of Charlotte, a term which is reminiscent of the centrality of inalienable material culture to the work of the anthropologist Annette Weiner. In her book *Inalienable Objects* (1992) Weiner studied the material culture of the Maori, and the famous Kula ring as participated in by the Trobriand Islands, best known from the work of Malinowski (1922). Weiner's starting point is that in contrast to many previous anthropological studies of exchange, there are certain forms of material culture that are profound objectifications of society itself, objects whose presence and constancy helps society to constitute itself as transcendent to individuals. These objects are inalienable because they cannot form part of exchange or be given away. Much of her interest is in the different capacity of objects to represent the inalienable, that bones, stones and cloaks lend themselves to different qualities. Cloth, for example, being ambiguous in its symbolism, as a second skin, is good for mediating the transition from human to larger cultural reproduction, as Henare (2005) has shown for the idea of Maori weaving ancestors together. These might contrast with, for example stone.

Weiner was unusual though in that she also conceded the role of similar processes of objectification to individuals as well as society. The term 'society' here may indicate the greater authority of social hierarchy, that is *taonga* the power of this inalienabilty that enhances chiefly power, or the authority of the sacred; what Weiner calls cosmological authentification. But it can also connote a commitment to one relationship (Weiner 1991: 54). Because in some cases there is quite a bit of contingency and personalization surrounding this *taonga* of objects. They may represent a particular chief or warrior, have individual names, be inherited by individual recipients, or be buried with a particular person. So in Weiner's work we come to recognize a quality of a material object—its potential inalienability. This may be employed to give sacred power to a sense of society that transcends individuals. But that same quality of inalienability can also be employed as the means by which an object personalizes an individual.

Weiner thereby provides a route from more traditional anthropology to the study of Charlotte, who has seen for herself that it is possible to exploit the different capacities of genres of material culture to represent inalienability and used this to constitute herself. It is hardly surprising that people show the same creative capacity in forming new processes of objectification that we see in our comparative study of societies. Objects too transcend these different registers from the more general to more specific. In another house, there lies on a bookshelf, grandfather's tin from the First World War. By now though this tin simultaneously represents the specific grandfather, England and history itself.

It follows from these observations that instead of seeing individuals in opposition to society, there was a possibility of regarding each individual or household as somehow analogous to that of a society. That we could appropriate those methods, developed over decades for the study of societies, and now employ them in the study of the individual. That both the holism and order once assumed to be properties of society might also be found at this level, and not necessarily because the individual was the microcosm to a larger macrocosm. In the vast majority of households there was very little sense that their aesthetic, that is the internal integrity of order within material culture and other relationships, owed very much at all to anything one could recognize as cultural traditions such as Kabyle or French.

I don't wish to exaggerate. In some cases there was evidence for the kinds of cultural transmission familiar from more conventional anthropology: the way an Irish couple organized their lives in a manner that corresponded to older Irish traditions. Even in their case, however, the result had an unprecedented and particular character as a result of living in London. A similar point could be made about family and parental influence. Often important—whether through systematic rejection or systematic reproduction—but rarely entirely determinant. Parental and cultural traditions joined with many other influences to produce what emerge as relatively unique configurations. This occurs under conditions within London that may be unprecedented, where households are granted a degree of privacy to more or less make themselves up as they go along. As I have argued elsewhere, they may also be subject to astonishing generalizations that transcend these differences (e.g. Miller 1998) but in *The Comfort of Things* it was the combination of internal holism and order set against the overall diversity of London that was emphasized.

Contra London

The other contributors of this volume either did not work in London, or as in the case of Bajić and Botticello, who worked with Diaspora populations, saw London from a very different perspective. Yet all of them share other concerns which lead us to a common focus on the issue of the individual in society. Firstly, all the chapters derive from ethnography carried out in accordance with the traditions of anthropological research. Most have a commitment to the study of material culture specifically through ethnographic methods. Although the chapters by Pertierra and Hosein are not employing this perspective, they share the underlying influence of Bourdieu's approach to the role of external forms of cultural order as socialization, which is at the core of this volume's contribution. All the chapters other than Olesen are also marked by an increasing use of individuals in the reportage of ethnography. While we retain our attachment to theory, there is desire to rescue this from the more obfuscating accretions to which it became subject over the last two decades and which tended to obscure our relationship to the people we work with. While this volume is committed to theoretical developments in the analysis of individuals, we also want to place in the foreground the role of informants in our ethnography and in our desire to convey these ethnographic experiences and results. Many of these chapters concentrate on one or two key informants who have played a major role in our ethnographic work. We hope there is an integrity implied in acknowledging this, and in turn giving them a more prominent role in the presentation of our work.

While the emphasis upon a key informant may arise as a desire to respect the realities of ethnography when writing up a thesis or article, it leads to the same set of issues. We are still confronted with questions about how the presentation of an individual stands for generalizations about a society within an ethnographic monograph. Hockey (2002) recently argued that, in situations such as urban Britain, the interview should not be regarded as a poor second best to participant observation, or a microcosm of society as a bounded unit. In some respects the interview comes closer to the occasional and disembodied partial presences that are the reality of modern urban life. This observation rings true for the research used in *The Comfort of Things* which is probably more interview based than any of the ethnographies presented here. But the other chapters represent different situations which may have different consequences.

Typically, in their more extensive writings, such as the PhD thesis, the contributors to this volume start some of their chapters with an extended example of one individual who stands for those generalizations with which the chapter is concerned. They then follow this with shorter extracts from other individuals that represent different possibilities, or caveats to emergent generalizations. This is a heuristic device that attempts to address the same contradiction which occurs when we are simultaneously trying to convey something about society and the individuals who live within them. But this is generally implicit. In this volume we make the relationship explicit.

We achieve this goal by concentrating on a middle ground between the extremes of specificity and generality. This may be found in the order that is discernible both for individuals and external to them. It has been introduced as the concept of an aesthetic. The point is that we are not simply telling a story about a person. The individual is used analytically to display a pattern of relationships that convey a sense of the cultural order the person lives by. The inferred relationship is between that order and the analytical order we implicate in presenting a society as a cultural formation. We can see the mediation between these two when that order is also apparent in external forms. In these chapters it may appear as the way a house is decorated, a cloth is designed, a person is expected to dress for a party or as a Pentecostal Christian, or behave in relation to gaining a livelihood or going out into the city at night. When the order is found in genres of objects we come close to Bourdieu's original observations on the way an individual inculcates that order through practical taxonomies of action. But we do not restrict ourselves to conventional material culture, because this order may be located in other relationships. These may be relationships to place, to persons, to the state and to discourse. They are the mechanisms that, in practice, bring alignment between the order we discern at the level of the individual and the order we discern at the level of society. What becomes evident in this volume is that in each setting different sources of order come to stand out as more or less significant in the formation also of individuals.

This allows us to discern a relationship between the individual and society that does not rest on an opposition between the two, or on being seen as mere microcosm of the macrocosm. Rather we see that individuals themselves represent a form of order in the world, and this emerges out of a creative and partial appropriation of the possibilities in the wider order around them. But what is very clear in these chapters is that the term 'appropriation' should not be reduced to some simple act of free will. It has almost always just as much to do with constraint, as with choice, with lack of power, as with creativity. The following chapters are organized in a sequence that starts with an emphasis upon objects, then moves to relationships to place, to persons and finally to the state. Even within the first section that concentrates on relationships to objects, we find considerable variation between relatively free appropriation as in Crăciun's chapter and considerable constraint in Olesen's chapter. Similar issues and comparable variations in the way people respond to the order and authority embodied in the state are noted in the chapters by Pertierra and Hosein. Even in Horst's paper on Californian youth the context is one of authority and constraint.

There is one final relationship between the individual and collective to be considered. This volume, as several precedents, arises out of a tradition in which we all took part. This comprises a monthly 'drinking group'[4] during which pre-circulated draft chapters are read and commented upon by all those represented here. So, unlike many edited volumes, there is an organic process behind this volume that arises from a conversation between participating academics over several years. The connotations of a 'drinking group' is one that favours critical dialogue rather than mere adherence to a common position. This in turn produces the diversity of these contributions; each concerned ultimately to use any insights from this conversation in the further understanding of the particular conditions of their own research project.

The first chapter by Crăciun concerns Fırlama, a trader in the Istanbul bazaar. He is an individual whose life only makes sense when we appreciate the way he uses a specific genre of material culture—the fake brand—as his primary instrument for self-objectification. It is the fake brand that allows him to construct a life devoted to the play between respectability and subterfuge, conformity and illegality. From her close reading of this relationship comes an observation echoed in many subsequent chapters. The roots to this trajectory lie in treating his life as a whole, especially his early relationship to his parents and to his schooling. These create the causes of his ambivalence, but it is his personal discovery of a propensity in this particular form of material culture, the fake brand, that provides him with an ideal mirror through which he comes to see and understand the contradictions of his own life. This is not some dry metaphor. Fırlama constantly celebrates the exhilaration and fullness of life that has been generated by this commitment to a small disruption in the overarching landscape of capitalism. As in many cases in *The Comfort of Things,* one might never have predicted Fırlama, but in retrospect one can make sense of his personal aesthetic. The word is appropriate because this life is a play: part tragic, part comic, part glorious insistency, upon what a life devoted to fake brands can come to represent within the modern world. The result is a sense of balance that occurs at many points, in many chapters in this volume, all the way through to the final chapter by Hosein who makes balance the subject of her contribution. Only in her case the balance between legality and illegality is that represented, not by an individual, so much as the consensual construction of 'fairness'.

There is a clear and striking contrast between Crăciun and Olesen despite the fact that they are both concerned with cloth. This contrast forms a parameter along which the other chapters find their niche. Fırlama crafts his life as a form of individualized creativity. But in the much more tightly socialized environment of Mali, people see creativity not as a simple expression of the individual, but as precisely that which determines the constraints on the degree to which individuals are permitted to interpret normative order. Again this is a common theme to many of the subsequent chapters. Olesen shows that none of our terms, such as 'originality', or even 'design', translate easily into a context where things are categorized in very different ways. We have a very clear idea of what copying means in relation to originality and design. The trouble is that the people Olesen studied have entirely different ideas about the meaning and implication of a copy. They see difference where we might see sameness and sameness where we might assume significant difference. But what matters more, is how, just as the fake brand objectifies a particular individual in Istanbul, so here the process of motif creation objectifies what these people understand by the very concept of an individual. Olesen thereby shows clearly how it is possible to have alternatives to the usual opposition between individual and society. For her, as in the work of Strathern (1988), and in Bajić's chapter, both individual and society are formed out of an aesthetic of relationships or relational ontology. But this is most clearly seen through detailed observation of this cloth and its associated innovation-through-copying.

The chapter by Dalakoglou neatly bridges between this emphasis upon the object as objectification and the source of order in space and place. Taking as his starting point the situation of mobility, he finds that the same object, the house, has to confront its differentiation by context, since a *Greek* house in Albania is quite different from a Greek house in Greece. One of the commonalities between these three chapters, which we can link back to Bourdieu, is the emphasis upon practice. Objects work as objectifications best when they are constantly being constructed. Each of these three chapters is also about people making a living—out of fake goods, out of designs on cloth, out of building houses. It is this which makes such objects central to their lives. In this case Fatos, Dalakoglou's informant, works out the permutations of his own identity around a house where the very terminology becomes an instrument in this task. A *Greek* house in Albania is a symbol of mobility of several kinds, aspirational as much as spatial. Again, a point common to many of these contributions is that material culture is rarely merely a reflection of contradictions. It is much more often an attempt at their resolution into something that a person can effectively live with and through. The aesthetic of order they feel is 'legitimate', a term that is later explored by Hosein. The house is not a fake brand, since this is an informal material culture that is not branded. But it is a hybrid creation that serves, as with Fırlama, to help an individual feel at home in the contradictory and complex world of modern mobility. The fact that the house Fatos doesn't live in does more work to resolve these contradictions of place than the one he does live in is typical of these little ironies, these plays of the comic and tragic that are found in these brave new worlds of self-creation.

In the chapters by Murray and Miller we confront the other end of the dialectic between the way a person is constructed as an objectification of place and yet has to be seen simultaneously as an individual. While the discontinuities of migration place the emphasis upon Fatos's own creativity through house decoration, these chapters have to deal with space that remains in place. In some ways my portrayal of the individual in Jamaica is the precise opposite of those I have presented within London. The presentation of Jamaica is based on a structuralist opposition, closer to the original work of Bourdieu. The two individuals described in this chapter objectify the opposing qualities of Pentecostalism and the highly amoral world of taxi drivers; an opposition which constitutes the landscape of Orange Valley itself. Here we almost retreat to the older anthropological trope of the individual-as-microcosm to society-as-macrocosm, which is common to structural anthropology. But not entirely. There is such a powerful aesthetic in the ability of these two persons to creatively embrace and convey the values that are inculcated by their respective and opposed cultural positions that inevitably we also come to an appreciation of them as specific persons in this structured landscape. They are not just a Christian and a taxi driver; they do Christianity and taxi driving with extraordinary aplomb. The chapter also looks backwards to the previous contributions in its emphasis on the capacity of the things themselves, the mobile phone and the taxi, to act as objectifications of these wider aesthetic orders.

Murray's chapter provides the perfect complement to Miller in that she tackles directly what is only alluded to by him. How, given this condition, by which a person exemplifies a place, does that person simultaneously gain his sense of himself in his specificity as a creative agent? Murray's paper starts in a highly socialized environment comparable to Olesen and ends with the self-crafting of an individual closer to Crăciun. This chapter shows clearly, along with every chapter in this volume, that we progress best by refusing to see this as merely some kind of opposition between constraint and creativity. Being original is not opposed to conformity when it is something that is expected of you. As Olesen has already demonstrated, this dialectic works in particular ways in particular places. In the case of Murray the attention to material culture has made visible an entity we can call 'Madrid' that goes well beyond anything previously designated by the term. This is a cosmological Madrid that exists in an aesthetic of order which a true Madrilenian seeks to convey in his way of life. It is there in his relationship to going out in the city in the evening, to setting up home and to having friends. So the individual Madrilenian has a clear consciousness of this burden of objectifying Madrid itself. As a result, perhaps more than the other chapters, Murray has to consider the place of individualism itself. Because as the chapter unfolds, this devotion to conformity provides a kind of foundation of security and identity. But once this bedrock is established, her subject Manuel then constructs an elaborate expression of individual difference, first in his hobbies and his clothing and then as perfected in his blog. But even this creativity and its associated individualism is one that at the same time becomes an expression of conformity. Manuel is only exploiting what have become collectively designated sites for individualism that, as Murray shows, can be understood best in terms of the long history which lies behind this creation of Madrid as practice.

If Manuel ends with his blog, then Horst's informants more or less start their search for individual creativity with their own presentation of the self in a virtual world. What is remarkable is that we have just been presented with the extraordinary conformity of Madrid and expect to see quite the opposite in the youth of California. California is the very seat of our notion of individualized self-expression as a kind of cult or ideology. The expectation here is that a youth will create an aesthetic form as an individual, if anything in repudiation of the collective. Yet in practice we encounter a remarkably similar issue of the tension between conformity and specificity. Horst's informant Ann seeks to ground her externalized representation of herself in social networking sites within her given relationships. These may be relationships to objects, such as the aesthetics of her bedroom, or later on in her relationship to her college roommate. But so far from being an expression of free 'Californian' choice, these actions are tightly constrained. Sometimes this is an expression of the technology itself, as when she moves from MySpace which, relatively speaking, encourages personalization, to Facebook, which keeps originality within tightly controlled genres of presentation. Sometimes the constraint comes from wider relationships. So far from being autonomous from wider social control, Ann confronts a parental pressure that manifests concerns with danger circulating in public discourse. This power seeks to close down her efforts again and again. The situation in California is thereby in some ways closer to that of the authoritarian state in Cuba portrayed by Pertierra.

The conflicting imaginations of mother and child are central also to the following paper by Bajić. Both her and Botticello's chapters focus on relationships to persons, but, as in all the previous chapters, there is also the clear influence of place and of objects in this creation of the aesthetic of the self. Both also engage with a particular context—the consequences of Diaspora. Bajić presents, with some compassion, the opposed perspectives of a mother in Serbia and her son Vladimir, now settled in London. The material culture of Vladimir's London home expresses his desire to maintain as much distance as possible from his place of origin. Not surprisingly his mother is unable to reconcile herself to this, and is therefore constantly looking for strategies to regain a foothold in her relationship with her son. He rejects all objects from his past, except a battery charger, while she, in good Maussian style, employs this in gifting to try and re-engage this relationship. Her conclusion looks appropriately to the work of Strathern (1988) who focuses upon the individual as constituted by relationships which only become apparent in the external aestheticized form of material culture and its exchanges. There is one important additional contribution. A reader cannot but be struck by the poignancy and nuances of Bajić's portrayal. What this, as also Crăciun's chapter, successfully convey are the contradictions of generality and specificity that emerge when anthropologists use extended portraits of individuals. Partly because this is not just analytical, they are also deeply meaningful to the people being discussed. These are contradictions experienced as tragic, in the case of Bajić, or as liberation, in the case of Crăciun.

For Botticello the tension is not between separated persons representing homeland and Diaspora, but a tension that now exists within the community of the Diaspora itself. While the Sebian Vladamir seeks to evade any identification with Diaspora, in the case of the Yoruba community there remains a powerful commitment to this collectivity. An individual might wish to creatively express his or her own version of the hybridity and cosmopolitanism that comes with Diaspora life, on a par with Dalakoglou's Fatos. But as Botticello's chapter shows, there remain vocal and effective constraints to the degree to which this is something that can be delegated down to the level of individuals. This is especially the case for public events. There is a forty-year-old woman who wants to wear unconventional dress to her own birthday, and other women who strive to assert their own balance between traditional forms and those they feel more appropriate to a London context. These both threaten the normative order of the London Yoruba community. But it is not so much constraint and disapproval that determine their practice, but the way in which that practice actively objectifies a wide range of social relations and commitments. As in several of the other chapters in this volume, what we learn is that while there may be a general acceptance that change is required to fit the dynamics of the world, there can still be passionate conflict over what is the acceptable unit which facilitates that change. As in the chapter by Murray, the individual is not simply the expression of individualism. The individual is better understood as the vehicle by which a larger social aesthetic achieves its dynamic.

One of the dangers of concentrating upon individuals, rather than society, for social science, is that it implies a turning of the lens. What was out of focus, invisible behind society, is now in focus. But potentially what was in focus now becomes the fuzzy and ignored background. Specifically it is the macro forces such as political economy and the state that can disappear from view when we focus down on the individual. This can be just as distorting a lens as that which previously ignored the consequences of such forces for specific individuals. The intention of this volume is to create a new kind of lens that can remain in focus when we look both at macro forces and at individuals, so we can inspect in detail the relationship between these two. Liberalism and humanism both claim to focus upon the ethics of the individual and thereby claim to enhance our understanding of individuals. But as many critical traditions within social science have pointed out, this can leave the individual detached from the wider context, and blind us to the forces that both create and constrain individuals, such as political economy or the state; in which case so far from enhancing, such perspectives actually diminish that understanding. Fortunately none of the chapters in this volume fall into that trap. None of them feel it is possible to appreciate persons without also colouring in the background context. This may be migration as in Dalakoglou and Bajić, commerce for Crăciun, Miller or Horst and in the final two chapters that of the state.

For the chapters by Perierra and Hosein the materialism that is pertinent is not the material culture of objects, but an external force that creates the material conditions within which people live. What these chapters achieve is precisely what is lost in those approaches that either turn the lens inwards to people or outwards to macrosociological perspectives. Both Perierra and Hosein start from the very evident simultaneity of these two aspects of the same conditions. Their ethnography was based on individuals, who they came to know very well, but in doing so they also came to understand the effect of an order that is based on authority. Indeed right from the first chapter by Crăciun we see that an individual who is quirky and eccentric may be just as good an exemplification of social order as a conformist.

Given this task, there is a fascinating contrast between Pertierra and Hosein, who work from two very different Caribbean islands. In the case of Pertierra, based in Cuba, we have one of the most controlling states in the world, one that seeks to order almost every aspect of everyday life. And yet it is one which seeks legitimacy partly by using the rhetoric of struggle by which an individual understands his or her task of getting by on a daily basis. In this discourse of *struggle* the state tries to link directly to the individual through a common aesthetic. What Pertierra reveals is how individuals are nevertheless able to assert themselves through quite different relationships to this concept of struggle. These may align with or against the state's own discourse. She concludes on a point central to all these chapters. 'The relative inability to become a "pure" individual in contemporary Cuba in no way curtails the capacity for individual Cubans to engage in ordering their sense of self.' Individuals still find ways of seeing themselves reflected in agency, even in the absence of much by way of individualism.

The conditions of Trinidad are very different from Cuba and allow Hosein to deliver on the promise with which this introduction started. I implied that this volume would address the issue that is posed when we transcend oppositions between society and the individual; that we would not just treat the individual as the microcosm of a macrocosm which is society. The intriguing thing about Hosein's concept of authority is that this is as much a product of persons as of institutions, because effective authority in Trinidad is based on legitimacy. So what comes to matter in the creation of social order is not just what institutions claim, or indeed what individuals claim, but what emerges from the grounds that each cedes to the other. This form of legitimate authority is an objectification of the constant and dynamic relationship that exists between them by virtue of their simultaneity.

As Hosein notes, these are structures of feelings as much as of materiality. The boundaries of where people can trade beyond the market are determined by what the market traders feel to be the limits of appropriate police authority—something very different from the legal definition of their authority. As we progress through her examples, whether the organization of a mosque, or the allocation of patronage, or the production of Carnival costumes, we see that morality itself has a shape and substance that either looks legitimate or has evidently gone beyond its accepted place in the world. Together these amount to what she calls 'aesthetic authority', because they constitute ultimately the order that people feel bound to live by and judge others by. People constantly compare the way things appear to be with the way they feel they ought to be.

This is the lesson of our volume: that people come to sense an order in the world which feels right, which looks right, and which comes to be taken for granted as the source of the normative. This is true whether the origins of that order are in states, in history or in their own creativity. To call it an *aesthetic* is to recognize that it has properties of balance and form and contrast. These may be in areas otherwise considered of the arts, as in Olesen's study of design or Horst on the Web pages of social networking sites. But they may equally be found in the struggle to get by on a budget, the identity of one's house, the oscillation of legality and illegality objectified in fake goods, trying to be a true Madrilenian or Yoruba, or compassion in relationships between mothers and children. This aesthetic may create an order homologous across different domains at the level of the individual, the family, traders in a market or the Yoruba Diaspora. But the very cohesion of this order and its points of identification for some may also alienate, harm or disempower others, who are excluded from or do not share this experience of the world. In some cases as the Jamaican Pentecostal and the taxi driver they may define each other by their opposition. Anthropology is the study of the normative; what comes to be accepted as the appropriate order of the world, and why people accept or reject this.

So what we have discovered is ultimately that the same issue confronts us irrespective of whether we are located at the extreme represented by Londoners who make up for themselves much of this order, almost as they go along, in their very private households. Or, at the other extreme, in Cuba, where the creation of order remains very much under the control of a state. This is why this is not a book about individualism or the concept of the individual; the two topics which dominate social science approaches to the individual. It is a book about individuals who have to be accounted for, whatever the nature and extent of individualism and its encompassing ideologies. Rather than an opposition between the order by which a person lives and orders created by institutions, we have discovered an aesthetic which may be understood as a balance between these two by Hosein, an alignment with dominant social orders as in Olesen, or a selective and contested co-option of order from various sources as Botticello, Crăciun, Dalakoglou, Murray and Pertierra.

We have found a means to study and understand this normativity through a specifically anthropological perspective. Approaches to order originally created by anthropologists, such as Bourdieu, to account for society are here applied to individuals. We give full acknowledgement to an individual's sense of order, which may be partly derived from parents and other social relationships, from their sense of place, and from their alignment with, opposition to, or compromise with the authority of the state. This order may represent a socialized *habitus,* their own personal *habitus,* or most often *habiti.* But for individuals, just as for Kabyle society, much of this order is constructed in and taken from material culture, rather than as a cognitive model. Order exists external to ourselves. People are found in this volume to have an endless creative capacity to explore the propensities of various genres of objects to create their understanding of themselves in the world, though they are constantly constrained and often frustrated both by the limits of these media and by the authority of others. Indeed the very concept of the creative person is found again and again to be a highly socialized construction that determines which media are permitted for individualized appropriation. Unlike phenomenology, we do not presume to emphasize any particular medium of things, whether the body or the landscape. Often it is objects we would not have anticipated highlighting—taxis, fake brands or mobile phones.

A final advantage of this direct confrontation with individuals is that it reflects also the integrity of anthropological fieldwork; that one starts with the empathy of ethnography, immersed in the lives of specific people, often friends, as much as informants. Many of us are touched by this encounter and wish to convey them; even as analytically we have to encompass the wider forces that we must also understand in order to account for those people as individuals. So this new application of traditional anthropological perspectives to the study of individuals is surely an extension, rather than a reduction, of the significance of the discipline itself. It stands as respect for the forces that create individuals as well as for the individuals that live with and through such constraints and potentials. In focusing upon individuals we enhance, rather than detract, from our appreciation of that premise for anthropology—the creative capacity of society.

Notes

1. The approach outlined in this introduction contrasts with most anthropological approaches to individuals, though some run parallel to the ideas explored here.

There is probably little overlap with anthropological approaches to individuals that have derived from various rapprochements with psychology that arise from time to time (e.g. Benedict 1974; Schwartz, White and Lutz 1992) through to more recent interest in cognitive approaches (e.g. Bloch 1998), psychoanalysis (e.g. Moore 2007), or psychology itself (e.g. Holland 2001). The most sustained concern in anthropology has probably been its relativist stance to our understanding of what we mean by the terms *individual* and the *self*. Extensive discussions follow from the work of Mauss (1985), for example Carrithers, Collins and Lukes (1985), and of Dumont (1992), for example Celtel (2004). This relativism has also been applied to the concept of the individual in industrial societies (e.g. Kusserow 1999). Brian Morris (1994) provides a useful summary of many such discussions. More recent approaches include the extensive impact of Strathern (e.g. 1979, 1988, 1992) both on the self in Melanesia and England. Also the work of Rapport (1997) building on that of Cohen (1994). There is an obvious analogy between this volume and Rapport's aspiration 'to give a comparative account of individual's meaningful experience' (2002: 9). The approach taken here is complementary and different but not necessarily a critique of their perspective. Finally there have also been anthropological approaches to the individual which arose either from methodological and philosophical issues or which followed a more biographical imperative such as Freeman (1979) or Shostak (1981). All anthropological contributions run parallel to many sociological rapprochements which include methodological individualism, the influence of economists such as Becker (e.g. 1996) and recent work on the rise of the individualism associated with Beck (Beck and Beck-Gernsheim 2002), Giddens (1991) and Putnam (2000). Within material culture, relevant approaches range from Hoskins's *Biographical Objects* (1998) to Gell (1998) on agency and, although not usually categorized in this way, I would suggest also Sennett (1992).

2. Bourdieu was not averse to the analysis of individuals, the best examples being his discussion of Flaubert (Bourdieu 1996a; Eastwood 2007) and Heidegger (Bourdieu 1996b). But this did not proceed through the direct analogy with his analysis of society as proposed here.

3. The use of the term 'aesthetic' here is not intended to connote its usual employment within the specific field of the arts, especially not contemporary art. It is also far removed from more philosophical concerns with the role of the aesthetic in the evolution of Western thought and ideology (Eagleton 1990). Many anthropological approaches evoke the relation of fragments to the whole (see Simmel 1968) as with the aesthetic of the microcosm implicated in Geertz or Bourdieu. But my use implies almost the opposite. Not the individual as a fragment, but the way an individual builds for himself or herself something that creates a sense of order which may or may not feel holistic for that individual. It may be based on his or her creativity, on the orders imposed upon him or her. More commonly it derives

from his or her selective co-opting of the orders he or she finds in his or her world, whether from family traditions, cultural traditions, institutions or others. As in all material culture approaches the concern is as much how these orders make people as how people make orders. What makes the word 'aesthetic' appropriate was rather a throw back to the pre-modern use of the term as expressing qualities that people wished to see reproduced in the arts, as they were assumed to have a bearing on the sense of beauty; principles such as harmony, balance and symmetry, but in the light of modernism, we could also add dissonance, contradiction and even edgy.

4. All the contributors to this volume were students for whom I was the primary supervisor of their PhD except Botticello and Dalakoglou for whom I was the second supervisor and Olesen who was formally supervised in Denmark but then settled in the Department at University College London as an Honorary Research Associate. We are all grateful to the comments on these papers over the years by other PhD students who overlapped with this 'generation' of students. We would also acknowledge the contribution of many visiting students from various countries who typically came to work with me for a few months and joined the drinking group for that duration providing comments on these papers and indeed drinks.

References

Beck, U. and Beck-Gernsheim, E. (2002), *Individualization,* London: Sage.
Becker, G. (1996), *Accounting for Tastes,* Cambridge, MA: Harvard University Press.
Benedict, R. (1974), *The Chrysanthemum and the Sword,* New York: Plume Books.
Bloch, M. (1998), *How We Think They Think: Anthropological Approaches to Cognition, Memory, and Literacy,* Boulder, CO: Westview Press.
Bourdieu, P. (1977), *Outline of a Theory of Practice,* Cambridge: Cambridge University Press.
Bourdieu, P. (1979), *Distinction: A Social Critique of the Judgement of Taste,* London: Routledge and Kegan Paul.
Bourdieu, P. (1996a), *The Rules of Art: Genesis and Structure of the Literary Field,* Stanford, CA: Stanford University Press.
Bourdieu, P. (1996b), *The Political Ontology of Martin Heidegger,* Stanford, CA: Stanford University Press.
Carrithers, M., Collins, S. and Lukes, S. (eds) (1985), *The Category of the Person,* Cambridge: Cambridge University Press.
Celtel, A. (2004), *Categories of Self: Louis Dumont's Theory of the Individual,* Oxford: Berghahn.
Cohen, A. (1994), *Self Consciousness: An Alternative Anthropology of Identity,* London: Routledge.

Dumont, L. (1992), *Essays on Individualism: Modern Ideology in Anthropological Perspective,* Chicago: University of Chicago Press.

Eagleton, T. (1990), *The Ideology of the Aesthetic,* Oxford: Blackwell.

Eastwood, J. (2007), 'Bourdieu, Flaubert, and the Sociology of Literature', *Sociological Theory,* 25: 149–69.

Freeman, J. (1979), *Untouchable: An Indian Life History,* Stanford, CA: Stanford University Press.

Geertz, C. (1973), *The Interpretation of Cultures,* New York: Basic Books.

Geertz, C. (1980), *Negara: The Theatre State in Nineteenth-century Bali,* Princeton, NJ: Princeton University Press.

Gell, A. (1998), *Art and Agency,* Oxford: Clarendon Press.

Giddens, A. (1991), *Modernity and Self-Identity,* Cambridge: Polity Press.

Goffman, E. (1975), *Frame Analysis,* Harmondsworth: Penguin.

Gombrich, E. (1979), *The Sense of Order,* London: Phaidon Press.

Henare, A. (2005), 'Nga Aho Tipuna (Ancestral Threads): Maori Cloaks from New Zealand', in S. Küchler and D. Miller (eds), *Clothing as Material Culture,* Oxford: Berg, 121–38.

Hockey, J. (2002), 'Interviews as Ethnography? Disembodied Social Interaction in Britain', in N. Rapport (ed.), *British Subjects,* Oxford: Berg, 209–22.

Holland, D. (2001), 'Developments in Person-centred Ethnography', in C. Moore and H. Mathews (eds), *The Psychology of Cultural Experience,* Cambridge: Cambridge University Press, 48–67.

Hoskins, J. (1998), *Biographical Objects: How Things Tell the Stories of People's Lives,* London: Routledge.

Kusserow, A. (1999), 'De-Homogenizing American Individualism: Socializing Hard and Soft Individualism in Manhattan and Queens', *Ethos,* 27: 210–34.

Le Roy Ladurie, E. (1978), *Montaillou,* Harmondsworth: Penguin.

Lindholm, (1997), 'Logical and Moral Problems of Postmodernism', *Journal of the Royal Anthropological Institute,* 3(4): 747–60.

Malinowski, B. (1922), *Argonauts of the Western Pacific,* London: Routledge and Kegan Paul.

Mauss, M. (1985), 'A Category of the Human Mind: The Notion of Person, the Notion of Self', in M. Carrithers, S. Collins and S. Lukes (eds), *The Category of the Person,* Cambridge: Cambridge University Press, 1–25.

Miller, D. (1987), *Material Culture and Mass Consumption,* Oxford: Blackwell.

Miller, D. (1998), *A Theory of Shopping,* Cambridge: Polity Press.

Miller, D. (2008), *The Comfort of Things,* Cambridge: Polity Press.

Moore, H. (2007), *The Subject of Anthropology: Gender, Symbolism and Psychoanalysis,* Cambridge: Polity Press.

Morris, B. (1994), *The Anthropology of the Self,* London: Pluto Books.

Myers, F. (1986), *Pintupi Country, Pintupi Self,* Washington, DC: Smithsonian Institution Press.

Putnam, R. (2000), *Bowling Alone,* New York: Simon and Schuster.

Rapport, N. (1997), *Transcendent Individual: Towards a Literary and Liberal Anthropology,* London: Routledge.

Rapport, N. (2002), 'Best of British: An Introduction to the Anthropology of Britain', in N. Rapport (ed.), *British Subjects,* Oxford: Berg, 3–26.

Schwartz, T., White, G. and Lutz, C. (1992), *New Directions in Psychological Anthropology,* Cambridge: Cambridge University Press.

Sennett, R. (1992), *The Fall of Public Man,* New York: W.W. Norton & Company.

Shostak, M. (1981), *Nisa: The Life and Words of a Kung Woman,* Cambridge, MA: Harvard University Press.

Simmel, G. (1968), *The Conflict in Modern Culture and Other Essays,* New York: New York Teachers College Press.

Strathern, M. (1979), 'The Self in Self-decoration', *Oceania,* 44: 241–57.

Strathern, M. (1988), *The Gender of the Gift,* Berkeley: University of California Press.

Strathern, M. (1992), *After Nature: English Kinship in the Late Twentieth Century,* Cambridge: Cambridge University Press.

Weiner, A. (1992), *Inalienable Possessions,* Berkeley: University of California Press.

–2–

Trading in Fake Brands, Self-creating as an Individual

Magdalena Crăciun

Since we first met, Fırlama has rearranged his shop three times. He is the only trader in this small Istanbulite bazaar who has allowed this anthropologist, interested in fake brands, to drop by any time she wants and to poke her nose into his business and his life. At first, the goods he is dealing in, that is fake branded underwear and, in a smaller quantity, fake branded perfumes and socks, were crammed into the attic of a glassware shop. Then, the glassware disappeared and the fakes took its place. A few months later, the shop was refurbished and a large selection of t-shirts, shirts, coats, sweaters, jackets and scarves, all fake branded, were displayed. When Fırlama and his neighbour became partners in a new business, he moved into a smaller place, further down the same alley, and has kept on selling fake brands ever since. 'I love this business. I have given it 25 years of my life,' he said one day, while playing absent-mindedly with a pair of bright orange boxer shorts, stretching them, checking the seams and stitches.

As for me, through sitting in his shop and coming to know him, an *imitasyoncu*, that is a maker and seller of fake brands, I often found myself in two minds. Sometimes, I shared with him my discomfort. 'You seem a quiet man, like the other traders. Could I say you are a typical tradesman?'. He remained silent for a while.

> I am not a quiet man, actually, but everyone has a different view on life. You may say 'I finished this school and I want to work at this place.' You draw a line for yourself to follow. Since my childhood, I have been used to living on high adrenaline. I don't like an unexciting life. If I didn't do imitation, I would rent this place, go and sit at home. I don't do this job only because I have to. This is my personality. I can't help doing it. You can see around other people doing imitations but they keep only a few products in the shop. I have a few thousands only in this shop. Plus the depots. Plus the factory. The others don't really take big risks. That's the typical tradesman, not me.

Explanations as such helped me to better grasp the particularities of this trajectory. At the same time, they pointed out that Fırlama himself must have experienced moments of discomfort and must have meditated on the contradictions inherent in his life.

Fırlama is an old nickname of my interlocutor, whose real identity I prefer, given his involvement in illegal activities, not to disclose. It is a nickname given usually to bold, impatient and practical minded children who demonstrate at an early age a keen sense of social manoeuvring. My encounter with Fırlama can be described as an instance of the 'complicity of mutual interest between anthropologist and informant, subtly but clearly understood by each other, that makes rapport possible—indeed that constitutes, even constructs it' (Marcus 1997: 89). After quasi-disappointing interviews with people exercising care when releasing information about their illegal occupation, I was looking for someone who was willing to reveal the juicy details an anthropologist wants to know regarding the quotidian of dealing in fake branded clothing in Istanbul. He, at the time slowly recovering from his most severe blow yet, a lawsuit that forced him to hide his goods and reduce the rhythm of his business, gradually welcomed the inquisitive anthropologist interested in listening to his ideas on this kind of business and its prosecution and the opportunity it presented for self-reflection and self-presentation.

Focusing on Fırlama's life, this chapter brings to the foreground the way an individual creates an understanding of himself and the order he lives by—practical, personal, moral—by exploiting the potential for fake brands as something that defies rules and flirts with illegality. The individual self-creates himself as a balance between conformity/legality and individuality/illegality, a balance that, despite its particularity, is very much in line with the idea Miller advocates in the introduction of this book, that of an aesthetic constructed at the level of the individual.

This balance materializes itself in the fake brand, a form of material culture that represents the 'principal locus for the objectification of the structuring principle' (Bourdieu 1977: 89) which governs the life of the protagonist of this chapter. The equilibrium between conformity and non-conformity is objectified in this ambiguous object, simultaneously conforming and disobeying, simultaneously inhabiting different 'orders of appearance' (Baudrillard 2001: 414). For the fake branded commodity might be seen as belonging to 'the first order of appearance', its relation to the officially branded goods being that of a counterfeit to an original. The first-order simulacrum never abolishes difference, its main characteristic being 'an always detectable alteration between semblance and reality'. A fake brand might be seen as the illegal version of a conventional form. At the same time, in a place like Istanbul, that is a major site of production in the global clothing industry, in which strategies are invented to make brands proliferate by escaping systems of control and in which it is not unusual to have the official copies and illegal versions manufactured in the same factory, even with the same materials, the fake brands might be also understood as belonging to 'the second order of appearance'. That is to say, the order of the serial production and the relation between the objects of a series is 'no longer that of an original to its counterfeit—neither analogy nor reflections—but equivalence, indifference. In a series, objects become undefined simulacra of one another' (Baudrillard 2001: 414). A fake brand might be thus understood as a legitimate object, another version of a conventional form. Put it in a nutshell, a peculiar project of assertion of individuality uses a contested object as its most fertile soil.

The Rebellious Son

Born into the family of a patriarchal tradesman, Fırlama is a son who rebelled. His father, whom he sometimes describes as a conservative man (*hacı hoca takımıydı*), and, at other times, as an uneducated person (*cahil*), mistrusted his family members' ability to execute important decisions, tried to make his children dependent upon his wisdom, experience and judgement and sought to imbue them with his own traits and values. For 'patriarchy entails cultural constructs and structural relations that privilege the initiative of males and elders in directing the lives of others,' a system Joseph (1999: 12) calls patriarchal connectivity.[1] Fırlama, the youngest among the six children, was terrified, wondering why his father treated him in a manifestly unfair way and whether he is an unwanted child (*fazlalık*). Kandiyoti (1994) argues male children in patriarchal systems are as powerless as women and, before they themselves become patriarchs, they are sons who have to obey seemingly all-powerful fathers. Such experiences might mutilate the psyche, some sons going so far as to promise themselves that they will never behave like their fathers.

Fırlama started coming to the bazaar at about the age of five, for the father wanted his boys in the bazaar after school hours, to earn their pocket money and learn the trade. Moreover, the father wished his youngest son to become an *imam*. Therefore, the boy was sent to an Imam-Hatip school, a choice probably motivated less by interest in education in accordance with Muslim beliefs and more by the positive evaluation of the school in terms of parental prestige and social mobility. With broad appeal to conservative families, these schools are state-run vocational institutions opened in the early 1950s, which prepare students to become knowledgeable about Islam and, preferably, to occupy religious functionary positions. 'In such a setting, students are expected to develop a sense of comfort in resigning themselves to accepting conformity, rather than developing the ability to recognise and confront their own complicity in the construction of their identities…The opportunities for the playful experimentation of the cultural milieu that marks the adolescent years in regular schools are curtailed in this environment' (Pak 2004: 336–7). Fırlama spent four years in an institution characterized by an atmosphere of discipline, where the duty of the students is to obey, and the task of the teachers is to inculcate moral values and compel students to be adherents to and practitioners of Muslim teachings.

Upon finishing this school, Fırlama left home. He knew how heartbreaking it had been for his parents, especially for his little sister who loved him dearly, when he left home for good, but Fırlama still could not help but suspect they had also been relieved deep down. He had to leave the house and pursue his own life of self-fulfillment. For six years, he lived a colourful life on the streets, encountered all manner of experiences and made the most of doing everything that was previously forbidden. His father knew nothing about him getting arrested at the age of sixteen and, again, at the age of eighteen. His decision to go out into the world was one of remarkable boldness, and through it he gained material and spiritual autonomy. Emancipation from paternal, religious and communal control came as an expression of a lust for life, an act of self-assertion, against a father who wished him to follow a path which Fırlama did not envisage for himself.

The masculine self had been, thus, negotiated within and against multiple sites and multiple relationalities for, although the 'son/parents relationship is certainly a central site for constructing identity, it is the convergence and divergence of this core relationship with other crucial relationalities that determine the sense of self' (Al-Nowaihi 1999: 238). After family and school, the other formative institution Fırlama entered was the 'street'. This was the space inhabited by *delikanlı*, literally meaning individuals with crazy blood, a term referring to adolescents and young unmarried men, who valorize the untamed and undomesticated. Among the popular classes, *delikanlı* is a desirable status of masculinity, 'a certain amount of deviant behaviour [being] accepted as an inevitable concomitant of this stage' (Kandiyoti 1994: 210). Fırlama crossed that line, rebelling against the father, traditionally regarded as the guarantor and protector of the normative order, and the state, the modern guarantor and protector of the order. He was imprisoned several times. Moreover, he was, in his words, 'political', that is actively involved in the political events of the turbulent 1970s.

He returned home in 1979, around the day he was supposed to start his military service. Hard as it was during this time Fırlama had managed and became, thanks to his excellent driving skills and bold manners, the personal driver and bodyguard of a high ranking officer. The army, one of the important institutions responsible for the production of masculinity in Turkey, played a major role in crystallizing his personal habitus. For there, demonstrating resourcefulness, wit and bravery, he began to value his 'difference' and to search for ways of combining his predilection for adventure with socially accepted modalities of earning a living and placing oneself in society.

> I love adrenaline. One memory I have...There is a distance of 12 km between Svelingrad and Kapıkule [the Bulgarian and Turkish border points]. At four o'clock in the morning, I ran the 12 km together with some wolves. As I reached and surrendered to the Turkish police, I heard the alarm sounds at my back. All my friends were caught back there, and they were all sentenced to 3 years in jail. My adrenaline was at its highest level there...You see, I have the tendency to do what ordinary people are afraid to do. What's interesting is that this is not in my genes. My parents, my grandparents, my uncles, no one has these genes. See, my brother, he is like a sheep. I am the only one in my family who does risky business.

He had only one wish for life, that is to prove himself. He could have chosen to enter deeper into the underworld or to become a spy, as the officer he worked for wanted him, but smuggling and faking seemed the best options, the 'cleanest' ones, preventing him from taking the path of marginality. Years of travelling all over Turkey, Europe and the Middle East followed, driving buses, smuggling watches, chewing gums, jeans, gold and silver, bartering with the Russians, doing imitations, or spending time in jails all over the region, only the stamps on the passport providing evidence for this exceptional way of life. He had an insatiable appetite for life, and availed himself of the opportunities that came his way, accumulating years full of all kinds of adventures that make one feel life was worth living.

One day, he returned to the bazaar and to the shop he inherited from his father. Work became his life: night shifts as a taxi driver; driving his van early in the mornings to the manufacturing sites; haggling with factory owners for every penny; carrying the goods to the shop; selling to customers; and carefully piling up his money. And so he established himself as a trader, with a stable capital. Fırlama married when he was in his late twenties, but divorced ten years later, bringing up his two kids on his own, being simultaneously, as he is fond of emphasizing, father, mother, cook and cleaner.[2] He swore to himself that he wouldn't subject his children to the inequities he had suffered at his father's hand. Today, even though he is in his late forties, he still calls himself and behaves like a *delikanlı* despite the fact that this stage in a man's life usually comes to an end with military service, marriage and fatherhood. At other times and in different contexts he enacts the authority of an honourable, honest and knowledgeable tradesman and the 'domesticated masculinity' of the responsible householder (Loizos 1994).

The Choice of Profession

> I wanted to make money everyday regularly. Some people say 'It's ok if I don't earn a lot as long as I don't get into trouble.' With me it's the opposite. I want to earn a lot but I don't care if I get into trouble. That is my character. Little by little, I came to realize smuggling, imitation are the kind of jobs I would make money everyday, even if they are dangerous ones. Before the military service, somebody asked for CK, for England, a big smuggling deal. I had already the tendency, I dived right in. I still haven't surfaced.

Since the early 1980s, Fırlama has been involved in the trade in fake brands, acquiring considerable expertise; learning the tricks; recovering after the blows, for betrayal and loss are frequent in this trade; searching for new connections and customers; getting to know who else is in this trade; evaluating which brand sells well, which colours are preferred, which models suit the taste of local and foreign clients, what technologies are most effective and what sources of excess products and leakages from the local textile industry are available. The gradual transformation of Istanbul into a site of production in a globalizing clothing industry and the city's recapturing of its historical role as a regional market, with trading routes spreading across a vast area, including the Balkans, Western and Eastern Europe and Eurasia, have offered good opportunities for the development of a business such as this one. And the rule of the left and right pockets, that is dividing money gained from sales into spending money, to be put in the right pocket, and money for the shop and factory, to be kept in the left pocket, has become his golden rule. He claims he learnt from the Jewish traders this rule that allowed him to remain on the market. In time, he has become *kaşarlı,* that is experienced.

> Effort must be put into making fraud too. Look at this pair of cotton boxers. I have made it nicely. The model and fabric are wonderful. If I don't sew this with mercerized fiber, it will be torn in less than two months. Soon, this model will be sold by others too, but it won't be the same quality, I can guarantee you this. The machine which weaves this comes from Italy. The machine is worth €105,000. Its brand is, let's say, Ferrari. The thread it uses has to be Ferrari too. I could make this 100 per cent synthetic and write the same thing, then I would sell it to you for €1.50. The only lie here is that it writes 'made in Italy'. Everything else is true. If I wrote 'made in Turkey', I wouldn't even have the chance to sell it. Then it wouldn't be imitation. It would be pointless... Sometimes I sign cheques worth 80–100 million lira per month. I don't really have that kind of potential. My working capital is like $300–400,000. If you saw my cheque list, you would say I have the courage of a crazy person or a fool. Actually, I have the courage of an honest person. I think some customer or another will buy these products and I will be able to pay for my checques... My experience, my investments, my honesty, the idea people have about me, these all make up my settled position in the business. As long as your products are good, nobody can touch you in this business. Except for the lawyers, of course.

He was first caught in 2001, due to a careless mistake. The number of the flat in which he had a deposit and the number of the building were the same. A team of lawyers was looking for the ground floor shop, in order to make a routine inspection. His employee happened to smoke a cigarette in front of the entrance at the wrong time and answered candidly to their question, indicating that number fifty-six was on the fifth floor. The lawyers entered the paradise, a flat filled to the brim with fake branded goods, and Fırlama faced a heavy fine and years in jail. The sentence was, however, suspended for five years, as this is the period after which the files are cleared, a legal loophole for whose application he generously bribed lawyers and judges. Thus, one day, his activity was redefined as 'illegal' and his relation with the state acquired a new dimension.

Consequently, he took more precautions, changing more often the location of his production sites, hiding the deposits even better, arranging for the bank to sequester some of his properties and strengthening his ties with local politicians, lawyers and underworld leaders. In the law courts, he always denied selling fake branded products, played stupid every time he went there, acting as if he did not have a clue about what happened. Lawyers paid impromptu visits also to the shop, but each time he kept himself out of trouble, half-bribing, half-threatening them. 'Isn't it a crime to sell what cost you €2 for €40? Or is it a crime to sell it for €3? You decide.' He for his part decided this is not a crime and he is not a criminal.

> I never try to take anybody's money. I don't have any bad records with banks or the tax office. I don't have a problem with the state or people in person. I don't mess with people, but with the brands. Because it is my major. Like you have your master's degree, I have this... I never sold drugs, I used them but never sold them and poisoned people. I never gambled. I did gamble only for fun, but I didn't put the gambling money into my pocket... I heard that nowadays, if you type a name on the Internet, all the lawsuits of that person will pop up. I have many, so many. One might think I am a bad person. But I do imitations.

These events and the growing attempts at enforcing intellectual property legislation did not discourage or frightened him. As the five-year period has come to an end, he is presently fully back in business, selling counterfeit goods in broad daylight, while keeping a studious lookout for authorities and rivals.

The Respected Trader

There is one thing Fırlama seems to never tire of: this is setting his shop in order. A short, big-bellied, middle-aged man, he swings by amidst the packages carefully piled up on top of one another on the floor but nevertheless occupying half of the twelve-square-metres shop. After standing motionless for a few seconds, as if nailed to the spot, scrutinizing everything, he lights another cigarette. The satisfaction he feels at what he sees is so evident that a neighbour cannot help but congratulate him for such an organized shop.

In this small bazaar, the mornings are busy, with big orders to be taken care of, goods to be sent to regular customers, bulk buyers to be served and trips back and forth with deposits to supplement the stock to be made. Everything must be done quickly, lest the client should be kept waiting. Accordingly, his apprentice is frequently scolded during these hours for failing to quickly select the requested items or for claiming that the ordered items are not available in the deposits. To this chatterbox of a boy, Fırlama feels bound to say over and over that doing business requires mind and moderation, permanent circulation of money and respect for the customers and that forgetting these principles might result in losing everything. In their world, a poor man is a nobody. Ideally, the trader must put his whole heart into his work, must be honest and thrifty. Consequently, he will prosper and his shop and deposits will be heaped to the brim.

Every now and then agitated shopkeepers rush inside, in urgent need of articles in a certain colour, size or brand, sometimes accompanied by their clients. Occasional customers make their way into the shop in a greater number around noon and late afternoon. They are welcomed with honeyed words, encouraged to rummage through the shelves and tempted with colourful underwear, in sixteen shades, as Fırlama is fond of telling, far more than the colour scheme of their officially branded counterparts. The naives, that is those who think they have made a lucky find, brands for a fraction of their price, are assured the goods in this shop are all imitations. The bothersomes, who imagine they can get a good discount for buying three pairs instead of two, are cut short and left alone to ponder whether they want to buy or not. The hesitaters are shown different items in the hope they would finally reach a decision, but sometimes their obvious pleasure in turning the shop upside down indisposes the shopkeeper. During these encounters, without exception, there comes a moment when both parties stretch the underwear, Fırlama to demonstrate their resistance and quality, the customers to check whether they suit them or not.

Business partners and other traders drop by from time to time, in search of information. The injustices they have suffered, usually unpaid debts, are eagerly shared, the men seething with indignation, uttering harsh but well-deserved words. Known as an honest person (*dürüst*), Fırlama is the best audience, his most trenchant criticism being reserved for the fickle characters, the ignorants and the blowers of bubbles. For the competition has become tougher, this profitable business attracting crowds of newcomers, who have no scruples about betraying other traders and threatening lawyers. From the gossip lavishly dispensed at these meetings, all participants distill pieces of noteworthy information. Business propositions are carefully pondered over, for everyone knows the local habit of bragging and promising, only to conveniently forget, a second later. Samples are carefully scrutinized, with expert eyes that know good trimmings and seams and experienced hands that can evaluate the fabrics. Financial issues might necessitate more than the simple act of giving or receiving cash or cheques. To solve the matters, appealing to every known tie and blandishments is one technique, but equally possible are threats and shouting, grovelling and haughtiness.

Fırlama for his part doesn't miss a chance to present himself as a successful trader. In those moments, as they say, his tongue is hung in the middle and wags at both ends. His numerous clients, the high-tech factory, the clever way in which his business is organized, the quality of the products, the models, the brands, the new arrivals in his shop, all eddy around in those torrents of words. To those who come in for advice, for they would also like to enter the trade in imitations but are afraid, he is fond of explaining the comical side of this business (his favourites being the following: policemen come and look for someone, they are told the guy disappeared, so they write in the register "unknown address" and leave, happy to get off cheaply; lawyers raid a shop, and in a second the whole bazaar knows, and the hunted goods vanish in the blink of an eye). Danger can be overcome with connections, money and intelligence, so the moral goes. The ridiculous and the serious converge, and this is something many but him find confusing.

The morality of his business is rarely an issue of concern for these visitors, with the exception of his rich and educated relatives. They have mixed feelings for Fırlama, a relative at whom they turn up their noses, for he is an uneducated man doing an unethical business and disobeying the normative order of the state that offered protection to his family, foreigners, Turks from Macedonia. To his arguments—fakes as free advertisement and a means of living for many people; the unjustified high price of the so-called original and the fair price and quality of the so-called counterfeit; the payment of taxes—they turn a deaf ear. Nevertheless, they do buy from his shop many items.

One day, lost in thoughts, he muttered under his breath to the anthropologist, watching her with friendliness:

> I became like this for I wanted to. Also life made me like this. But I am happy with the way I am, for I always had money this way. I have twelve, fifteen more years to live, I smoke and drink, let's say I will die at seventy. I live by my own rules and I will stay like this till then... I will drown not in a lake, but in the ocean. I will be eaten up by sharks or whales in the ocean, but I will not die in a lake.

In the bazaar time flows by. Everything the shopkeeper does in here—sipping tea; smoking; chatting to the neighbours; gossiping about passers-by and common acquaintances; eavesdropping on chats ebbing and flowing with the inclusion of new participants, often never to be concluded or completed; haggling over the prices; putting things back on the shelves or dusting the merchandise—not only has he certainly done many times before, but is also liable to repetition infinite times in the future. For Fırlama, however, the daily routine is interspersed with doses of excitement, for adventurous episodes might occur, in his case, even in a bazaar immersed in languor.

Concluding Remarks

One of the predominant themes of the Middle Eastern novel is that of the individual rebelling against the social norms, triumphing over a hostile, uncomprehending undifferentiated collective (Al-Nowaihi 1999; Altorki 1999; Muhidine 2006). Such novels portray individuals ready to explore and determine matters on their own, to formulate their own set of values rather than accept what is being handed down to them. Central to such works, it has been pointed out, is a perceived tension between two models of self, that is the individual self who values autonomy, independence and being unique, and the relational self who has relatively fluid boundaries and derives its sense of worth from being part of, rather than apart from, a collective entity and significant others. Even though their fictionality casts a shadow on their validity as sources of knowledge, for it might be argued that the purpose of creating these exceptional characters is that of contaminating the readers and causing them to question the social order, such novels, nevertheless, emphasize an important characteristic of the Middle Eastern societies, namely, 'the tenuous waters that a person must navigate with and against the family to create the self' (Al-Nowaihi 1999: 262).

In the Muslim Middle East family and community have been valued over and above the person, connective relationships becoming not only functional but necessary for successful social existence. However, persons in these cultures have often resisted and constructed alternatives, for the embeddedness in relational matrices that shape the self does not deny distinctive initiative and agency. Connectivity can thus co-exist with individualism in the same culture and perhaps even in the same person (Joseph 1999: 189). Though crucial for the construction of self in the Middle East, experiences in the family are but one instance of a whole range of institutional arrangements which go into the definition of what it means to be a man or a woman (Kandiyoti 1994: 202). In a society such as Turkey, it is worth keeping in mind the possible influence on identity construction of the modern masculine and feminine ideals of nationalism (Kandiyoti 1997: 122). In brief, as a sense of the self has to be formulated within and against the constructions of personhood available in a society, the peculiar balance between conformity and individuality discussed in this chapter could have nevertheless taken root even on thick communalist soil. This struggle for self has unfolded in a culture that valorizes kin structures, morality and idioms, resulting in an unconventional but fulfilled life.

Fırlama started his life under very strict rules, but responded by systematic rejection and needed illegality to confirm himself as individual rather than the mere product of these rules. His rebellion can be defined as opposition to conformity but without the desire for changing the social order that conformity supports. Rebellion from paternal, religious and communal control, the formative institutions he entered during his life, his ability to cross different social milieu, all 'predisposed him to a broader view of the space of possible and hence to a more complete use of the freedom inherent in its constraints' (Bourdieu 1996: 208).

He has found a niche that allows for the possibility to construct himself in terms of a morality he is comfortable with, which has much smaller oscillations between conventional morality and illegality and which he can envisage as expressing his own moral position. After a big oscillation between conformity and illegality, he has engaged in an activity that guarantees the exciting experiences he has always been fond of and that allows him to be not only an honest trader, who sells quality at a fair price; but also a good citizen, who pays his taxes. These are his moral acts, and, as Asad (2003: 95) emphasized, they are not necessarily the responsible acts of a free agent answerable to God, society, or conscience. The agency can be traced back to his habitus, and to that part of it Asad calls 'ethical sensibility', acquired, in this case, especially in religious school. Thus, he was able to reconcile himself with his primary experiences and take them upon himself, to assume them without losing anything he subsequently acquired. The multiple but antagonistic determination of his personal habitus has been successfully channelled into constructing a balance, however fragile, between conformity and nonconformity, conventional and illegal.

And it is the fake brand, the kind of object he is dealing in for the last twenty-five years, which objectifies this peculiar process of self-making. In a way that parallels

Bourdieu's description of the Kabyle house (Bourdieu 1977), the ambiguous nature of the fake brand might be understood as reflecting a particular habitus and reproducing its constitutive elements for the inhabitant of this 'very very small society' (Miller 2008: 295) that is Fırlama.

Notes

1. 'Patriarchy entails cultural constructs and structural relations that privilege the initiative of males and elders in directing the lives of others. Connectivity entails cultural constructs and structural relations in which persons invite, require, and initiate involvement with others in shaping the self. In patriarchal societies, then, connectivity can support patriarchal power by crafting selves responding to, requiring, and socialised to initiate involvement with others in shaping the self, and patriarchy can help reproduce connectivity by crafting males and seniors prepared to direct the lives of female and juniors and females and juniors prepared to respond to the direction of males and seniors' (Joseph 1999: 12–13). Though this concept is used for understanding selving in the Arab/Muslim world, it is taken here as being also relevant for another Muslim society, the Turkish one.
2. In almost all the Middle Eastern states, family law has upheld men's property in their children, so that, upon divorce, control of the children is given to the father (Joseph 2000: 21).

References

Al-Nowaihi, M. M. (1999), 'Constructions of Masculinities in Two Egyptian Novels', in S. Joseph, (ed.), *Intimate Selving in Arab Families: Gender, Self, and Identity,* Syracuse, NY: Syracuse University Press, 235–63.

Altorki, S. (1999), 'Patriarchy and Imperialism: Father-Son and British-Egyptian Relations in Najib Mahfuz's Trilogy', in S. Joseph (ed.), *Intimate Selving in Arab Families: Gender, Self, and Identity,* Syracuse, NY: Syracuse University Press, 214–34.

Asad, T. (2003), *Formations of the Secular: Christianity, Islam, Modernity,* Stanford, CA: Stanford University Press.

Baudrillard, J. (2001), 'Simulations', in R. Kearney and D. Rasmussen (eds), *Continental Aesthetics: Romanticism to Postmodernism. An Anthology,* Oxford: Blackwell Publishing, 411–30.

Bourdieu, P. (1977), *Outline of a Theory of Practice,* Cambridge: Cambridge University Press.

Bourdieu, P. (1996), *The Rules of Art: Genesis and Structure of the Literary Field,* Stanford, CA: Stanford University Press.

Joseph, S. (1999), 'Introduction: Theories and Dynamics of Gender, Self, and Identity in Arab Families', in S. Joseph (ed.), *Intimate Selving in Arab Families: Gender, Self, and Identity,* Syracuse, NY: Syracuse University Press, 1–17.

Joseph, S. (2000), 'Gendering Citizenship in the Middle East', in S. Joseph (ed.), with a foreword by D. Kandiyoti, *Gender and Citizenship in the Middle East,* Syracuse, NY: Syracuse University Press, 3–30.

Kandiyoti, D. (1994), 'The Paradoxes of Masculinity: Some Thoughts on Segregated Societies', in A. Cornwall and N. Lindisfarne (eds), *Dislocating Masculinity: Comparative Ethnographies,* London: Routledge, 197–213.

Kandiyoti, D. (1997), 'Gendering the Modern: On Missing Dimensions in the Study of Turkish Modernity', in S. Bozdoğan and R. Kasaba (eds), *Rethinking Modernity and National Identity in Turkey,* Seattle: University of Washington Press, 113–32.

Loizos, P. (1994), 'A Broken Mirror: Masculine Sexuality in Greek Ethnography', in A. Cornwall and N. Lindisfarne (eds), *Dislocating Masculinity: Comparative Ethnographies,* London: Routledge, 66–81.

Marcus, G. E. (1997), 'The Uses of Complicity in the Changing Mise-en-Scène of Anthropological Fieldwork', *Representations,* 59: 85–108.

Miller, D. (2008), *The Comfort of Things,* Cambridge: Polity Press.

Muhidine, T. (2006), 'L'individu inquiet de la littérature turque', *Cahiers d'etudes sur la Méditerranée orientale et le monde turco-iranien, Cemoti*, no. 26: L'individu en Turquie et en Iran, mis en ligne le 20 mars 2006, http://cemoti.revues.org/document34.html (accessed 16 July 2008).

Pak, S.-Y. (2004), 'Articulating the Boundary between Secularism and Islamism: The Imam-Hatip Schools of Turkey', *Anthropology and Education Quarterly,* 55(3): 324–44.

–3–

'Making Things Come Out': Design, Originality and the Individual in a Bògòlan Artisan Community

Bodil Birkebæk Olesen

While the study of design is closely linked to that of individuals, the study of decorative patterns tends to focus instead on their relationship to or significance for collective entities. Within the field of textile history terms such as 'Kuba cloth' or 'Ewe textiles'—classifying a group of textiles by referring to the ethnic or cultural group that made them—speaks to a scholarly legacy of conceptualizing material culture and its stylistic elements somewhat tautologically as indices of such groups. Research in anthropology and art history has of course shown that the social and cultural significance of patterns far transcends such indexicality. Washburn (1999), for example has argued that the symmetry of decorative patterns may embody central cultural concepts, while Gell's (1998) theory of art's agency demonstrates how patterns can be viewed as material extensions of socially constituted agency. Recent innovative approaches, for example Stafford (2007) and Küchler (2005), see patterns as loci of cognition external to the human mind. As these studies have demonstrated, anthropologists (and art historians) have only begun to grasp the manifold, complex role of patterns in creating and sustaining social process.

Like all the contributors to this volume I wish to explore how an anthropological focus on individuals may provide an innovative starting point for exploring and understanding the relationship between the individual and society, and for exploring the cultural orders they live by. Thus, the question that ultimately concerns me here is what we may gain from expanding the focus on patterns and their significance for collective entities—for sustaining collective values, extending generalized social agency or visualizing and maintaining cognitive structures—to focusing on the significance they may have from the perspective of the individual. In the following, therefore, I shall explore a body of patterns by focusing on the design process in which they come into being. More specifically, I focus on *bògòlan* cloth, a handmade, hand-decorated cloth from Mali, and the design practices within a community of *bògòlan* artisans that I observed during my doctoral research on the cloth and its contemporary significance.[1] What emerges from my analysis, however, is not an account intended to redress the collectivist orientation in the study of decorative patterns. I do not intend to show the idiosyncratic meaning or significance that the experience of designing a pattern by definition has to the individual. Rather, starting with the design process allows for an exploration of an aesthetic order in which the individual and society are not treated as two distinct analytical perspectives, but instead appear as aspects of each other.

The use of plant and mineral dyes for cloth decoration has a long history in the area that today is known as the Republic of Mali. One type of such cloth, known as *bògòlanfini* (Brett-Smith 1982a,b, 1984; Duponchel 2004), has historically played an important role among the Bamana, the dominant ethnic group in Mali. Bamana women used plant dyes and mud rich in iron oxide to decorate cotton cloths with intricate, symbolically significant motifs, wearing them during significant stages of their life such as excision and childbirth, and Bamana hunters used the technique to decorate their hunting garments. In both cases the cloths were seen to facilitate life and prosperity through the containment and control of the powerful life force that was believed to permeate the world. This use of the cloth and its concomitant cosmology has diminished steadily throughout years of French colonial rule, increasing numbers of conversions to Islam, modernization and national independence. Today the production and use of *bògòlanfini* is limited to some of the more remote parts of the country. In the wake of this diminishing significance, however, the dyeing technique has proliferated into a number of new incarnations, which are generally referred to as *bògòlan*. The technique has been used by artists as a new, creative medium and by a number of artisans who produce cloth for sale both within Mali, where it remains a popular fabric for garments, and internationally where it is appreciated for its African-ness. Awareness of the cloth has been established by a number of Malian musicians who wear the cloth during concerts, and by fashion designers. It has become an emblem of Mali as a modern nation-state and is a ubiquitous visual element in the street life of many urban settings as it is worn by the fashion-minded Malians or displayed by vendors catering to tourists (Duponchel 1995; Rovine 2001).

The provincial town of San, where I carried out a large part of my research, has a population of around 30,000 people and is the centre of commercial *bògòlan* production. All the major *bògòlan* merchants—whose biggest market is the export market—commission a large part of their stock in San, and the town's artisans are appreciated by the merchants for their large and ever-changing range of cloth designs. Brett-Smith has suggested that San's geographical location and political economic history were important factors in its development as the centre for contemporary commercial *bògòlan* production (Brett-Smith n.d.: 150). Historically the town occupied a prominent position in the regional and supra-regional exchange of salt, kola nuts, gold, horses and slaves (Mann 2006: 24), and its present-day strategic position—close to the intersection of Mali's main highway and the road leading south towards Burkina Faso—is a decisive factor for the continued importance of trade to San. The sporadic sources suggest that San's commercial *bògòlan* production started in the late 1960s or early 1970s when local Marka women began using vegetable and mineral dyes in innovative ways to produce and sell fabric intended for apparel, as well as buying and re-selling cloth from rural Bamana women living on the other side of the nearby Bani river.[2] The concentration of production in one particular neighbourhood in San, the Misira, is no coincidence: the artisans of the Misira are relatives of these original Marka traders and have maintained and expanded the commercial relationships that their kinsmen established years ago. There are more than a hundred workshops in San, but many of them produce only sporadically as supply far outstretches demand. The artisans in Misira, however, are always busy.

One of San's oldest neighbourhoods, lying directly north of the town's beautiful mosque, the Misira consists of the characteristic adobe houses, laid out in the strict grid pattern—series of squares of rectangular blocks of compounds, surrounded by unpaved streets—that are common in former French colonies. A mere seventeen blocks, the neighbourhood is nevertheless home to more than twenty workshops. Within just one block are eight different workshops, and in the immediately surrounding blocks another five, all run by kinsmen of the Marka traders who first took up production and trade in the 1960s and 1970s. Walking through Misira is an intense visual experience. *Bògòlan* production requires space—to decorate cloths or to leave them out to dry during the various stages of production—and for the successful artisans working on commissions of more than a hundred pieces of cloth at a time, the space of the compound will not do. The open square in the neighbourhood, which every Thursday is the arena for local football matches, also provides the luxury of an abundance of space for those artisans whose houses are located right on the square, while others have to contend with working in little shacks outside their compounds. They, along with anyone else who has run out of space in the compound, leave their pieces out in the street either on the ground, where the chicken will traverse them frequently, hanging over a low wall, draped over an old horse cart that is not in use, or hung over the occasional clothes line. Thus everywhere one encounters the familiar sight of cloths and their characteristic earth colours. Walking through the Misira one constantly passes artisans working outside their compounds, catches a glimpse of them carrying out their various chores inside the compounds and now and then passes a door left open to the storerooms full of the dried *n'galama* leaves and *wolo* bark that are used to make the yellow and red dyes. Every Monday and Thursday the merchants send commissions to the artisans in San on the bus, and one catches the familiar sight of a white canvas sack, with a workshop patron's name and the quantity of the commission written on it, on the donkey carts that take the sacks from the bus station to the workshops. Monday is also market day in San, and rural women, carrying their large sacks of *n'galama* and *wolo* on their heads, go from workshop to workshop in the Misira hoping that some of them need to buy fresh supplies this week.

This ubiquity of visual elements and the bustling carrying back and forth of materials that was such an integral part of the Misira's street life is one reason I find Rosalind Krauss's (1986) concept of an aesthetic economy so compelling. As decorative features of the neighbourhood that gives it its distinct character, their presence also speaks unanimously to many people's dependence on creating aesthetically pleasing cloths for procuring a livelihood. And in this process stencils, cloth, labour and materials circulate continuously between kinsmen and neighbours in the different workshops, tying them together in bonds of economic reciprocity that made my attempts at conducting income surveys and calculating workshop profits something of a challenge. But Krauss's notion is also useful for enabling a more complicated understanding of the creative practices involved in production, however commercial and economically crucial it is. Krauss used the notion to expose the rhetoric of the avant-garde—and modernist art in general—and its self-celebratory claims to originality. Such claims, and their concomitant contempt for repetition, she argues, were not only bound together in a particular aesthetic economy, 'interdependent and mutually sustaining, although the one—originality—is the valorised term and the other—repetition or copy or reduplication—is discredited' (Krauss 1986: 160). But they also, by extension, entail a certain blindness or refusal to address the endless instances of material and conceptual replication that were the necessary precondition for originality, as for example when Rodin's genius was celebrated posthumously through the replication of his work (Krauss 1986: 151), or when various modernist artists 'enact [their] originality in the creation of grids' (Krauss 1986: 160). Krauss's argument, that it is the artist's own self rather than any property of the artwork that guarantees its originality, resonates with other scholars arguing that the very notion of the lone artistic genius, and the dichotomy between originality and repetition, is closely tied to the rise of a peculiarly modern conception of the human subject that may not be particularly well suited for understanding personhood and creative practice as they exist elsewhere in time and space (Ingold 2000: 350; Ingold and Hallam 2007). But her notion of an aesthetic economy is also a useful analytical construct for grasping the configuration of repetition and originality in the context I describe, where the terms 'innovation' and 'copying' are used so frequently but with very different connotations than those familiar to most Western readers.

The artisans in San place great value on designing a cloth pattern. This value, however, is restricted to the design process as an intellectual process and does not necessarily include its material execution, which, in fact, is preferably left to those of junior status. The term used for this intellectual endeavour is 'innovation' and its materialization as a finished piece of cloth is referred to as a 'model' (*modèli*). The connotations of this term are different from the conventional Western ones which, as a quick survey of the *Oxford English Dictionary* will confirm, are to a conceptual, mental or material representation or depiction of something else. A model among the artisans denotes instead this act of invention itself. I often witnessed people, who entered a workshop and encountered a design that was unknown to them, asking who had 'made' a particular piece of cloth, a question that was always framed as *jòn modèli don?,* 'whose model is it?', *not* who made it (*jòn y'a kè*). The person who has 'authored' a design is referred to as the *natigi,* literally the head from which it comes.

The value of designs clearly has a commercial component. Patrons, those who have a workshop and employ others to make cloths, may achieve a name for themselves among artisans and merchants as capable of providing a variety of new designs, something which is believed to appeal to clients, thus acquiring fame through a process of exchange in ways that seem to resemble the Kula exchange described by Malinowski (1922). But there is an additional aspect to the notion of a model that pertains to the ontology of design as a creative process. Although all the artisans insist that the *natigi* of a particular design can always be traced, they all admit that such an endeavour would require significant time and effort, and no one really ever embarks on such a task. The relevance of articulating authorship by designating a design a model arises instead within a socio-spatial matrix as it posits that a model is designed by a particular person and *not* by somebody else. The significance of this seemingly banal claim to originality becomes clear when it is placed in its practical-material context. There it becomes evident that the terms (model and innovation), as they are used to refer to the design process, articulate copying as the foundation of originality, while simultaneously insisting on the uniqueness of the design arrived at. Let me explain what I mean by this.

As already mentioned, cloths are dyed and then decorated with hand-drawn or stencilled motifs. When making designs by hand the artisans use a paintbrush and mud to draw thick lines on the cloth which has been soaked in a natural dye that acts as a mordent for the mud, fixing its contents of iron-oxide onto the cloth as a black colour once it is washed. The cloth is made of pieces of strip-cloth that are stitched together, and the artisans use the stitch-lines that consequently run down the cloth as a grid for the design. As they work on the design from one corner of the cloth, they start out by dividing it into borders by applying straight lines on top of the stitch-lines. Within these borders they create geometric features by drawing rectangular and diagonal lines and repeating them across the border. They then elaborate these further into particular motif elements and then either combine two different borders or repeat the same border across the cloth (Figure 3.1).

Stencilled motifs are applied to the cloth by cutting a shape in plastic, placing it on the cloth and applying mud on top of the stencil (Figure 3.2). It is at this stage of the production process, when the mud is applied, that the structure of the finished designed is determined. Additional colours are applied to the cloth once the mud has been washed off and it has dried. But when the artisans talk about a model they are referring exclusively to this basic structure of the design that is made with the first layer of mud. And while they refer to this process as innovation, the application of the other colours is instead described as imitation because, as they explained to me, the person carrying out the work is merely executing a design according to the *natigi*'s intentions.

The nature of the decorating process has particular implications for the replication and consequently the dissemination of motifs and designs: acquiring the necessary decorating skills for applying the first layer of mud and thus making a model is

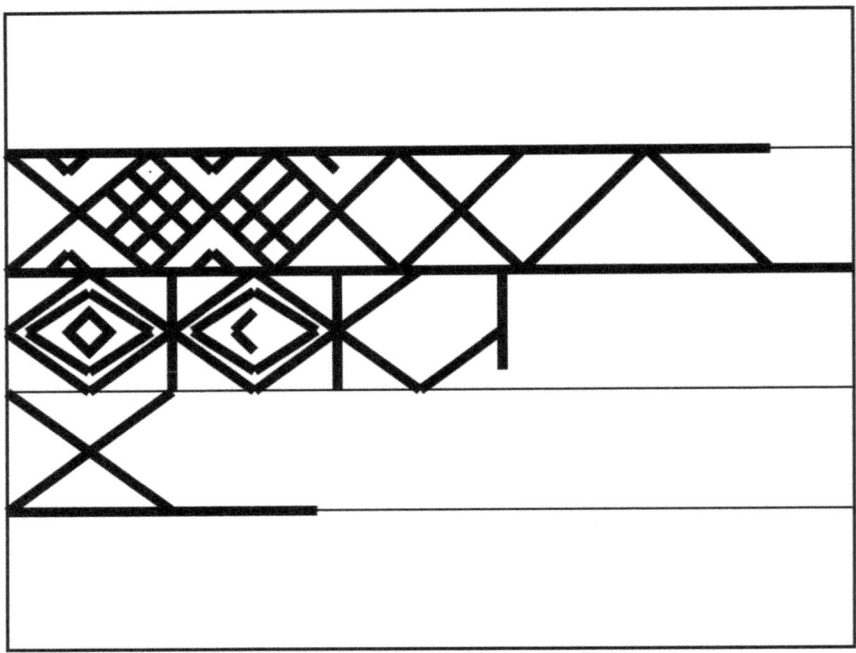

Figure 3.1 A schematic rendition of a piece of cloth and its patterns, consisting of five pieces of strip-cloth. The thin black lines within the cloth are the stitch-lines, upon which the artisans draw a line with the mud (thicker black line) to make up borders across the cloth. Within these borders they combine rectangular and parallel lines to make up various motifs, which they repeat across the cloth.

relatively simple, and experienced artisans possess the skills to replicate any hand-drawn design they encounter. Stencilled motifs are easily reproduced, since although harder to copy just from sight, the actual stencils circulate constantly between workshops (Figures 3.2 and 3.3). Moreover, the visibility of the cloths in the Misira means that motifs are not only technically replicable but also accessible for the artisans. And in fact motifs are constantly replicated and disseminated. Within workshops the recurrence of the same motifs in different artisans' designs is high, and one can generally map the social distance or proximity between workshops (i.e. whether there are kinship ties or ties of neighbourliness between them) by looking at the recurrence of motifs in designs.[3]

That this recurrence is the result of active practices of copying elements from other artisans' designs is clear from watching the work going on in a workshop and the interaction between workshops: artisans, when starting a new design, always look up and around, see what other artisans are working on at the time being and then copy elements of their designs and combine them with elements of their own previous designs (Figures 3.4 and 3.5). Likewise, close kin or neighbours come into

Figure 3.2 An example of how stencils circulate between workshops, and kinsmen and neighbours. The artisan is using stencils borrowed from her patron's son, thus copying motifs from one of the latter's models, the one seen in Figure 3.3.

a workshop, look around, and often elements seen in one workshop begin to appear in this other workshop.

The models depicted in Figure 3.4 and in Figure 3.5 are decorated by two different artisans working in the same workshop within a time-span of 45 minutes. Hawa decorated the cloth depicted here and then put it out in the sun to dry. As she did this, Koti started working on the model shown in Figure 3.5. As we see, she has used the X-shape from Hawa's design as well as the cross-hatched shapes, then changed the additional elements slightly and combined them with a different, thinner border between the main borders.

Previously unseen motifs occasionally enter this aesthetic economy as some artisans occasionally do look beyond this proximity for new motifs. The nature of this process is beyond the scope of this chapter, and I have discussed it in more detail elsewhere (Olesen 2007), but suffice to state here that although such new motifs quickly undergo the same process of being incorporated into new design configurations, their interest in introducing such motifs is marginal compared to the interest in copying already existing motifs. By the same token, while the artisans could design new cloths exclusively by re-combining the elements they have been working with already, they never do that. And although all patrons have piles of stencils tucked away in their houses, such stencils are never brought out into the courtyards for everyone to rummage through. Rather, only a few stencils at a time circulate

44 • *Anthropology and the Individual*

Figure 3.3 Another example of how stencils circulate between workshops, and kinsmen and neighbours. A young male artisan decorated this cloth using stencils that he later lent to one of his mother's workers (Figure 3.2).

'Making Things Come Out' • 45

Figure 3.4 An example of the innovation-through-copying that I am describing.

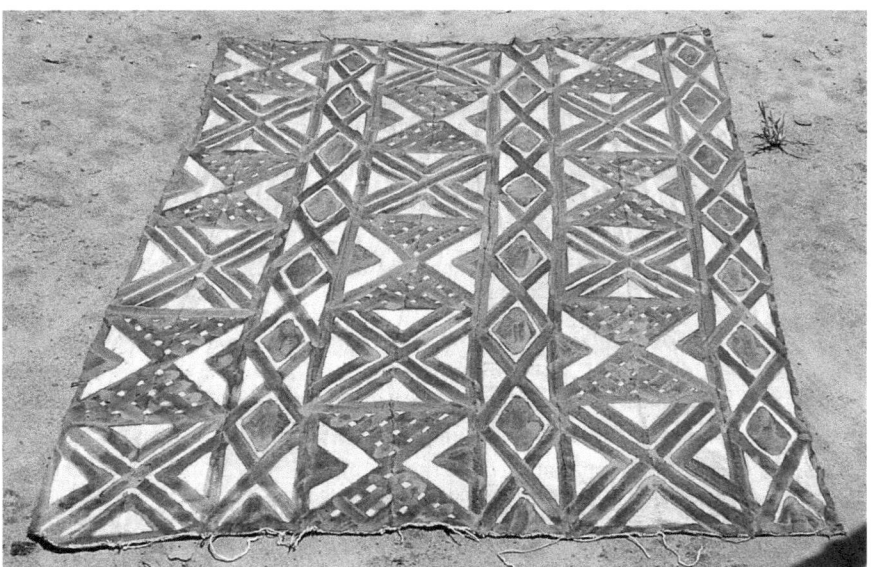

Figure 3.5 Koti's model, made shortly after Hawa finished the model depicted in Figure 3.4.

between artisans. Thus, to sum up, the orientation in the design process is towards artisans in one's social proximity.

At the same time, the outcome of this design process is articulated, as already mentioned, as innovation as well as with reference to difference or uniqueness rather than similarity. In the beginning of my fieldwork, when I was struggling to understand the logic of this creative process I had numerous discussions with the artisans in which I tried to frame my enquiries into the rationale of innovation by pointing out that many models looked a lot alike, an argument that never failed to surprise them since, in their eyes, all the designs were different. When I qualified myself by pointing out that many models contained the same decorative elements, some of them eventually began to grasp what I was trying to say. But in the end, they always qualified their agreement by stating that *a bè bòlen, nka kelen tè,* that is they look like each other—but they are not the same. In their view, although the same motifs appear over and over on different models, they always appear in new combinations, and they see no contradiction between this fact, the uniqueness of all models, and the way in which they describe their design practices as innovative.

Anthropologists working in West Africa often use phrases such as 'relational self' (Piot 1999) or 'relational individualism' (Shaw 2000) to describe the conceptions of self that prevail in the social life of the people with whom they work, and to how an individual self takes an explicitly relational form in many African settings. The point is not that people experience self only in terms of a de-individuated collective, as suggested in some earlier work (e.g. Tempels 1959), but that local conceptions of the individual self entail a sense of inherent existence within a larger relational field. This ontological priority of social relationships, it has been argued, makes the analytical distinction between individual and society highly problematic for understanding these life-worlds. A profoundly modern (and Western) dichotomy, some have argued (e.g. Carrithers, Collins and Lukes 1985; Kondo 1990) it also posits society as consisting of a group of individuals defined by their inherent properties. As Adams and Dzokoto have argued, by granting the individual analytical primacy, 'social relationships are treated as a secondary product, not necessarily in the sense of being less valued but nevertheless as being *derived* or manufactured' (Adams and Dzokoto 2003: 346, my emphasis). Shaw's comparative discussion of bodily metaphors among the Temne in Sierra Leone provides an exemplary illustration of the difference between a Western conception of individualism and the relational individualism found among the Temne. The Temne use a number of metaphors, such as being bad-hearted (i.e. jealous), a characterization that at first seems no different from the Anglo-American description of someone as hard-hearted. However, where the latter is thought of as a 'personality trait', an inner tribute of that person, bad-hearted-ness is seen as an attribute that derives from the capacity for relationships, a person's capacity to relate to others, rather than from an inner essence (Shaw 2000: 40–1).

There are numerous works that demonstrate the implications of this relational ontology and the way in which no interior entity exists which sets apart the experiencing self and exterior, as it pertains to people's relationship to other people, to place and to spiritual forces (e.g. Fortes 1949; Jackson 1982). This, however, is not due to some innate, homogenous African-ness but is differently configured throughout the continent and often the historical product of slave trade and warfare (Miers and Kopytoff 1977). And neither does such a relational ontology preclude individualistic behaviour. In fact, competition and emphasis on individual difference are prevalent among the Mande, the cultural group to which most of Mali's ethnic groups belong.[4] Bird and Kendall argue that competition is dynamic and inherent to Mande identity. The terms *fadenya* (father-child-ness) and *badenya* (mother-child-ness) articulate the social foundation and dynamic of this competition and the conflict arising from a hierarchical social structure where status is valued yet attained through the control of others and one is supposed to succumb to the needs of the social group. Thus, attaining status almost necessarily involves a measure of selfish behaviour and disrespect for the demands of one's kin. Likewise, the terms articulate the inherent tension in a polygamous patrilineal society where rivalry between half-siblings is inevitable (Bird and Kendall 1980). The term *fadenya* is used generally to refer to competition in Mali today, and the *bògòlan* artisans often use the term to describe how they work. Interestingly, Grosz-Ngate has suggested that in everyday life among the Bamana of Sana a common instantiation of such competition is the assertion of selfhood through a principle of differentiation. Thus, she argues, 'an individual does not become a person on his/her own, but by differentiating him/herself from others in her/her conduct and activities' (Grosz-Ngaté 1989: 172). People who stand out in their relations with others and in being sincere may acquire the name *maa sebe,* a sincere person, just as a woman can rise above the disadvantages of her gender by excelling in her tasks and earn the appellate *muso seben.*

These discussions of relational selves and relational individualism cast interesting light on the design practices that I have described and the aesthetic economy in which they take place. What may at first seem like a contradiction between copying and originality may instead be viewed as what one could call a relational originality where the particular or unique is conceived as a product of a totality and where origins is sought with reference to a wider social field. The notion of model itself actually nicely illustrates this. As mentioned earlier on, a model is by definition innovative and by extension different from everybody else's. But when the artisans elaborate on the innovative nature of models their explanations always articulate the uniqueness of a model as a relational phenomenon. Often such explanations emphasize an almost extreme uniqueness of a model as derived solely from the individual. As one artisan put it, 'when you sit down to make a design you draw what is in your head. And what is in one person's head is different from what is in another person's—that's why models are all different.' Yet the same artisan would interchangeably emphasize the relational nature of such difference by explaining that 'if someone makes a design and somebody sees it and copies it then we say that this is that person's model.' Thus, while designs are considered unique, this uniqueness is articulated with reference to other models or, more precisely, to other people's models. That such articulations reflect a relational ontology is perhaps best illustrated by the term that the artisans used for innovation. It is *ka fènw bò nyògòn ma*—to make things come out from the others.

These insights are additionally interesting because of the light they cast on the individual practices of innovation-through-copying that I described earlier on, that is the very conscious and intentional copying of motifs from artisans in one's social proximity. As I also described, there is a general concern among the artisans, their kinsmen, friends and neighbours, basically anyone in the Misira who is familiar with *bògòlan* production, towards the origins of cloth designs. People constantly enquire about the *natigi* of models that are unfamiliar to them. Likewise, in cases where particular models are reproduced over longer periods of time, mainly because they had been commissioned by a client, the artisans would keep referring to such models with reference to their *natigi*. In one particular instance the head of a workshop wanted to know if one of her workers knew a particular model. Since she had no photo of it she described it briefly and then added that it was the one that was Hawa's (one of her workers) model, but the one that Sarata (another worker) usually made. As I described there is little interest in incorporating new (i.e. previously unseen) stylistic elements into the design process. Rather, innovation takes place through copying those in one's social proximity in a way that resonates with the principle of differentiation described by Grosz-Ngaté in which the assertive behaviour of the individual is competitively oriented towards socially relevant others. In Grosz-Ngaté's account these socially relevant others are those of the individual's own gender or own age set, over and against whose actions one may assert oneself as a good woman or a good youngster. As I have described, the source for the artisans' models, their originality, are exactly those with whom they interact or work closely. And, by extension, those against whom their work can, and will, be evaluated and ascertained as different and therefore innovative. The orientation towards others' work and the concern with copying *their* particular work in the creation of one's own unique model thus both reflect the relational nature of selfhood and creative practice as well as the assertive nature of selfhood that defines itself against socially relevant others in ongoing competition through differentiation. The result is the continuous production of constantly reconfigured designs that are celebrated as being different.

I began this chapter with the observation that while the study of design is closely linked to that of individuals, the study of patterns tends to focus on their significance for collective entities. Focusing instead on the individual and the design process involved in making *bògòlan* cloths, I showed how an ensemble of seemingly very similar patterns is the outcome not of individual execution according to visually prefigured designs, or collective values about what such designs should look like, but of individuals' creative practices, their assertions of individuality. Yet, the similarity between patterns is not culturally and socially arbitrary. As I showed, the modality of innovation, of copying motifs from those in one's social proximity, when placed within a context of relational individualism and assertive competition found in the Mande world, reveal themselves as profoundly social assertions to individuality.

Notes

1. The material included here derives from fieldwork carried out between 2003 and 2005 for my Ph.D.
2. In San the ethnic label 'Marka', or 'Markadialan', refers to those of the town's population who consider themselves its indigenous inhabitants but nevertheless are of diverse ethnic origins (Kamian 1959). My Markadialan informants are less concerned with origins than with asserting an urban, Muslim and trading identity that distinguish them from the surrounding rural, often Bamana, farming population.
3. While the Bamana term for neighbour (*siginyògòn*) denotes people occupying an adjoining or nearby house or dwelling, the notion of neighbourliness (*siginyògònya*) designates the bonds of reciprocity that people develop with the neighbours and others in their social vicinity.
4. 'Mande' is a broadly inclusive term for labelling peoples, languages and cultures with common origins in the Mali empire of the thirteenth and fourteenth centuries in the Western Sudan.

References

Adams, G. and Dzokoto, V. A. (2003), 'Self and Identity in African Studies', *Self and Identity,* 2: 345–59.

Bird, C. S and Kendall, M. B. (1980), 'The Mande Hero: Text and Context', in I. Karp and C. S. Bird (eds), *Explorations in African Systems of Thought,* Washington, DC: Smithsonian Institution Press, 13–24.

Brett-Smith, S. (1982a), 'Iron Skin: The Symbolism of Bamana Mud Cloth', PhD thesis, Yale University, New Haven, CT.

Brett-Smith, S. (1982b), 'Symbolic Blood: Cloth for Excised Women', *RES,* 3: 15–31.

Brett-Smith, S. (1984), 'Speech Made Visible: The Irregular as a System of Meaning', *Empirical Studies of the Arts,* 2(2): 127–47.

Brett-Smith, S. (n.d.), 'A Language of Power: Bamana Mud Cloths', unpublished manuscript.

Carrithers, M., Collins, S. and Lukes, S. (eds) (1985), *The Category of the Person: Anthropology, Philosophy, History,* Cambridge: Cambridge University Press.

Duponchel, P. (1995), 'Bogolan: From Symbolic Material to National Emblem', in J. Picton (ed.), *The Art of African Textiles: Technology, Tradition and Lurex,* London: Barbican Art Gallery, 36–39.

Duponchel, P. (2004), *Collection du Mali: Textiles Bogolan,* Neuchâtel: Musée d'Ethnographie, Neuchâtel.

Fortes, M. (1949), *The Web of Kinship among the Tallensi,* London: Oxford University Press.

Gell, A. (1998), *Art and Agency: An Anthropological Theory*, Oxford: Clarendon Press.

Grosz-Ngaté, M. (1989), 'Hidden Meanings: Explorations into a Bamanan Construction of Gender', *Ethnology*, 28(2): 167–83.

Ingold, T. (2000), *The Perception of the Environment: Essays in Livelihood, Dwelling and Skill*, London: Routledge.

Ingold, T. and Hallam, E. (2007), 'Creativity and Cultural Improvisation: An Introduction', in E. Hallam and T. Ingold (eds), *Creativity and Cultural Improvisation*, Oxford: Berg, 1–24.

Jackson, M. (1982), *Allegories of the Wilderness*, Bloomington: Indiana University Press.

Kamian, B. (1959), 'Une ville de la République du Soudan: San', *Les Cahiers d'Outre-Mer*, 47(Juillet–Septembre): 225–50.

Kondo, D. K. (1990), *Crafting Selves: Power, Gender, and Discourses of Identity in a Japanese Workplace*, Chicago: University of Chicago Press.

Krauss, R. E. (1986), *The Originality of the Avant-Garde and Other Modernist Myths*, Cambridge, MA: The MIT Press.

Küchler, S. (2005), 'The Modality of Time-Maps: Quilting in the Pacific from Another Point of View', *RES*, 47: 179–90.

Malinowski, B. (1922), *Argonauts of the Western Pacific: An Account of Native Enterprise and Adventure in the Archipelagos of Melanesian New Guinea*, London: Routledge.

Mann, G. (2006), *Native Sons: West African Veterans and France in the Twentieth Century*, Durham, NC: Duke University Press.

Miers, S. and Kopytoff, I. (eds) (1977), *Slavery in Africa: Historical and Anthropological Perspectives*, Madison: University of Wisconsin Press.

Olesen, B. B. (2007), 'Crafting Selves, Circulating Images: Engagement, Transformation and Relationality in Malian *Bògòlan* Cloth', PhD thesis, Aarhus University, Aarhus.

Piot, C. (1999), *Remotely Global: Village Modernity in West Africa*, Chicago: University of Chicago Press.

Rovine, V. L. (2001), *Bogolan: Shaping Culture through Cloth in Contemporary Mali*, Washington, DC: Smithsonian Institution Press.

Shaw, R. (2000), '"Tok Af, Lef Af": A Political Economy of Temne Techniques of Secrecy and Self', in I. Karp and D. A. Masolo (eds), *African Philosophy as Cultural Inquiry*, Bloomington: Indiana University Press, 25–49.

Stafford, B. M. (2007), *Echo Objects: The Cognitive Works of Images*, Chicago: University of Chicago Press.

Tempels, P. (1959), *Bantu Philosophy*, Paris: Présence Africaine.

Washburn, D. (1999), 'Perceptual Anthropology: The Cultural Salience of Symmetry', *American Anthropologist*, 101(3): 547–62.

–4–

Building and Ordering Transnationalism: The 'Greek House' in Albania as a Material Process

Dimitris Dalakoglou

This chapter addresses two major themes: migration from Albania to Greece and the ordering capacities of material culture in the transnational[1] practices of Albanian migrants. It examines a house built in Albania by an Albanian migrant who resides permanently in Greece. This house belongs to Fatos[2] who calls it 'a Greek house'.[3] Despite the semantic and material contradictions embedded in it, Fatos's house in Albania and its construction brings the totality of his contradictory, fluid and sometimes paradoxical migratory everyday life into a unique and sensible system of reference. The ordering of this fluid everydayness through these houses explains in part why so many Albanian migrants build dwellings in Albania even though they do not reside in the country or have any intention to return there permanently.

Space–Culture Isomorphism

Until recently, most anthropologists classified cultures and their socio-cultural formations (e.g. artefacts, kinship systems or *habiti*) according to statically perceived spaces.[4] This static and universal type of space was named 'isotropic' and 'infinite space' by Lefebvre (1991: 1–9) and 'neutral space'[5] by Tilley (1994: 7–11).[6] Gupta and Ferguson (1992) have termed this close deterministic association between static spaces and cultural formations 'space–culture isomorphism'. The legacy of space–culture isomorphism implies a theoretical problem for anthropology until today. During the 1990s Gupta and Ferguson (1992: 14) explained: 'The problem for anthropologists is to use our encounter with "them", "there" to construct a "critique of our own society", here'. But a further puzzle was added: what happens when 'they' are not 'there' anymore, but 'here'? Or if they are both 'here' and 'there'? What happens when the anthropological subject migrates? The space–culture isomorphism of the past suggested that members of a group have common characteristics and behaviours due to their origin or residence (or other associations) in a static place.

So, according to an 'old-style' reading of space–culture isomorphism, a *Kabyle* builds a *Kabyle* house (Bourdieu 1973); an Albanian normally builds an 'Albanian house' and a Greek a 'Greek house'. According to several authors (e.g. Urry 2007), however, we are today in an era of extended spatial mobility where increasing numbers of people have multiple and mixed spatial–cultural references, causing spatial–cultural paradoxes.

An example of these paradoxes is Fatos's house in Northern Albania, which Fatos occasionally calls 'a Greek house'; this house expresses a dynamic relationship between the two sites. Part of the same contradictory picture is the extensive number of houses which are constructed in Greece but by Albanians, as construction is the main form of employment for Albanian migrants in the country,[7] including Fatos. While the phenomenon of the multiple and mixed spatial–cultural references of Albanian migrants in Greece is more complex than the way it has been presented above, this text aims to illuminate some of these complexities in the case of home and house-building process.

This becomes the point of entry for a material culture analysis. Focusing not only on the person but also on one of the key components of their material culture—the house and domestic aesthetics—allows us to go beyond a dualism of 'Greek' versus 'Albanian', the individual against the collective or the single location against mobility. In the process, we can hope to achieve a more nuanced sense of the relationships between these elements. This chapter views the house as the main instrument with which, in practice, Albanian migrants resolve the tensions implied by these dualisms (regardless of whether these dualisms are fictional or pragmatic). In celebrated examples, such as the Kabyle (Bourdieu 1973: 98–110, 1977) or even Gell's (1998: 251–8) Maori meeting house, the house is perceived as the very basis of our sense of spatial immobility. Carsten and Hugh-Jones (1995: 37) put it explicitly: 'the buildings are portrayed as relatively fixed and permanent.' The case presented here is somewhat different: it follows a perception of the house as a material process, an idea that was suggested by several authors (e.g. Carsten and Hugh-Jones 1995; Buchli 1999; Miller 2001). In the case of the current chapter, it is the house as process that symbolizes, facilitates and incorporates mobility but also a type of fixity. The individual; the family and larger community; the migratory experience in both the destination and the place of origin and the maintenance of transnational networks between the two all find a material articulation within this house. When it is seen as a process the house of Fatos in Albania becomes an ordered and ordering articulation of a spatially mobile and multi-sited migratory life.

Migration to Greece

Fatos was born in a small Christian Catholic village near Shkodër (Northern Albania), thirty-seven years ago. Although his family's immobile property was confiscated in the 1940s, they kept their pre-socialist stone-built[8] house where he grew up.

Eventually, in 1990, when the borders with Greece opened, he went there on foot. Poor, exhausted and with no papers (not even a passport), yet still optimistic, he initially accepted any job offered to him for very little money.[9] After travelling around Greece and experiencing the aggression of Greek police, he ended up on the periphery of Athens where he worked as a builder, eventually starting his own construction firm a few years later.

Before leaving Albania, he married Adelina, a girl from his village, who was pregnant when he left. A few years later when, after much delay, the Greek government finally established a migration policy, he was able to legalize his existence there. Consequently, his professional life became more stable and in due course he arranged the necessary documentation for his wife and daughter to join him. In Greece they had one more child, a son, and today they live permanently in one of the southern suburbs of Athens. In Greece, Adelina works as a cleaning lady, sometimes in the houses that her husband has built. Their children are at school. The entire family visits the village in Northern Albania three times a year on average, but Fatos returns more frequently for building work on their house.

The Table

For many years, the family has been renting an apartment in Greece that Fatos renovated himself. He agreed with the owner of the building that he himself would refurbish it in exchange for a reduced rent. The layout of the building does not differ much from most other lower-middle-class homes in the area. Their first- (and top-) floor apartment comprises two sitting-rooms, two bedrooms, a kitchen, a bathroom, a storage room, balconies along a backyard and a garage. The ground floor is a shop, used by the Greek owner of the building. Fatos and Adelina's apartment already had some decoration and furniture, which the couple then supplemented. Out of all the decoration in the apartment, this discussion will focus on a coffee-table. In the room Adelina calls the 'everyday sitting-room' (in contrast to the 'good sitting-room'[10] which is used when they have visitors), there are sofas, armchairs, a television and a short coffee-table (Figure 4.1). This table is identical to one they have in their home in Albania (Figure 4.2).

This house, in Albania, which they own and is built partly with his own personal labour, is, as he calls it, 'a Greek house', while Adelina talked about 'Greek aesthetics'[11] in reference to it. It has been under unceasing construction for the last ten years: it is three stories high, but at present only the ground floor is finished, and while the other two floors have a solid framework with plumbing and electricity it so far constitutes a small apartment within what will become a bigger house. This smaller, completed section of the building has a similar layout to the apartment in Athens and the great majority (if not all) of the decorative elements, from the kitchen furniture and appliances to the floor tiles and the paint on the walls, have been brought from Greece by Fatos over the previous eleven years.

54 • *Anthropology and the Individual*

Figure 4.1 The coffee-table in the home in Athens.

Figure 4.2 An identical table as *sofra* in the home in Albania.

Among these items from Greece is the low table, identical to the one the family has in their apartment in Greece. In the house in Albania the coffee-table is not located in front of sofas, like its 'twin' in the Athens apartment. Instead, it is located in one corner of the sitting-room, where there is a low-built bench (35cm high) covered with cushions purchased in Greece and wrapped in "traditional" Albanian woollen covers (Figures 4.1 and 4.2). This is a reproduction of the traditional *sofra*, found not only in the Balkans but also in places such as Anatolia, the Middle East and North Africa. Usually the *sofra* is a round low table, which was typically found in much of rural Albania until the 1970s and was used by people squatting or sitting on cushions, low benches or short-legged chairs. In urban areas, even before socialism, the *sofra* was gradually being replaced by tall tables. The *sofra,* according to Fatos and Adelina respectively, is an 'Albanian thing'[12] and a 'traditional Albanian table'.[13]

This 'Albanian thing' appears to be the most mobile piece of furniture in their home. The table is regularly moved from the corner where the low benches stand to the other corner of the room, and is thus transformed into a coffee-table in front of the sofa, as is its twin table in their home in Greece (Figure 4.3). Adelina, when in Albania, does this habitually, and even when Fatos is there without her he is compelled to move the table, sometimes under her instruction via telephone depending on the occasion. A similar process takes place in relation to the cushions, bought from a well-known domestic soft furnishings chain in Greece but covered in Albania with woollen pillowcases. Ultimately, the entire domestic space *itself* is like this little

Figure 4.3 The table moved in front of the sofa where we are sitting. In the background is the corner where it is used with the *sofra* layout. The picture also shows Fatos's parents.

56 • *Anthropology and the Individual*

table which is frequently moved from its position next to the low benches, then to the sofa, and then back again, depending on the particular aesthetic result the household members prefer. Sometimes it has an 'Albanian' layout, at some other times a 'Greek' one; however, it dynamically incorporates the experiences of the couple in both Albania and Greece. There is also a direct link with the very materiality of their house. Its gradual and fragmented construction on the one hand means that the couple do not hold the necessary capital to complete the house at once, yet on the other hand this gradual and constant building develops in parallel to what happens in their everyday life in Greece. For example, the more they earn in Greece at certain times, the more they spend on their house, and vice versa.

Materials, Techniques, Walls and Technicians

This house is created according to developments in Greece but also has direct links with the migratory destination: its administrators and actual constructors live there while the money and the building materials flow from Greece. In fact, the entire house is gradually flowing in from Greece, part by part. Occasionally, Fatos travels with the materials and not the materials with Fatos, as he often argues that there are times he goes to Albania only in order to carry some of them.

Over the last ten years, he has organized more than ten large-scale expeditions to transport materials,[14] renting trucks along with his own professional vehicle, which he fills with tons of materials before driving them to Albania. At the same time, he always brings something 'for the house' (i.e. construction materials or furniture and decorations) along with gifts for his people when he travels there for holidays. As a building contractor, he is able to buy the materials at a good price. The transportation incurs additional costs despite the better prices for materials, because the trip between his village and the suburbs of Athens takes more than ten hours by car, but Fatos dismisses this cost. When the issue of transportation costs came up, Fatos claimed that another reason he prefers materials from Greece is because he has greater faith in the Greek market, arguing that in the recent past it has been difficult to find the proper 'good materials' in Albania.

However, there is a pattern here reminiscent of the Greek cushions covered with Albanian woollen cases. Although most of the materials came from Greece, one material important for the appearance of the house comes from Albania—the stone on the surface of the external walls of the house. Today, the ground floor's external walls are covered with stones (Figure 4.4.), and in the future Fatos plans to cover the entire house in stone. These stones are the result of the extensive excavation of the hill where the house is located. They are used both in the surfacing of the house walls and also in the large enclosure. Although this house is being built with materials coming from Greece, it is covered with 'Albanian' stone, yet at the same time the same 'Albanian' stone is used for the enclosure wall which distinguishes it from its

Building and Ordering Transnationalism • 57

Figure 4.4 The '*Greek house*' in Albania. The foreground shows the vegetable garden and a corner of the swimming pool. The background shows the surrounding fence and wall.

Albanian surroundings. This repeats the scheme of the table aesthetics: this house may be given a clear-cut characterization as 'Greek' but it combines both Greek and Albanian elements, occasionally in a contradictory pattern.

Besides the 'Greek' materials, there are also the 'Greek' techniques used in Fatos's house. Fatos was not a builder in Albania; he learned the craft in Greece from a Greek '*mastoras*',[15] named Kostas. Generally, in Greece, formal training in the construction sector is very limited. The majority of builders learn the craft from someone who has been in the profession longer. Later, Fatos taught the craft to his brother and his Albanian best man, and today they co-own a small building firm in Greece. Occasionally, other men from his village work under Fatos's supervision in Greece when he runs larger projects. Fatos's small business is successful, partly because he has competitive prices but mostly due to his good reputation. He is aware of his reputation and he explains that his own house is 'Greek' because he has a superior knowledge of the construction techniques used in the neighbouring country. He accomplishes further 'technical' links between Greece and his house. He often relates particular decorative or technical features of his house to projects he has built in Greece. For instance, the interior walls of the ground-floor apartment are painted with a technique which he calls '*technotropia*'.[16] He presented to me the *technotropia* he applied on the walls of his house by referring to a lawyer's house on the island of Paros and a pharmacy in Omonoia Square in the centre of Athens where he had also applied it.

Fatos even visualizes the technical link between Greece and his house in Albania. In his car, he carries a photo album of his buildings, which in Greece he uses for displaying his projects to his clients. However, when he travels to Albania the album also travels in the car; he has displayed his '*technotropia*' and other techniques to me and to relatives but also to his Albanian colleagues, whom he appoints to complete numerous projects in his house. Fatos has one main group of builders he chooses to complete parts of his house: these are returnees who have previously worked for him in Greece. He usually supervises them from a distance, for example he often pays them some extra money in order to send him SMS photo messages of the various projects and he calls them to remind them about details.

The materials he uses in his house are produced in or imported via Greece. Remarkably, Fatos ignores the distance between Athens and his Albanian village when he carries the materials. Arguably, this neglect bridges the distance between Athens and his village, attributing proximity between the two sites. At a metaphorical level, this neglect of distance makes his house look like it is located in Greece. However, he covers his house with Albanian stone, the same stone used in order to distinguish his house from its Albanian surroundings.

Moreover, the 'Greek' techniques he refers to are not exactly located in Greece. Probably the techniques themselves have continuity and carry agency, yet this agency has mixed 'national' character because it is closely linked with the human agency. Although earlier versions of the various building techniques were initially taught to Albanian builders by Greek master-builders in the early 1990s, in Greece today the techniques' contemporary versions are usually applied by both Greek and Albanians, because construction is the main employment of Albanians in Greece. In some regions of the country, the majority of builders are from Albania. Although Fatos follows what he considers the more proper 'Greek' techniques, such as the '*technotropia*', these techniques are in fact shared practices because they are applied in both countries, by technicians of Albanian origin. In other words, it is not only the materials which flow from Greece to Albania. It is also the analogous techniques and knowledge, even though these cannot have a clear-cut nationality. Probably the most characteristic example of this phenomenon is linguistic. All the building terminology Fatos's team uses while at work is in Greek, although there are Albanian terms for some of the same items or practices; however, the rest of the discussion which involves these Greek terms is conducted in Albanian.

Landscape and Infrastructure

Fatos appears to want to give the house a type of autonomy from its physical surroundings, yet at other times uses the same spatial detachment practices to 'relocate' it back to its physical surroundings in Albania. The house is located on a hill, next to the home of his parents, where he grew up. This hill is part of the land which used to belong to his kinship group (*fis*) before 1945. When he first proposed building his house in the 1990s, this hill was very steep and heavily wooded, and everyone in his *fis* tried to discourage him from building on it. Despite their misgivings, he insisted and eventually managed to build it on the hill. The area now occupied by the house had always been a wooded hill on the periphery of the village and at first it was impossible for a bulldozer to reach it. Making it fit for a home required extensive manual work, i.e. digging and deforestation; in fact, Fatos made this place from scratch. He likes to emphasize that he created this house and land completely by himself, as he has everything else in his life, such as migrating to Greece, arranging the papers for his wife to join him, setting up the construction business and so on.

Fatos also likes to highlight the difference between his home and plot in comparison to its environment, which he does both verbally and in practice. Spatially, for instance, he has his house on a hill encircled by a high stone wall or wire netting, sometimes with trees planted parallel to it. He has extended the municipal road into his own plot and, although the municipal part is unsurfaced, he had his road section paved with cement and gravel. As one experiences the passage from the rocky ride on the unsurfaced and often muddy drive through the village towards his house, to the smooth feel of a cement-covered road heralded by a gated and fenced area surrounded with high trees, the difference is striking. Furthermore, the building is not connected to the public running water system: it has its own independent water reservoir, and no telephone land-line.[17] Nor is it connected to the public electricity network like the rest of the village; instead, it has its own petrol-fuelled electric generator. Due to its location 'above the village',[18] when the area has one of its regular black-outs and Fatos is there, he likes to turn on the powerful spotlights in the yard; during these black-outs, his father calls the house 'the island'.

Nevertheless, there is a contradiction embedded in these practices. When there is a black-out, the generator and the house's position on the hill makes it the only visible house in the village, thus transforming it from its spatial and physical isolation to a central position in signifying its spatial surroundings. However, as it is the only house with electricity, this again implies a type of detachment. The same applies for the road, because although the surface is different, it is still an extension of the vehicular network of the village where he was raised. Moreover, although his plot is surrounded by a wall and a fence, it is located on a high hill on a plateau 'above the village' and therefore its physical isolation visually dominates the landscape of the entire settlement.

This simultaneous and interchangeable detachment and relocation of Fatos's house in its physical surroundings also has a historical dimension. Although this is a 'Greek house', it is very closely linked with the history of Fatos's family, and with the history of this plot in Northern Albania. This hill is part of a large expanse of land owned by Fatos's *fis* before the war, after which the socialist regime confiscated it. Fatos's house affirms the social prestige of the entire kinship group through reclaiming their private immobile property and consequently his personal prestige as the most powerful man of his cohort. Today, the *fis* of Fatos is not taking any possible type of legal action to reclaim their title to this land formally. Instead, they base their claim on the customary respect for immobile property in Northern Albania,[19] as Fatos explained in 2006: 'We do not have to, everyone knows that it belongs to us. Hoxha[20] took it [the land] for forty years, but it belongs to us for a thousand years, nobody can claim it since we are here'. Indeed, the 'here' in this statement means the 'Greek house', as Fatos himself is in Greece most of the time.

Building and Ordering Transnationalism

People often use language derived from conventional static spatialities, for example terms inspired by the concept of the nation-state such as 'Greek' and 'Albanian', and consequently the ethnographer must also use them, although we are all aware of the potential paradox when these are employed within an increasingly mobile and transnational world. Fatos, for as long as he continues to work on his home in Albania, will add features which he presents as 'Greek'. In 2007 for example he planted olive trees in his garden for future olive oil production and vines have been growing around the fence of the plot for the last two years. He plans to buy a barrel to begin producing *retsina*[21] (a type of Greek wine). He recently added a sizeable swimming pool in the yard, which is a popular architectural element in the seaside southern suburbs of Athens. Yet, next to the swimming pool, one finds something not seen in the Greek seaside suburbs' bourgeois houses: a small vegetable garden cared for by his father, which Fatos finds amusing (Figure 4.5). Emphasizing the aesthetic irony of this co-existence, he said to me once, laughing: 'An Albanian vegetable garden next to a Greek swimming pool […] at least the garden contains some seeds and plants which are brought from Greece'. In a recent telephone discussion, Fatos spoke about his house in Albania and said jokingly: 'It has become a piece of Europe in Albania; I may rent one of the floors to an International Organization.'[22] The space-culture associations of his house have been upgraded from simply '*Greek*' into '*European*', and perhaps in the future will become even more '*Western,*' like the café '*Americano*' I saw in Tiranë. Despite the vast amount of resources and energy put into this house, none of the family currently intends to return to Albania permanently, especially not the children. Therefore this dwelling is not built for the purpose of settling down, or at least not in the near future.

In the 1990s, many Albanians migrated to Greece, as well as to other countries in smaller numbers. In 2005, the number of Albanian migrants in Greece and Italy was estimated at a total 800,000 (Barjaba and King 2005: 13–15). Amongst their first priorities, after accumulating some cash from their work abroad, was to build or refurbish their homes in Albania. For instance, in a biographical survey of Albanian

Figure 4.5 The swimming pool and the vegetable garden. In the background is the village on the plateau.

migrants in Greece (Nitsiakos 2003), the great majority of interviewees refer to their goal of building a house in Albania (e.g. 2003: 131, 169, 195, 219, 255–6, 277). Other qualitative surveys on Albanian migrants such as de Soto et al. (2002) and King and Vullnetari (2003: 49) emphasize this relationship between the house and migration.

The association between new houses and migration is epitomized by these newly built dwellings, which remain uninhabited for most of the calendar year, like the house of Fatos and Adelina. In this sense, there are two categories of migratory dwellings: those which are not lived in most of the time and those in which only one or a few members of the original household group reside. The southern prefecture of Gjirokastër is typical of most Albanian prefectures today. In quantitative terms, the census of 2001 (INSTAT 2004: 12) reported a total of 34,268 dwellings in Gjirokastër, but 7,528 of them are referred to as 'uninhabited'.[23]

Why should Albanian migrants build houses in Albania when they do not live, or even expect to live, there? It is, I argue, because these houses combine multiple, diverse and contradictory elements—which are present in their migratory everydayness—in one single tangible material entity that makes sense to them and makes all this dynamic, multi-sited and multi-cultural everydayness a logical system of reference for the individuals involved. Fatos's house is an example of these ordering capabilities of multiple and even conflicting elements. Fatos builds a house physically located in Albania, but he calls it 'Greek'. When we approach his house as a material process, we see that he builds it with the very same materials he uses for the houses he constructs in Greece; he even carries these materials from Greece, journeys which often amount to dramatic expeditions that scorn the distances involved. But he wraps this house up in an 'Albanian' stone surface, a material which is also used to build the fence that distinguishes his plot very visibly from its Albanian surroundings. He builds his 'Greek house' using the same techniques that he applies to his professional building projects in Greece, but in both cases the actual builders are Albanians. Greek decorations adorn his house in Albania, but occasionally the same decoration is joined with Albanian elements creating a hybrid layout. He locates his house on the top of a hill, isolated from the rest of the settlement, but in doing so he is using this 'Greek house' to reclaim his family plot in Albania. He has his house disconnected from all utility networks, but this disconnection is exactly what relocates it occasionally in its Albanian environment.

What can appear as a paradox or irony to someone else actually reflects the everyday lives of Fatos and Adelina, pivoted somewhere between Greece and Albania. This mobility and flexibility of the house and its material culture reveals the way individuals take their sense of order from diverse sources and create for themselves a hybridized pattern of life, which makes sense for them given the objective dislocations to which they are increasingly subject. They may not live in this house, but they are building an aesthetic, a cosmological order by which they can live. This house may be a source of semantic and material contradictions, but at the same time is an element of comfort, it is the main point of reference for the everydayness of Fatos and Adelina. It is where they like to spend their savings, time (in Greece) and energy. However, while they reside in Greece they have this house as a point of reference for their practices, but obviously they are not physically located in Albania, and yet the construction process as such makes perfect sense to them, perhaps because the house as such is a 'Greek house'. This house incorporates more or less everything going on in their lives in Greece and wraps it into an Albanian cover which internally reproduces a Greek-based 'technotrope' but one performed by Albanians, combining elements of a single-sited past and a multi-sited present.

Notes

This chapter is based on my PhD research (Dalakoglou 2009); my fieldwork in Albania took place between August 2005 and September 2006 and I would like to thank my informants for their help, although for reasons of anonymity I cannot name them. For this chapter, thanks are due to Victor Buchli, Daniel Miller, Caroline Humphrey, Dimitra Gefou-Madianou, Eliana Lili, Antonis Vradis, Rigels Halili, Fereniki Vatavali, Bodil Birkebæk Olesen, Ivana Bajić, Catherine Baker, Liz Abraham, Vicky

Beresford and Chris Simotas for their help and their comments on earlier versions of this text; any errors in this chapter are my responsibility. My doctorate received financial support from the Hellenic State's Scholarships Foundation (programme for post-graduate studies in social anthropology). I would also like to thank the Marie Curie European Doctorate Programme for the Social History of Europe and the Mediterranean for additional financial assistance.

1. Albanians living in Greece represent a distinctive case of transnationalism (see Mai and Schwandner-Sievers 2003; King, Mai and Schwandner-Sievers 2005). The term 'transnationalism' has usually referred to other diaspora communities and their links with the country of their origin, for example the Hindu diaspora living in South America or the United Kingdom, West Indians living in the United Kingdom and the United States or African diasporas and Mediterranean migrants living in Western Europe. For an overview of anthropological works on transnationalism, see Schiller et al. (1992); Kearney (1995); Marcus (1995); Mahler (1998); Vertovec (1999); Bryceson and Vuorela (2002); Eriksen (2003). The main distinction between all these aforementioned transnationalisms and the case of Albanians in Greece is the geographic proximity between the migratory destination and the place of origin, combined with what one could call 'cultural proximity'—that is the fact that the territories which are today known as Albania and northern Greece were both part of the Ottoman Empire until 1913 and that, in fact, a common Albanian–Greek border only strictly materialized after 1944.
2. All names in this chapter have been changed.
3. '*Shtëpi Greke*'. One should bear in mind that the Albanian language does not distinguish between 'home' and 'house'; the word '*shtëpi*' is used for both terms. There is also the more formal term '*banesë*' which means dwelling. Since the interviews were carried out in both Albanian and Greek, one should also note that the situation is similar with the Greek language, where the term *'spiti'* also stands for both home and house (my transliteration of the Greek alphabet follows Green 2005).
4. One of the most typical examples is the *habitus* theory of Pierre Bourdieu, where the Kabyle habitus, for instance, is located statically in Algeria and the distinctive *habiti* of French society are, of course, located in France. The *habiti* of both Kabyle and French society were presented in association with static isomorphic places–cultures. The increase in mobility has made this model less realistic today, yet one cannot be sure that it was realistic even when Bourdieu studied the Kabyle. In Bourdieu's photograph album from his Algerian fieldwork (2004), one can see that part of his research actually took place in settlements of prefabricated houses, along the national road. One wonders whether the roads visible in the background of the photos may have played a rather greater role in Kabyle aesthetics than can be gleaned from Bourdieu's analysis. This question could be supported also by the celebrated question of Carsten and Hugh-Jones (1995:

40) who challenged the notion of inside/outside suggesting the introduction of movement as an extra dimension of Bourdieu's scheme.
5. This division of humanity based on particular territories owes much to the German Romantic philosophy of the nineteenth century, which inspired the foundation of nation-states and the ill-founded separation in space of ethnic groups. In this sense, it is no coincidence that the German-trained Franz Boas became a pioneer in establishing anthropological subjects and their cultures according to the space they occupied. In 1910, for example Boas created his first systematic study of what he called 'culture areas' by mapping the North American Indians, dividing them into seven culture areas and directly linking clear-cut bounded spaces with respective cultures (Stocking 1974: 257–67). It was Boas who criticized the layout of the ethnographical collection of the American National Museum (1887a,b). He suggested that what was then the innovative layout of ethnographic collections into a 'room per culture' should replace the prevailing layout at the time, 'room per artefact' (evolutionarily classified from the most primitive to the most advanced).
6. In fact, the problem with the prevailing perception of space at that time was that it was understood as mathematical, objective and fixed. The critique by Lefebvre and Tilley argued that space was not objective or solely physically defined; rather, space was subjective and always depended on the socio-cultural framework in which it was embedded.
7. The International Organization for Migration (Chindea et al. 2007: 15; de Zwager et al. 2005: 16) has estimated that the highest percentage (49%) of male Albanian migrants in Greece are active in building and construction. Lamprianidis and Hatziprokopiou (2005: 104) found that the highest percentage (36%) of male Albanian migrants who returned permanently to Albania had been working in building and construction whilst living in Greece. One should also add to these figures people who are active in the construction sector but are included in the self-employed or professional categories. Fatos, the main informant of this paper (who is technically self-employed, yet in the construction sector), is a typical example. An earlier survey of Albanian migrants of Thessaloniki by Lamprianidis and Lymperaki (2001) found that construction and building employed the highest percentage of the male Albanian migrants of that city.
8. Stone was the most typical material used for building houses in rural areas before World War II. Cement and bricks emerged as popular materials during the socialist period while those material industries in Albania flourished. In postsocialism, buildings are constructed almost exclusively with cement and bricks, but today these materials are mostly imported because the productivity of the contemporary Albanian industry is limited.
9. This was—and frequently still is—the usual situation of many Albanian migrants in Greece. The Greek state's migration laws gave migrants without documents very limited chances of obtaining permission to stay: therefore, during the 1990s

most Albanian migrants became a very inexpensive labour force for Greece, especially in rural areas. In fact, the Greek state not only prevented migrants legalizing their residence in the country, but state authorities (e.g. the Greek Police) had a leading role in construction of negative representations about Albanian migrants. A dimension of these processes was reported ethnographically by Lawrence (2007) in the case of Argolida area of south mainland Greece.

10. The interview was conducted in both Greek and Albanian, yet at that point she used the Greek terms '*kathimerino kathistiko*' and '*kalo kathistiko*'.
11. '*Estetika Greke*'.
12. '*Gjë Shqiptare*'.
13. '*Tavolinë tradicionale Shqiptare*'. During my fieldwork, I researched what happened to the *sofra* during the projects of socialist modernization. It seems that, in most of the villages, the old *sofra* was moved out of the sitting room into rooms not frequented for public activity, such as the kitchen, the storage room or even the yard. In other instances, I learnt from some of my informants that their living-room modernization was achieved partly by transforming the low *sofra* into a tall-legged table. The *sofra* continues to be used in Fatos's parents' home, and was the only table in their home until the mid-1980s, when they got a tall-legged table.
14. Almost everything needed to build a house—from cement, bricks, iron rods, tiles, paint and tools to doors and windows and sanitary ware—came from Greece.
15. In Greek, '*mastoras*' refers to the master builder. The *mastoras* organizes and accomplishes the most advanced parts of the building process and he supervises and teaches newcomers to the profession, who initially enter the hierarchy as his 'assistants' (*voithos/oi*). '*Mastores*' are usually divided according to their expertise, e.g. '*betatzis*' (an expert in cement concretes) or '*petras*' (an expert in laying stones).
16. The term '*technotropia*' is generally used in Greece by wall painters. Sometimes it refers to the same technique Fatos displayed, a heterogeneously coloured surface which results from spreading colour on the wall using gloved hands or a rough brush. However, the term also refers generally to other techniques of colouring walls which do not produce the homogenous smooth surface achieved with the typical paintbrush and roll technique.
17. This is not rare in rural Albania, since people occasionally went from having no telephone at all to using cell phones during the 1990s. However, it has significance here within this framework of general physical disconnection.
18. '*mbi fshat*'.
19. The power of customary law and land notions in pre–WWII Albania is well reported by the two major pre-war ethnographers of the Albanian North, Margaret Hasluck (1954) and Mary Durham (1979, 1985).
20. Enver Hoxha was the leading figure of the Albanian Communist Party (which later was renamed Party of Labour of Albania); occasionally Albanians when

they refer to the socialist period, they use terms such as the age of Communism or the age of Enver.
21. For more details on the anthropological examination of *retsina,* see Gefou-Madianou (1992).
22. '*Po ndërtohet një copëz Europe në Shqipëri; Mund tia jap me qera një nga katet një Organizate Ndërkombëtare*'.
23. In fact, it can be claimed that the number of uninhabited dwellings in 2001 was much higher. This irregularity can be explained by most of the buildings being under slow construction in Albania. Most of the time, the 'making' of houses is perpetual. Even when the houses are being built relatively quickly, they still have semi-completed sections or additional rooms or floors can be attached. In such circumstances, some of these 'houses' have a few rooms built, while the rest of the building is under construction for up to a decade or longer. Often, these two or three so-called closed rooms (meaning that they have been completed, with doors and windows) are on the ground floor of a two- or three-storey building. Thus, although these 'closed rooms' can be a completed small house within a potentially bigger house, they are not being reported as dwellings in the census. Furthermore, the census is a quantitative research tool which can miss qualitative aspects: for example the census reports a house as 'inhabited' when only one member of the original household group lives there while the rest are abroad. Therefore, in a town of approximately 34,000 houses, at least 7,500 of them are uninhabited but are being continuously refurbished. Here one should add that many commercially built apartments remain empty because there is not an analogous demand for them. This limited demand for flats and apartments built by construction firms is due, first, to Albanians' extended preference for building their own house themselves (for reasons which will be analyzed below) and, second, because some firms, encouraged by the 'building fever' for accommodation, invested in blocks of flats, but did so in vain because they failed to discern the private nature of this construction boom and its character of personal projects. Moreover, some accommodation is empty because certain buildings have been used for money laundering so that nobody cares how these properties are used as long as they are built.

References

Barjaba, K. and King, R. (2005), 'Introducing and Theorising Albanian Migration', in R. King, N. Mai and S. Schwandner-Sievers (eds), *The New Albanian Migration,* Brighton: Sussex Academic Press, 1–28.
Boas, F. (1887a), 'The Occurrence of Similar Inventions in Areas Widely Apart', *Science,* 9(224) (20 May): 485–6.

Boas, F. (1887b), 'Museums of Ethnology and Their Classification', *Science*, 9(228) (17 June): 587–9.
Bourdieu, P. (1973), 'The Kabyle House', in M. Douglas (ed.), *Rules and Meaning*, Harmondsworth: Penguin, 98–110.
Bourdieu, P. (1977), *Outline of a Theory of Practice*, Cambridge: Cambridge University Press.
Bourdieu, P. (2004), *In Algeria*, Graz: Camera Austria.
Bryceson, D. and Vuorela, U. (eds) (2002), *Transnational Families*, Oxford: Berg.
Buchli, V. (1999), *An Archaeology of Socialism*, Oxford: Berg.
Carsten, J. and Hugh-Jones, S. (1995), 'Introduction', in J. Carsten and S. Hugh-Jones (eds), *About the House*, Cambridge: Cambridge University Press, 1–46.
Chindea, A., Majkowska-Tomkin, M. and Pastor, I. (2007), *The Republic of Albania Migration Profile*, Ljubljana: IOM & Republic of Slovenia.
Dalakoglou, D. (2009), *An Anthropology of the Road: Transnationalism, Myths and Migration on the Albanian-Greek Cross-Border Motorway*, PhD thesis, University of London.
de Soto, H., Gordon, P., Gedeshi, I. and Sinoimeri, Z. (2002), *Poverty in Albania: A Qualitative Assessment*, Washington, DC: World Bank.
de Zwager, N., Gedeshi, I., Germenji, E. and Nikas, C. (2005), *Competing for Remittances*, Tirana: IOM Tirana.
Durham, M. E. (1979 [1928]), *Some Tribal Origins, Laws and Customs of the Balkans*, New York: AMS.
Durham, M. E. (1985), *High Albania*, London: Virago Press.
Eriksen, E. T. (ed.) (2003), *Globalization: Studies in Anthropology*, London: Pluto.
Gefou-Madianou, D. (1992), 'Exclusion and Unity: Retsina and Sweet Wine', in D. Gefou-Madianou (ed.), *Alcohol, Gender and Culture*, London: Routledge, 108–36.
Gell, A. (1998), *Art and Agency*, Cambridge: Cambridge University Press.
Green, S. (2005), *Notes from the Balkans*, Princeton, NJ: Princeton University Press.
Gupta, A. and Ferguson, J. (1992), 'Beyond "Culture": Space, Identity, and the Politics of Difference', *Cultural Anthropology*, 7(1): 6–23.
Hasluck, M. (1954), *The Unwritten Law in Albania*, Cambridge: Cambridge University Press.
INSTAT (2004), *Popullsia e Shqipërisë: Gjirokastër/2001*, Vol. 6, Tiranë: INSTAT.
Kearney, M. (1995), 'The Local and the Global: The Anthropology of Globalization and Transnationalism', *Annual Review of Anthropology*, 24: 547–65.
King, R., Mai, N. and Schwandner-Sievers, S. (eds) (2005), *The New Albanian Migration*, Brighton: Sussex Academic Press.
King, R. and Vullnetari, J. (2003), 'Migration and Development in Albania', DRC Working Paper C5, Development Research Centre on Migration, Globalisation and Poverty (DRC), Brighton: University of Sussex.

Lamprianidis, L. and Hatziprokopiou, P. (2005), 'The Albanian Migration Cycle', in R. King, N. Mai and S. Schwandner-Sievers (eds), *The New Albanian Migration,* Brighton: Sussex Academic Press.

Lamprianidis, L. and Lymperaki, A. (2001), *Albanian Migrants in Thessalonica,* Thessalonica: Paratiritis [in Greek].

Lawerence, C. M. (2007), *Blood and Oranges,* Oxford: Berghahn.

Lefebvre, H. (1991), *The Production of Space,* Oxford: Blackwell.

Mahler, S. (1998), 'Theoretical and Empirical Contributions: Toward a Research Agenda for Transnationalism', in M. P. Smith and L. E. Guarnizo (eds), *Transnationalism from Below,* New Brunswick, NJ: Transaction Publishers, 64–100.

Mai, N. and Schwandner-Sievers, S. (2003), 'Albanian Migration and New Transnationalism', *Journal of Ethnic and Migration Studies,* 29(6): 939–94.

Marcus, G. (1995), 'Ethnography in/of the World System: The Emergence of Multi-Sited Ethnography', *Annual Review of Anthropology,* 24: 95–117.

Miller, D. (2001), *Home Possessions,* Oxford: Berg.

Nitsiakos, V. (2003), *Testimonies of Albanian Migrants,* Athens: Odysseas [in Greek].

Schiller, N. G., Basch, L. and Blanc, C. S. (eds) (1992), *Toward a Transnational Perspective on Migration,* New York: The New York Academy of Sciences.

Stocking, G. W. (1974), *The Shaping of American Anthropology 1883–1911,* New York: Basic Books.

Tilley, C. (1994), *A Phenomenology of Landscape,* Oxford: Berg.

Urry, J. (2007), *Mobilities,* London: Polity Press.

Vertovec, S. (1999), 'Conceiving and Researching Transnationalism', *Ethnic and Racial Studies,* 22(2): 447–62.

–5–

The Christian and the Taxi Driver: Poverty and Aspiration in Rural Jamaica

Daniel Miller

Pressed: The Christian and His Mobile Phone

There are creased trousers and there are Pentecostal creased trousers. There is the way individuals living in poverty somehow appear every day with their white shirts and their neat clothes, and then there is Sunday best. At a Jamaican Sunday Pentecostal service the clothing looks too perfect to be of this world. The creases are so sharp, the starch so crisp, the effect is radiant; speaking for the aspiration to heaven rather than of earth. The signs of the saved and of the saints that bring a person closer to the state of angels. Indeed the seven- and eight-year-old children in their stunning frocks and suits and their immaculately braided hair with shining baubles seem about as angelic as human beings ever get to be in this life.

Yet one cannot separate out the creases of Pentecostalism and poverty in Damian's trousers or in any other part of his life. This neat and clean clothing exemplifies how other-worldly aspirations are constantly manifest in his world. Damian is five-foot-six or seven, with dark brown complexion, a winning smile. In his case the big ears help him look appealing rather than odd. His short hair is, of course, as neat as his clothes. Yet Damian's smile, which is pretty much a constant, has a Job-like quality, because of the way it accompanies every new misfortune. It indicates the way he turns his problems into divine tests, each thereby providing a further step towards bliss. So, too, his unfailing good manners, his courtesy, that seems so natural to him, and so contrived in others.

Whatever happens, he knows exactly what he is going to become and how he will reach that goal. Indeed he feels he is about to reach this goal anytime soon. He will be a Pentecostal Pastor just as his father is now—which is why to describe him as a seventeen-year-old is so misleading. Where I live, seventeen-year-old boys are as shapeless as my trousers. Mostly, infuriatingly relaxed, playing computer games, playing at school, playing at being this or that personality. Uncertain of who they are, or who they want to be and fluctuating from caring too much to not caring much at all. Damian was never young in that way.

Damian's father is a pastor to a few small churches built by farmers that could never provide 'a living'—this is a million miles from Trollope and Jane Austen. His mother is a market vendor. As a child Damian lived in about six different tenement buildings. His parents never wanted so many children, they just didn't have family planning. They left him and his brothers and sisters with a helper, who used to beat him regularly. Although he passed all his exams, he still had to learn to work the markets to pay for his school fees, together with a scheme he developed for re-selling sweets to other school children. He lived with an aunt and commuted thirty miles to school, but always helped her with her church duties. He insisted on being baptized (saved) before his elder siblings, since he knew he was ready. Today, quite apart from the regular Sunday prayers, Damian goes to a prayer meeting on Monday night, a bible meeting on Wednesday night and on Friday night he organizes the youth programme. Other matters were secondary. He had had a girl friend for six months but they had separated, partly from differences in their religious feelings and partly because she was unfaithful to him.

Damian genuinely believed in his own aesthetic aura, that he was a beacon of light, literally radiant. He was nominated President for the inter-school Christian fellowship group, an executive member of this youth society and a leader for that one; vice-president for peer counselling, and eventually, inevitably, head boy of the school. He had started a Christian club, a fellowship for students that mirrored the Pentecostal churches of the elders. School children would come together for prayer which started to include speaking in tongues, healing and revelation. The club was a success; attracting twenty, sometimes even forty, school children.

But then, according to Damian, one young man received a revelation from God that they should all pray for the school, because some serious thing was going to happen in the school. He said they should pray for the Principal who was in danger, which put some of the children into a panic. There follows a long story, but the upshot was that as soon as the exams were over Damian left school, with the mutual feeling between himself and the Principal that his real vocation lay elsewhere. His economic affairs were even more complex. As with many people in poverty he juggled multiple debts and multiple potential sources of income, including a rotating credit scheme, with his market work making up the shortfalls. After completing school he began helping to serve two churches and consider schemes that would allow him to develop his own flock. Even now there was no real separation of church and living. The money that he earned was often intended for the constant needs of the church, while organizing a youth event was as much an entrepreneurial as a spiritual venture.

Damian's first phone, a Panasonic, was bought in spring 2003 for J$3,000 (£30). When at school he was trying to keep monthly phone bills to J$300. Later on, with all his church responsibilities, this was creeping up sometimes to more like J$500 a week. As with most Jamaicans, even this cheap low-level cell phone is much more than just a communications device. This is his watch and his calculator. It's where he keeps his vital information, especially his diary. On his phone he can play games when he is bored, using a mouse like a navigator key, and he plays most days. It can store some 200 numbers. When we first met in 2003 he had only 65, but by the summer of 2004 this had grown to 136.

About seventy of these names are young men and women in approximately equal numbers. Many are fellow school children, especially those who formed his Christian club. Many others, especially young women, are people he met at periodic church camps. Fourteen of his contacts are people who could potentially provide music for his church activities. He also has eight relatives listed, but almost no-one that connects to him through his market activities, other than relatives. A major part of his phone address book then consists of those he works with in the church. Some are just called church sisters or brothers, but there are also pastors, youth camp leaders, and counsellors. Almost always when it comes to a younger person, the basic description he provides of them is in terms of the state of their religious relationship. So he will say 'Oh that's Peter; I witnessed to him in school' or 'That's Nadine, she is saved', 'That is Deneal; he is a backsliding man', or simply 'Kenaisha, she is a Christian.' Commonly what he remarks upon is the interaction between his Christian relationship and the potential for other kinds of relationship. So there is 'Jodie. I like her spirit in the sense of a young lady who loves God, so I took her number to call and encourage her' or Kelly: 'She had a big, big crush on me. Yes I phone her very often because I crave her vulnerability to minister Jesus Christ to her; being that she is so vulnerable to me I just use that to minister to her.' There is Dwain: 'He is very spiritual, someone I consider to have an anointing of the mind. He plays the drums.' He uses the categories feature in the phone to organize the names. There are 'friends', 'family', 'witness'—those he will call or text about Jesus Christ—and the largest group which is called 'church people' that he works with in the ministry.

Damian was quite clear on the benefits of the cell phone:

> If I am feeling down, or when I feel depressed I can call a person, and hopefully they can cheer me up or change my mood. Often people call me when they are down and I encourage them. Or I might just randomly send a text, a scripture of encouragement, to them or to my church helpers. I compose a piece of scripture. And then there is a system called user message on the phone, so you can send it to ten church brothers and church sisters at the same time. Especially on special occasions such as Christmas and New Year's Day. You could send 'May the joys of the Season fill your life with love and with righteousness.' My aunt is in the choir and sometimes they don't meet for practice, she would call her church sister and say 'what song you have in mind that we could sing for this service.'
>
> I also do counselling by phone. The other night this girl called me, and she said she just did something bad. She had sex with her boyfriend, and her grandmother came and caught her in the act. And she said she just wanted to kill herself or run away. And I

encouraged her and prayed for her and she went to bed. Then I saw her in the morning and she said she felt much better. Another time, another young lady called me and told me they are spreading rumours about her and her close friend, that she is a lesbian.[1] And she went away from her community for a period of time because of the rumours. And I encouraged her and told her not to let what people say do this to you. I always try to influence the environment in a positive way. And she felt much better and went back home. I can spend a whole card on this, and someone might call me seven times in one hour till their credit finish. So I can reach people more easily. It's a friend indeed since it's always there when I am in need.

The word of God says 'Be not confounded to this world, but be transformed by the renewing of your mind.' I think personally that many souls are going to be saved, and the phone is a medium in which we can help persons who don't know Jesus Christ, to help them find Jesus Christ by this partnership of prayer and encouragement and counselling. I think the phone is a blessing from God since this is the medium through which I can help many persons.

On the other hand Damian sees a darker side to this technology:

People's phone does go off during a service which is very disturbing. Most churches encourage members to put their phone on vibrate or turn it off. Once my pastor stood up and said that God is not pleased when we allow the phones to disturb the service, and that once you are serving God he won't allow anything bad to happen such that a person has to call you urgently. The phone can also be a route to temptation. It is capable of much evil. It can lead people to have phone relationships. They don't know the person, but they can be girl or boy friend because of the phone. They call it voice lovers, or phone lovers. They will do phone sex. One of my friends tried that. There is not much affection in it though. If the phone connects to the Internet they can download pornography. Then they would want to get a better one, a newer model that would even allow him to watch a sex movie live.

I think the phone is part of the prophecy of the Mark of the Beast. Because when I first had my phone, the phone company representative called me and started giving me information. And they can tell how much you use, when you made your last call and your text. Then they can even put a chip in it and know your whereabouts. In the Christian religion, we believe that in the last days there will be devices of the devil to stop God's people from going to heaven. They will have the mark on their forehead or on their right hand, and you won't be able to buy or sell without the mark. So I would conclude that this chip in the phone will encourage advancement in the way of the Mark of the Beast and that's how they will get to know different information about different people. I heard there is a chip called a Digi-angel that can pick up 2,000 informations on one person in about one second. Fortunately at this special time, approaching the last days, the phone can also be summoned against the works of the devil. According to Mathew 24, Mark 13 and Luke 21, in last days the enemy will be going about his work with ever more concentration and energy since he knows he has little time left. This is why God has now granted us the technology to move his work within the spiritual system. So we can spread the gospel more effectively, more quickly with the instruments that have been provided.

Overall, as the year progressed, Damian became clear that the phone is not in itself either an instrument of good or evil. It depends mainly upon the state and motivation of the user. The phone even starts to come into his preaching. He says in a sermon 'Before you run to the phone run to the throne. When something happens to some people they will call their friends and say some bad thing happened at church. They call and create mischief. But they should first run to God and talk to him first before they talk to anyone else.'

Damian does not worry that his phone will be stolen since he has 'covered it under the blood'. That is, he has prayed to God to protect his phone under the blood of Jesus against the deeds of Satan. That's why he does not feel the need to back up the numbers in the phone. In any case, he notes he could easily get back most of these numbers, because he is involved with most of these people directly, not just by phone. That is not the only way a phone can be Christianized. At first Damian was tolerant of secular ringtones, but as time went on he increasingly saw these as an abomination, not surprisingly, given the racy titles and lyrics of some Jamaican dancehall tunes that are popular as local ringtones. Fortunately there are Christian alternatives. He has several on his phone, which also has the facility to record music directly and turn these into ringtones. These include 'No matter what they say I made up my mind I am a fool for Christ', and 'My God is an awesome God; he reigns for evermore', but also, entirely without irony, 'Oh God you are the only one, that's why I am holding on so long.'

Damian never seems to stress the phone's application to his business activities. Although, observing and listening to him, this does actually seem to be quite an important part of his use of the phone. Sometimes he will ask his mother or a friend to make purchases when church business prevents him from coming to Kingston. Sometimes he returns such favours, again being alerted to the indisposition of others by the phone. But if Damian plays down the importance of the phone in this regard it is because he plays down such secular activities in general. For him, two uses in particular seem to stand out. One is the development of his actual counselling by phone and the fact that he doesn't have to take a taxi and travel to be with those who need his prayers and counselling. Damian regards himself as rather like a doctor. A patient suffering from sin needs certain, what he most often calls 'encouragements,' to be dispensed. If this can be done via the phone, so much the better. The other blessing is the use of the phone to organize meetings, especially his youth meetings. The phone, and its internal system of categories, helps him in these organizational tasks. He goes through his contacts, summoning those most relevant to the various tasks: of providing music, or merely turning up as the congregants to his meetings. He is aiming for an attendance of 120 at his next youth day. So his work is reduced down to the fine art of scrolling through this very organized phone address book. In this way the phone has become an ally in his constant struggle; a variant of that found in so many parts of the world, to maintain respectability, dignity and finally salvation, in conditions of constant struggle and poverty.

Driven: The Taxi Driver and His Van

You are hurtling down a mountainside. There is no lighting; the road is full of potholes; it is narrow, twisting, precipitous; and the van you are in is not small. The driver sitting beside you smells strongly of beer, hardly surprising, since you recently watched him consume his fifth in the last two hours. It's not as if you even enjoy those video games which throw at you a twisting road with sudden obstacles and challenge you to keep within its limits. At least with those, when disaster strikes, you only have to put your 'avatar' on the screen back to its proper position. Yet actually you are also aware of your own awe at your companion. Because while this is certainly not sensible, you have been driving long enough to realize, perhaps for the first time, just how skilled an activity this can be; that this is quite possibly the best driver you have ever known. There is no hint of hesitation, doubt or concern. There is simply a kind of magical understanding of the relationship between driver and machine. Diamond loves his vehicle, with a sometimes painful intensity. It may be reassuring to know that even if he is not overly concerned with your hide, he is desperate not to scratch its body. Having just completed a three-hour interview, during the course of this journey, you are aware that this van hasn't suffered a single scratch in the two years since he purchased it.

As for the advanced state of inebriation, this too is hardly novel. It's what this van drives on. Diamond needs alcohol just as much as the vehicle needs petrol. He simply doesn't do driving sober. This is not just the odd drink; you can't recall an evening when he wasn't pretty close to what for you would have been blind drunk before he goes off driving. This trip has had only one stop so far to refuel that van, but it has had plenty to refuel the man. In the end, I am no Hemmingway. This is still an art I would rather admire from a distance than stake my life on. I am very relieved when we get home.

The car, and by extension the taxi (with its money-making capacity), has become one of the most common foci of aspiration among young boys in rural Jamaica. A symbol of mobility, the taxi is a more affordable and attainable dream than migration or the building of a house, goals that have traditionally occupied high esteem in Jamaica. Diamond's own rise came slowly, over a decade of tedious work and dedication. Unlike today's well-groomed vehicle, Diamond's first vehicle, in which he started out as a conductor collecting fares, was a chipped blue van with a maroon hood and ripped seats which he shared with his cousin who drove the vehicle. As a 'ducta', he learned how to work out how many school kids could be crammed into the rows to compensate for their discounted fares (only $J10 compared to $J30 for full fare). He learned who had it hard and discerned who to let get by with a free ride.

And he also learned that all-important axiom: it is not the cost, but how much each person can afford to give, or have taken.

Just as his skills on the road developed so did his handling of girls and women. No longer did he content himself with lurking in the right places or communicating his attraction through awkward stares, followed by such unmemorable statements such as 'mi like yu'. In its place, he learned to hold onto a hand a little longer as a person paid her fare or entered and exited the bus. He learned to linger in the corners and out of sight and to place the good-looking girls in the front seat next to him where he could catch a glimpse of their thighs or breasts as the vehicles jerked around the corners. He gained the confidence and the luck to find his own vehicle by negotiating a deal to purchase his own taxi, a vehicle which outside of Jamaica would have constituted a four- to five-person vehicle, but could easily carry six adults in Jamaica.

Working the route from Orange Valley to Everton five to six times per week, he developed a regular clientele who asked him to carry them to and from the airport(s) as well as for special days such as outings to the beach. He also started to develop relationships with a number of girls and women who he 'checked' when he had the opportunity to pass by. Some worked in bars or were old friends or contacts from his youth. During this time, Diamond drove his car hard and learned the fastest routes across the island, the best places to stop, where the police hid, and who could be bribed. But he still was not content and could see that his taxi was not going to get him big money. No, the passenger van which could hold up to fourteen people was certainly much more lucrative and he began saving his partner's[2] money and working on his mother to help him finance a van so that he could collect his mother and all of her goods from the airport and wharves, or carry her to church rallies and other events in distant parishes. Within two years of hard work and savings, he managed to obtain the used white van with grey vinyl interior that he owns today.

As soon as Diamond collected the van, he started to feel and to believe that he had arrived. No more torn seats, dirty floors and mats, dents or missing items; this van was meticulously maintained. He kept a chamois cloth in his vehicle to clean the windows and to wipe off the steering wheel which had its own special 'bumpy' covering. He became extra careful in not spilling his beer or the corn-on-the-cob he occasionally stopped to eat when on the road with passengers. When travelling the routes, he was keen to make sure that the school kids were not marking up his vehicle with pen or that those women who chose to eat a patty or have a lunch didn't leave crumbs. He hired both a 'ducta' to recruit passengers as well as one of the men from his district to clean the car almost daily.

With skinny legs and a concave chest, Diamond never really had the brawn to command a lot of women. But his mother equipped him with Nike shirts, a Kangol hat, trainers and other elements that suggest money and 'connections'. Diamond decided to take on a common-law wife who he kept fitted in new clothes, wigs and pedicures. He also purchased a series of thick gold braided necklaces (probably admired less for quality and more for thickness and quantity) as well as three gold rings which bore his initials. He also put gold caps on his teeth, one of which was fitted with a diamond (or cubic zirconia). This 'bling' aspect of Diamond's new life as a 'taxi driver' also made him feel more adventurous. He took on more girlfriends, some in those distant parishes that he travelled to on chartered journeys to the airport.

Taxi drivers are of critical importance to the wider life of this rural area. They represent the core to a rural 'public sphere'. There are certainly people who would put themselves forward as the more public face of Orange Valley, and who would feel they have the experience and responsibility to consider its affairs and take them forward. There is a town committee consisting of the leading figures: headmasters, doctors, shopkeepers and so forth. But for the most part, the population who live in the villages regard such people as distant. These are people they may need and may depend on, but they experience them as a powerful and sometimes oppressive hierarchy.

By contrast, it is the taxi driver who has become the critical figure that unites and brings together the community, since it is the taxi driver who carried news as well as individuals from place to place. It's not just that they deliver the school children and the people coming to market. They help supply the shops with their goods; they deliver parcels and produce. But above all in a society that pivots around one phrase that defines Jamaica: 'whagwaan', they are the people in a position to know what's-going-on, whether it is the latest dancehall event or the real reason behind last night's murder in Arsenal. To become successful in the way a taxi driver succeeds is not to create any distance from others. Taxi drivers do not grow up and above others in the way of the town's elite. They remain about the most accessible people in the town. You see them every day except Sundays. They are central to the wider 'communicative ecology' of the place (Slater and Miller 2007; Slater and Tacchi 2004). They are the people who will take a parcel for you to a friend further down their route, without charging you for it. They are the ones who will turn up in an emergency to take your sick child to the clinic. They are the ones who can save old limbs from treacherous muddy paths back up to the village. It is the taxi drivers who know that the old man, who used to be a tailor, dreamt last night of cats. And so by seven o'clock in the morning a significant proportion of the town can bet on the 'right' numbers in today's 'cashpot' lottery.

Furthermore the taxi driver represents the kind of success that most ordinary people can and do aspire to. They have a regular income that, where possible, is invested in their own transport. They are the entrepreneurs that can generate a certain amount of security and constancy in income. But, unlike other forms of investment, this is the one that seems to have little of the negative—the entrapments, that people, especially young people, also associate with such success. They haven't passed over to another side, gone to live down Babylon.

Unlike other symbols of mobility (homes, church, etc.), the taxi doesn't seem to tie one down in the way a shop might, or even another steady job. If anything it seems to actually accentuate the freedoms of an individual who retains his autonomy, his choice to work, his time of work. While other jobs seem like a boulder that drags a person down to a fixed place, this is more like a light and useful carapace that he can carry with him, and that carries him wherever he wants to go. To be a taxi driver is the resolution of work and freedom (Miller 1994); a freedom that finds its definition in the relationships, the women, it brings in its wake.

In Jamaica women have children to show that they can, to show they are mature, to demonstrate that they are indeed properly women, and because in various ways they must (Sobo 1993). Diamond is happy to represent himself as the victim of this cycle. 'Like if you go court, them charge you to how you work. If you have a woman and she have pickney for you; if dem know say you inna a good work dem demands money from you. Mostly the younger one dem prefer talk to a married man. Them get more benefits, like them get money, and things like that. And seem when them deh wid a married man and so, them nah do nutten for the man, cause them no have to go home to wash, cook, or something like that.' Actually it is clear that Diamond is as much concerned to demonstrate his own masculinity through having women bear children for him. This is a vicious cycle at the heart of Jamaican sexual life.

If a fifteen-year-old has a child in order to try and 'fix' a man, and fails in this venture, then however bad the situation for the fifteen-year-old, the child is a victim from birth. A remarkable number of babies are indeed looked after, cared for, loved by other women, who actually have no real obligation to care. But there are other children who are not really cared for, have no secure sense of being mothered or looked after; who become old enough to go to primary school, but have no money for lunch or school books. At a local primary school, perhaps a third of the pupils do not attend school with any regularity for precisely this reason. And these are the girls who grow up knowing that the only real hope, the best bet, is to have sex and, better still, have a baby for a taxi driver, who has a secure income, and just might be prepared to provide for the baby and the baby's mother (for the background to this see Chevannes 2001; Mohammed 2002; Reddock 2004).

These two individuals, Damian and Diamond, define in turn the aesthetic of the town itself. Orange Valley is something of a façade. Because the bustle represented by sixty shops, augmented by around twenty small temporary stalls, set up anew each day, and selling snacks or clothes, means that, at first, one hardly notices the lack of residences. There are probably no more than sixty or seventy houses, less than the shops. It simply services the local rural area. The main institution that constitutes the town is a primary school and especially the secondary school with more than 2,000 pupils. When the school day ends, these children don't just descend into town, they swarm. They erupt with the force of their release from a place they regard largely as a space of constraint, if not oppression. Orange Valley turns instantly from a quite dusty coloured backwater to a carpet of white and maroon, the school uniform.

The swarm does not last long. Just as Orange Valley looks completely overrun and doomed, the other major feature of the town comes to life as taxis whirl and swoop like birds of prey to pick off the swarming children; a feeding frenzy that whisks them off in all directions, returns and feeds some more, until within an hour only the stragglers remain. For this hour, the two, the dominant imperatives of this town, meet and give reason to the place: the educational institutions that garner children from all over the district and the taxi system that brings and returns them, and spends the rest of the day linking up the inhabitants of this straggling region, who emerge to go about their daily business and then filter back to their homesteads. So the core relationship of Orange Valley has become that of the taxi driver and the school child. At first glance, it seems so innocent. And there are taxi drivers who go out of their way to care for school children, who ferry them to distant sites, watch over them, know their parents and often share some kinship with them. But as is clear both from Diamond's conversation and his actions, there is another side to this relationship, based more on mutual exploitation and sexual predation.

Discussion

Is this a chapter about two individuals, or is it a means to convey something called Jamaican society or culture? What is implicit, but needs to be made explicit, is the process of selection, the decision to use these two people to write this chapter. My starting point is that it has entirely different implications from the description of another two individuals, Charlotte and Malcolm, presented in the introductory chapter to this volume. Those individuals were specific to themselves, characteristic only of the diversity of society at an individual level. But the way I have employed Damian and Diamond imply the much older anthropological tradition of the person as microcosm, who stand for the macrocosm. They are society writ small.

Damian stands for Pentecostalism, the dominant ideology of contemporary Jamaican Christianity. A significant percentage of the Jamaican population, mainly older people who have settled down as child carers, or young people still under their influence, largely give their lives to these ideals. Unfortunately for Damian, religion becomes much less important as people move into their late teens and twenties. They then tend more to share aspirations with Diamond. But the way Diamond was described in the context of the central relationship between taxi drivers and school children in Orange Valley showed that he too represents, not just an individual, but the structural core to the town itself, its contradictions and values. Both come from similar conditions of poverty and both have clear aspirations, conventional to their immediate peers. Both are unusually successful, for their age, in fulfilling those aspirations.

The macrocosm—the cosmology that creates society—is not a single normative form, to be represented by a single person. As in much of the work of Bourdieu (1977 and 1984) these two represent a systematic and structural opposition which constitutes that larger structural whole. This should not be reduced to a single representation of Jamaican society. This is many worlds apart from the middle-class of Kingston, for example. But it can apply to the specific area of Orange Valley.

These are not individuals chosen at random. They are selected because they do the job of exemplification particularly well. Damian is not just any Christian. He performs what he strives to be with unusual clarity and commitment. Diamond does the same for a completely opposed set of values. They stand as ideal types in an almost Weberian sense. Yet they do actually exist as two individuals encountered during fieldwork, described without requiring exaggeration. That really was my recollection of Diamond's driving.

There is a wonderful monograph on Jamaican Pentecostalism by Austin-Broos (1997) that carefully explicates the logic within the cosmology of this faith. But this chapter argues that a similar potential exists for material worlds. As in the previous chapters of this volume by Crăciun, Olesen and Dalakoglou the logics implicated in these persons derives in some measure from that which is external to them. The phone and the taxi are not incidental. They are central to the contemporary manner by which individuals construct themselves. It is impossible to even imagine Diamond, except as partly an emanation of the existence of taxis. The number of ways Damian finds to Christianize his phone, or for Diamond to subsume his life within the ideals of taxi-driving are astonishing. Similarly the way Diamond seems to stand for Orange Valley itself; the taxi driver's relationship with school children as the very raison d'être to the place. They were brought up in this place with these material things and again, following Bourdieu (1977), it is possible to see them as socialized through the way they inculcate the order found in objects and places. The objects no more represent people than people merely represent objects. It is a process of objectification (Miller 1987).

Both individuals use objects in a manner close to Gell's (1998) notion of an aesthetic as the external expression that allows a person to extend his agency in order to secure the interest of others. Both use objects for this art of seduction, quite literally in the case of Diamond's desire for multiple sexual relations, and figuratively in the case of Damian's desire to attract a flock from which he can form his church. The 'bling', the taxi, the numbers of youth at a church event are the evident signs of personal achievement for Diamond and Damian respectively. But the concept of aesthetic as outlined in the introduction of this book is not that of Gell. It is a much more holistic device. It is the order and structure that makes sense of the wider values being expressed and the larger opposition that constitutes these values as society and structure. The evidence presented in this chapter is in support of the contention that an aesthetic holism can be discerned analytically, both at the level of the individual, and at a level that transcends them as individuals and is found in Orange Valley itself.

This is therefore not at all a chapter about individualism. It might have been. Jamaican individualism is a fascinating topic. Colleagues working with traditional fishing communities report that a fisherman expects to sell his fish to his wife who then markets them. Similarly people were giving up telephone landlines partly because of their antipathy to a shared expenditure as opposed to their individualized payments for mobile phones (Horst and Miller 2006: 73–8). In Jamaica money is used to express the internal relations of families in a way that most English people would see as far too individualistic. So there certainly is a form of individualism in Jamaica that derives from long-standing features of Jamaican society and has nothing to do with contemporary neo-liberalism. One could therefore engage in long debates as to whether Jamaicans or Londoners were more or less individualistic. But the degree of individualism is a different topic and argument. It is not the concern of this chapter. That individualism in no way detracts from the ability of individuals to act as a microcosm in relation to the wider Jamaican aesthetic in a manner that I have suggested would no longer be possible in a place such as London. As the introduction suggests, and as the chapters of this book demonstrate, we can examine the individual as one of the media being used to objectify social orders, irrespective of the degree of individualism.

This becomes still clearer when we juxtapose this chapter with that of Murray. Madrid is a modern urban centre, far removed from rural Jamaica, and yet Murray indicates how an individual objectifies Madrid in a manner that corresponds to the case from rural Jamaica, not that of London. By comparison with the rural poverty of Jamaica, most people in London have considerable resources, support from, but also autonomy from, the state. I suggest in the introduction that this allows them to construct a heterogeneous aesthetic, taken piecemeal from the sheer diversity and heterogeneity of their surrounding and influences. The people in Madrid have comparable resources to Londoners. Yet they retain a homogeneity that means an individual makes sense only in relation to an aesthetic that is objectified by the place itself—Madrid. So the diversity of London cannot be reduced to the wealth of London. The economic conditions may allow for the emergence of an aesthetic of household described in the introduction for London, but comparative anthropology shows they do not determine it.

So neither situation, Madrid, London or Jamaica should be regarded as more authentic, or more modern, or more central to anthropology, per se. Rather, in combination, they help us to appreciate another concept of aesthetic as an analytical tool. One that may be found in the portraits of individuals: the way they comb their hair, the way they talk to women, the things that give them confidence and the need to incorporate each and every object within a particular style. This aesthetic is the very shape and form of struggle and hope in Jamaica. Without the skills to fully embody these aesthetics they have very little chance of success.

This aesthetic quality is even clearer when the two figures are juxtaposed. Because whatever they have in common, they are also systematically opposed. Damian's mission in life is to persuade his generation not to take the path represented by Diamond, which he represents as a fundamental choice between heaven and hell. While each island is specific, there is a pattern to such dualistic oppositions that seems characteristic of the Caribbean more generally (starting from Wilson 1966). Such dualisms have been criticized for the way they present gender (e.g. Besson 1993), but my evidence from Trinidad (Miller 1994) does not support these criticisms. In this chapter the opposition is portrayed through two internally consistent individuals. But it is entirely possible for this situation to change. One day Diamond may find God, but without losing his ambition to accumulate women. Or Damian may become so successful as a preacher that temptations will arise to which he may succumb. The chapter could still have rested on these two individuals but would have had to work through the analysis of their internal contradictions.

The aim would remain the same. There is a cultural order here, as in the classics of anthropology from Malinowski through to Geertz and Bourdieu. It is an aesthetic that people see and express through the material and other orders around them, and gives them their style and aspirations. It is not freely chosen; its roots are often in poverty and historical oppression. It doesn't just make sense of life; it is their lives. By focusing upon the phone and taxi we can see how fully it saturates everyday actions and aspirations. There is a wider holism, but we can also explore the internal logics, consistencies and contradictions that can be discerned, at the level of both individual and of society. In this volume we try to make explicit the implications of trying to convey this aesthetic both of the person and of the wider society within which they live; what it means and what is at stake when one makes theoretical and analytical points through portraits of individuals.

Notes

Both of the individuals discussed in this chapter were introduced to me by Heather Horst, with whom I conducted fieldwork on the impact of the mobile phone in Jamaica. I am entirely indebted to her contribution, without which I could not have participated in the fieldwork. All my observations and insights depended upon continual discussion with Horst, whose fieldwork was much more extensive than mine. We are still considering a more extensive volume of these portraits which would be an entirely collaborative work. All names and places have been anonymized. A considerable amount of additional context is available in Horst and Miller (2005, 2006), but for a sense of the wider background also see Austin-Broos (1997) and Besson (2002).

1. Jamaica remains in general virulently homophobic.
2. 'Partner' is Jamaican for a rotating credit scheme.

References

Austin-Broos, D. J. (1997), *Jamaica Genesis: Religion and the Politics of Moral Orders,* Chicago: University of Chicago Press.

Besson, J. (1993), 'Reputation and Respectability Reconsidered: A New Perspective on Afro-Caribbean Peasant Women', in J. Momsen (ed.), *Women and Change in the Caribbean,* London: James Currey, 15–37.

Besson, J. (2002), *Martha Brae's Two Histories: European Expansion and Caribbean Culture-Building in Jamaica,* Chapel Hill: University of North Carolina.

Bourdieu, P. (1977), *Outline of a Theory of Practice,* Cambridge: Cambridge University Press.

Bourdieu, P. (1984), *Distinction: A Social Critique of the Judgement of Taste,* London: Routledge and Kegan Paul.

Chevannes, B. (2001), *Learning to Be a Man: Culture, Socialization, and Gender Identity in Five Caribbean Communities,* Mona: University of the West Indies Press.

Gell, A. (1998), *Art and Agency: An Anthropological Theory,* Oxford: Oxford University Press.

Horst, H. and Miller, D. (2005), 'From Kinship to Link-up: Cell Phones and Social Networking in Jamaica', *Current Anthropology,* 46(5): 755–78.

Horst, H. and Miller, D. (2006), *The Cell Phone: An Anthropology of Communication,* Oxford: Berg.

Miller, D. (1987), *Material Culture and Mass Consumption,* Oxford: Blackwell.

Miller, D. (1994), *Modernity: An Ethnographic Approach,* Oxford: Berg.

Mohammed, P. (2002), *Gendered Realities: Essays in Caribbean Feminist Thought,* Mona: University of the West Indies Press.

Reddock, R. (2004), *Interrogating Caribbean Masculinities: Theoretical and Empirical Analyses,* Mona: University of the West Indies Press.

Slater, D. and Miller, D. (2007), 'Moments and Movements in the Study of Consumer Culture', *Journal of Consumer Culture,* 7: 15–23.

Slater, D. and Tacchi, J. (2004), *Research: ICT Innovations for Poverty Reduction,* New Delhi: UNESCO.

Sobo, E. J. (1993), *One Blood: The Jamaican Body,* Albany: State University of New York.

Wilson, P. J. (1966), *Crab Antics,* Prospect Heights, IL: Waveland Press.

–6–

How Madrid Creates Individuals

Marjorie Murray

The intention of this chapter is to demonstrate through an extended essay on a single figure, Manuel, how the concept of individualism is actually rooted in the constraints and possibilities that are given by the experience of living in Madrid. What is encountered here is very different from that which is usually meant by the term 'individualism' as employed in anthropology (e.g. Dumont 1986; Strathern 1992). Rather than individualism per se, what is encountered in the figure of Manuel is a route to the study of how certain elements of Madrid as cosmology manifest themselves through the individual person. Analysing Manuel's attitudes and interests shows why it is necessary to focus first on a cosmology that emerges as much from the study of Madrid as from the observation of this individual. We can then come to appreciate how this requires a delicate analysis of overlapping levels of the order that Madrid provides, the spaces and domains that enable this particular expression of the individual. More specifically, I focus on the areas within which Manuel is able to make sense of conformity and creativity respectively.

A Coffee with Manuel

When I met Manuel in a café while visiting Madrid three years after having originally met him, he was wearing his underground train driver uniform, which gave him an air of adult seriousness that he hardly transmitted otherwise during my time in the field. This attitude was no doubt related to the imminent and very expected moving out from his parents' into a flat of '*protección oficial*' subsidized by the government, which would be ready by the end of the year. Apart from this, his relationship of two and a half years with Eloisa, a Madrilenian waitress he met in a bar during my time in the field, gave an impression of a present life that was in many ways different to that which I had observed during my ethnography. In the course of our meeting he explained to me how things have changed since then: how he feels less keen on partying as he used to and how he is much more interested in going out for lunch and strolls with his girlfriend during the day, or taking her dog to the countryside during the weekends. He made clear that his life is moving on; a reason for pride and perhaps relief. This surprised me, as he had hardly manifested either frustration or anxiety in his days as a regular informant. These desires and wishes I knew, but he was always stoical enough to avoid expressing frustration or anxiety apart from the times of common place complaining with others that is usual in Madrid.

He told me about his projects. For example, he is keen on finally buying a car in order to take the dog more often to the countryside, and spend more weekends outside of Madrid. He now has the necessary justification for this long-term dream of his, which he has quietly been waiting to achieve. He has not changed his cautious attitude though. He told me he might wait until the end of the year for the current models to drop their price. When I asked him if he had purchased furniture and ornaments for the new flat he told me he would rather wait until it is ready, as he already has enough things, including the art history book collection, the many shells and his photographs. He knows he has to be very careful at the time of selecting what to buy for this small two-bedroom flat, that will most probably be his definitive home, or at least one for a long term.

The current and coming changes are the biggest ones since Manuel got this job five years ago. This is his first stable and likeable job after years of working as a plumber's assistant. It has allowed him to save enough money and fulfil the requirements to apply for the subsidized flat in a brand new fashionable neighbourhood in the north of Madrid, for which he pays roughly half of its market price. It has also given him a sense of security and stability that many of his peers would like to have and even an attractive air, as people are always curious about his work. Now at thirty-five, adulthood appears imminent with the departure to his own home, hopefully in the company of his girlfriend. Consistent with his personality, he told me he would not talk about these things with her until he first moves to the new place.

Knowing him, I was not surprised by this, or by his claim that he does not want to ever get married, as he does not believe in marriage. What I was more surprised to hear was that he does not want to have children and that, happily, it seems that Eloisa does not want children either. He said that he is much more keen on adopting a Chinese girl, as do many other people these days in Madrid and Spain.[1] The explanation he gave was based on humanitarian grounds, plus that adopting is qualitatively less complicated than having children of one's own, and a different kind of responsibility. This decision is partially related with his concern with global issues including the environment, overpopulation and the suffering of innocent children. More interesting is his argument about the responsibility of involved in becoming a father and a mother. He does not feel prepared and does not like the role of a father as he knows it; he also does not trust Eloisa's abilities as a mother. But he believes them both capable of giving shelter and love to a child and enabling that child to have so much more from life than she would otherwise experience.

In hearing him discourse on topic after topic, I felt that time had not passed in vain and Manuel sounded much clearer and more confident in this preparation for fundamental change. At the same time, I realized he had become even more individualistic than before, as evident in his self-centred attitude, and the increasing detached and judgemental attitude to the world around him. But the concept of individualism is always of a particular and usually ill-defined kind. The take Manuel has on individualism is one out of certain quite specific ways in which one can be individualistic in Madrid.

Madrid and Spanish Individualism

Manuel has always been known and he refers to himself as someone that goes his own way (*va a su bola*). This is a very common term to describe those people in the city that have a more detached attitude to other people, others' activities, and who decide independently what to do and with whom. This is characteristic of several of the city characters—who are to be found in the literature and vocabulary of the city—such as the '*chulo Madrileño*,' the proud man that goes 'his own way' and succeeds in conquering women. What is usually neglected in the description of this proud and independent attitude is its counterpart; a huge range of practices that are followed with a conformity and rigour that one might never have expected to find in a capital city. As is the case with many of my informants, there is a complex background of stability, routine and order that allows him to go his way without anxiety or sense of anomie. The strength of normativity and the expectations that people have of these roles in Madrid formed a fundamental part of my PhD thesis. Unusually I approached these individuals and the specific categories of characters that they appeared to represent through the study of several relevant genres of material culture, using a broad range of informants in the city. In the larger work I provide the evidence for a very specific regime that is objectified by the city of Madrid itself; one that seems to preserve order and conformity in many areas, but also allows domains for the specific expression of individuals.

Roughly speaking, when we say that individualism is held or practiced as a value in a certain society, '*we mean that its people hold the individual to be as important as, or more important than, clan, case, estate, race or nation, and that they act in ways that enable us to infer that they assign that significance*' (Béteille 1986: 121). It is a concept rooted in the understanding of modernity, and assumed to be characteristic of the (Protestant) West. Different societies have their own versions and emphasis: Tocqueville and egalitarianism in the United States, for example. Madrid is out of the picture here, both theoretically and ethnographically. In a nutshell, this is because of the emphasis on kinship, religion and folk traditions in the anthropological study of Spain. There is, however, a relevant discussion that emerges from historical analysis. Contemporary individualism in Madrid may correspond in many respects to what essayists and travellers have described as Spanish individualism (e.g. Menendez-Pidal 1966; Unamuno 2005; Williams 1929). The same as the already mentioned *chulo*, several characters from Cervantes's Quixote (Weiger 1979, Williams 1929) onwards have been described as individualistic, but in a sense that is quite different to that of the 'traditional' settings where individualism has been described. Individualism is generally assumed to be one of independence, and a lack of interest in communitarian or group organization. At its best, it is related to the brave spirit of *conquistador*. At its worst it has also been described as simple atomism (e.g. Wright 1957). It is closely related to the well-established Mediterranean syndrome of 'honour and shame' (e.g. Peristiany 1966); the assumption that the core values in this cultural area were the defence of (virile) honour in the case of men and of shame in the case of women as its counterpart in a 'cultural area'[2] with a strongly gendered division of values.[3] Some aspects of this account still seem pertinent to the individualism that is found in Manuel. This is partially built upon the defence of pride and dignity that is close to that described in the classical ethnography. It is manifest in the absence of need for 'others'. As Manuel puts it 'I don't like depending on anyone, I like being self-sufficient'.

The following section describes some aspects of Manuel's everyday life, first when out with acquaintances and then certain aspects of his life indoors; the neglected intimate circle of support and the set of rules that are fundamental to an understanding of his individualism. From there I suggest that this individual's cosmology combines the heavy weight of Madrid's ways of being and doing with other more creative personal oeuvres. At first these seemed contradictory. They certainly would be if we were looking for an integrated aesthetic as proposed by Miller in the introduction to this volume. They make sense, however, if instead we look for their integration at the level of Madrid, the city itself. From the perspective of the city conservatism and innovation are not opposed, because the latter presumes the former.

Manuel and His Manners

Manuel is a charming man who feels at ease in his city streets. He naturally follows Madrid rules of courtesy, for example speaking to strangers in the street by using colloquial common places. His companions at work, and the people he has hung out with throughout the years, would certainly describe him as *'majo'*, a sympathetic and easy-going person with whom it is good to spend time. In his case this means a lot of people, as he has hung out with many different groups throughout his long years of nights out, which have migrated according to where the fashionable '*marcha*' areas are, and the kinds of people he feels more comfortable with. As a first-class connoisseur of every corner of Madrid, he also knows several waiters, waitresses and bar assistants in the central areas of the city, who would guide him to where the best parties are or possibly give him an extra free drink. His openness and ability to 'meet' new people was an extreme version of the not exceptional search by young informants for company at hand, acquaintances. This practice of getting to know—and politely exchanging phone numbers—with people to '*quedar*', to meet for a drink or coffee, fulfils a very different role from what my informants would call making friends. Having people to *quedar* with is a necessity—to share a beer and enjoy the city in avoidance of physical isolation. 'I used to *quedar* with this and that but not anymore', was a very common phrase amongst my young informants when I went through their mobile phone contact lists. Manuel's case is extreme; his knowledge of the territory and rules of the game allows him to turn up at bars and places where he knows there will be acquaintances, or at least well-known bartenders to talk to. Occasionally he would text an acquaintance in order to make sure they would be at the same place, same time.

When I asked him in the coffee place about the four people he hung out with the most during my time in the field, he told me he had lost contact with two of them—who he never considered his friends—and that only Mar, a twenty-six-year-old art teacher, has remained as a friend. Cecilia, a journalist he used to talk with in different bars they both frequented, he now meets only occasionally. When he feels like talking to her, he goes to her boyfriend's bar, where she spends most of her evenings these days. Manuel did not hesitate in assuming it was absolutely natural that being in a relationship implies a substantial decline in meeting with other people. This is the common '*se echó novio/a, pasa de nosotros*' (now he/she has a girlfriend/boyfriend and doesn't care about us). In his case, he was simply happy to hang out with his girlfriend's friends. This is perhaps the best evidence of how little Manuel relies on friendship. Most of the people he knows and hangs out with are providers of companionship, which can be readily exchanged for alternative companions when circumstances change.

In order to understand Manuel it is necessary to grasp that which he does rely on, that which is taken for granted, as well as his beliefs. Manuel is the elder of two of what many locals would call a *castiza* Madrid family. The term *castizo* literally means pure and in Madrid refers to those that are thought to be 'the real Madrilenian characters'. His father Pepe is a sixty-year-old plumber and his mother Sara, fifty-eight, is a nursing assistant. Manuel lives with them in a small two-bedroom flat in a block in Vallecas, a traditional working-class neighbourhood in the city. They have lived there since before he was born, apart from a period of three years in the 1970s in which the family migrated to Switzerland in search of work. The flat has experienced an interesting rotation of people. For example Sara's mother lived there with them before she passed away, then they rented the second room in order to get some extra money. For three years now it has been just the three of them, after Manuel's sister Clara left. The couple follow the division of labour that is typical for people their age in Madrid: even if both work outside and share expenditures, Sara is the one in charge of cooking, washing, shopping, cleaning, ironing, etc. The men of the family are committed to paid work outside the home, and mostly to relaxing while indoors—watching TV and drinking beer in the case of Pepe and watching films and pursuing his hobbies in the case of Manuel.

The Sierras share dinner almost every evening unless something exceptional happens. At thirty-five, Manuel is expected to call or text his mother to let his parents know if he is not coming, which most informants living with parents, did. They enjoy their meal without speaking much to each other apart from commenting on television programs, the news, or the telling of some anecdote or story from work or to complain on the current state of affairs. They spend long hours together in the living room in front of the widescreen television which has been placed in the traditional wall-to-wall *mural* piece of furniture. On Saturdays, Sara prepares one of the family favourites, a *cocido madrileño* (traditional Madrilenian dish) or seafood and Manuel joins them in time even if he has stayed out at Eloisa's flat. It is extremely hard to identify even small acts of resistance to their own rules.

Sara, Pepe and Manuel agreed that their flat, its furniture display and its standards of cleanliness are 'not too different to that of the people around'. This idea had drawn my attention since the beginning of my fieldwork: I had to understand that, like many other families, their perception was that most homes of Spaniards in Madrid shared quite a lot or were expected to fulfil certain standards of possessions and display, together with their associated routines and habits. The difference perceived is one of quality rather than substance: it relates to the standard of these possessions or the number of rooms available in the flat, but not about the home's essential organization. This was made even clearer with the Sierras' and other families' explanations of their home interiors, possessions and customs, which they could relate to other families in the city, and teach me about the way things are done and held in Madrid, which was the fashionable piece of furniture or kitchen implement that everyone now has. There is a sense of pride and dignity regarding this common tradition toward which much effort is put, compared with originality or specific taste, certainly expected, but something to deal with once the former is secured. In many respects the Sierras assume that their first aim is to be 'normal' (meaning, average, expected), an adjective that my informants used with an amazing regularity to describe themselves, others or the way things are and ought to be like.

At the same time they describe their family as being a 'strange' one (*rara*, meaning eccentric, out of rule). They assume that in contrast to most households, their expressions of affection are weaker, as well as their relationship to their extended family and the several family festivities that take place through the year. For example, they place less emphasis on Christmas celebrations than most people. They conduct the basic series of rituals and meals, but they hardly ever meet with their extended family or friends and are less excited than many. It is true that the Sierras are not particularly expressive in their feelings to one another—the most frequent object of cuddles and sweet words is indeed the cat. In their own everyday routine interactions romantic expressions of love are absent. It is through everyday shared routines of contiguity and ritualized activities that they experience and reinforce their sense of family, much of which depended upon Sara's devoted effort. Not surprisingly it was Sara that complained most—albeit quietly—about the family routines and organization of which there seems to be no way out. She refrained from criticizing what might have been regarded as excessive and unfair housework duties and the lack of help she has in accomplishing them. Like other women her age in Madrid she complained more about how boring her husband was, and how little time they spent out together, if at all, which is felt as abnormal in a city in which life out is a fundamental ingredient for self-fulfillment. As with other informants in a similar situation, she managed to escape by finding a way to spend some time out in the city, in this case with her sister.

Even these days out with her sister had become another routine, as are most of the activities each of them engages in. For example during my time in the field Sara and Pepe went every Sunday to visit Sara's sister in a close-by *pueblo* (town). There they would buy the bread for the week and often some other extra quality foods. During our more recent coffee together Manuel told me that these days they do the same, but they have changed destination—now they go to their daughter's place in another *pueblo*. Certainly, they have their own quirky and particular customs, which identify them to other families. But overall it is their tendency towards routine and to accepted ways of being and acting that tie them to a sense of conformity I observed in Madrid's families when taken as a whole. They are impressive in their tendency for repetition and homogeneity.

Manuel himself is sceptical of many things around him and declares himself to be someone who does not like the society he lives in. He does not believe in politics, the corporate world or the media. He also distrusts the apparently profound intentions of the people that surround him. Given such a world of appearances he develops relationships and encounters that are functional to the achievement of the company at hand rather than committed friendship. The exception to this is his girlfriend in whom he focuses his time and care, cautiously, as his reluctance in her becoming a mother or moving in with him show. This does not mean that he is cynical though. There are a few things he does believe in. As it is to be expected, the one person he does believe in is his devoted mother. She is the one person in the world that will be there for him until the day she dies. This relationship comprises a very specific mixture of devotion and slavery, which is implicated in the concept of motherhood in settings where devotion to the Virgin Mary has taken place (e.g. Warner 1985). This is condensed in the phrase *'ay las madres'* (oh, mothers) which celebrates a mother's devoted work and is employed whenever they do a remarkable action of what is expected from them. It is a devotion that is two times secured as successful: experienced both as a mother's love and care for her child and also the strict social sanction that surrounds the role of proper motherhood in this society. These make it impossible for Manuel to doubt her loyalty, which is reinforced in the security and continuity found in the everyday preparing of meals, ironing and sharing the watching of television together in the evenings after dinner. This is the basic, taken-for-granted sense of stability. Life behind the flat's door is safe. This is a trend in a society clearly oriented to patrimony, one that is less related to ancestral inheritance, financial security or investment, but to a sense of safeness in a hostile, changing world.

Manuel was no exception in feeling a compulsion towards this achievement of stability through the unquestioned aims of property, stable work and a partner. This is true for him to the extent that when he finally got the flat he joked, saying he was now 'sorted' and might get bored from now on. In this context, the impact of having achieved a stable job five years ago had radical implications for his status as citizen. This is not surprising in a society where a large number of my younger informants aim to obtain a permanent work of different kinds in government or public institutions for which they can spend years studying—this is after formal education—in order to achieve a post in one of the most competitive fields.

In Manuel's case, this job gave him a certain respect within his family and among his peers, as well as the possibility of saving money and applying for the already mentioned State-subsidized property that he will soon move into. Overall, what has traditionally been considered a contemplative attitude of people in this area (e.g. Unamuno 2005; Menendez-Pidal 1966) is manifested today in the way that even with regard to the core things he is expected to achieve, Manuel and his family both believe in and rely on fate. There is nothing like a narrative of effort behind these achievements. The job he found through the government job agency; a good job was available at the right time, luckily. The flat he has been allocated is luckily located in the right—brand new, middle class—neighbourhood. These are occurrences that he, his peers and family attribute to his luck, his 'good star' that has allowed him to achieve things more easily than others. His strong belief in fate and luck supports his stoical attitude to his own life, which he can now take pride in given his growing list of achievements, but which could have very easily led to a completely different fate of precarious work and income and no prospects for moving out from the parental home.

Yet there is something else he strongly believes in, and which might seem of a completely different order, far from this bedrock of conformity. Manuel is confident about his taste. From clothing to art and cuisine, his taste constitutes a pivotal expression of who he is in the world. And, as many of my informants, he is quite judgemental of those he wants to repudiate or be distinguished from, through this individual taste. And it is through his hobbies that he objectifies this personal sense of taste.

Manuel and His Aesthetics: Clothes, Photography and Blog

Manuel has always been concerned with clothes and has always liked adding some special touch to his youthful looks of which he has always been proud. This has involved considerable creative effort in keeping up with his own taste; one that is intended to avoid what 'most people are wearing' as well as preferring quality and originality to quantity. This is hard work in the Madrilenian context of exceptional high street homogeneity and even harder for someone with a very tight budget, which has been Manuel's case all his life until very recently. Through the years he has developed several strategies to keep up his well-known good taste and originality in patterns and design. In particular, he has found several small shops—including designer shops and outlets—to go to during sales times, which he visits and then carefully decides upon one or two garments to add to his wardrobe.

Because of his sense of care and keeping of clothes and shoes, and of not having changed size since he was a teenager, Manuel has accumulated a quantity of clothes that allows him to wait until the sales begin before he spends the first euros, without risking a loss to his style. At the same time he manages to wear clothes again even after a few seasons of storing them, which makes for his unpredictable outfits. In the last few years, during which he has started travelling abroad on holiday, he also enjoys finding original clothes and trainers, which he brings back and recombines with the old ones.

Overall, his way of wearing and combining clothes is braver and more playful than most of the people I know, in a society with strict rules of propriety when it comes to clothing. My analysis of clothing in Madrid suggests that this is a place where fitting people into stereotypes through their looks is a widespread activity and where many actually make their claim to belong to specific groups through their use of identifiable kinds of clothes. Manuel allows himself to use colours and patterns that few others employ, including slight glittery touches that make him playful with his sexuality, particularly when he goes out in the gay area of the city. It is not, however, a claim to eccentricity; rather, it is a need for a kind of self-affirmation in the world through his outfits and hairstyle. These make him original, while at the same time elegantly manifest either affinity or avoidance with respect to the different styles of the city. This was clear in the way in which a particular purchase of his would usually be admired through the comments of those he would meet on the street or by friends.

Just like many Madrilenians Manuel's real interests and devotions are to the time spent outside of work. In his case, he has been devoted to collections of comics, to downloading music and film and to sharing these with workmates and other acquaintances. His favourite hobby in the last years, however, has been photography, particularly after he invested in a quality digital camera. He spends hours in the streets taking pictures of the city, the flowers of the *'rosaleda'* (rose garden) in spring, of friends, or of insects in the countryside and more recently also of his trips. He then spends long hours in his room in front of the computer, working on these images, employing different software that he enjoys discovering and searching for applications as a crucial part of the overall process. It has become a very personal way of dealing with the transformation of nature in a comparable way to what Chevalier (1998) has suggested for gardening in the case of the English and cooking in the case of the French. He captures creatively what is found in the outside world and crafts it in the search of a personal outcome that causes in this case, aesthetic pleasure. A lot of this work is kept in his computer files, while other photographs hang in the walls of his room. However, I realized at an early stage of my acquaintance with Manuel that his satisfaction with this activity is most fully achieved when he shows his creations to others. On many occasions he gave his work as presents to people he believed might appreciate it even if there is a risk that some will not value it. He even tried to exhibit his photographs in one of the bars in the city that regularly displays artwork.

It is as an expression of this last point that we can appreciate the attraction of his most recent activity as a blogger, and why it has acquired such an importance for him. Following his cautious way of proceeding in life, it took him several months before he finally set up his page. He had researched different platforms and questioned whether he really wanted to have one. Once he started, it was clear that he had thought of every detail thoroughly, from the name to the epigraph and the overall design and colours. It claims to be a blog constructed by someone dissatisfied with his society but thankful to those that make things a bit better. This is perhaps the best description he could have made of himself: a fatalist that wants to get the best of what is around. A miscellaneous space, his postings range from pictures—simple takes on the street but from an innovative angle, microscopic insects or a crafted set of pictures in the train tunnel (see Figure 6.1)—to thoughts on topics that vary from curiosities to politics and promoting his friend's clothes shop, for whom he did the photos of the autumn collection. Comments on art exhibitions, uploads and comments on YouTube videos of politicians he criticizes, as well as promoting bars and venues in the city (see Figure 6.2), are also part of the picture. This is the place where different aspects of Manuel's life, his interests and opinions about his surroundings, and the people he cares for are present. It is here that Manuel's desire for care and expression manifest with pride—easily observable in his will of others to visit it. In this space his sense of ethics and aesthetics are synthesized. It is here that he feels he is useful to others and where he can live his involvement with his city and society to the greatest extent.

Individualism in Madrid

Most of the chapters in this volume concern the individual but not necessarily individualism, for reasons given by Miller in the introduction. But in the case of Manuel we have to directly confront the issue of individualism; because this is a designated component of the person that is clearly given a specific position within Madrid society. It is Manuel that describes and assumes himself to be individualistic. As he puts it 'I need a space for solitude in which I can find silence and tranquillity; plus, I don't like to depend on anyone, I enjoy being self-sufficient.' The analysis of Manuel's sense of individualism places us at the precise point where—in order to

How Madrid Creates Individuals • 93

Figure 6.1 Madrid's Metro tunnel from the train.

understand it—it is necessary to see how Madrid as manifested through the family meets Madrid as manifested through independent individuals and where creativity meets conformity. As a European capital Madrid is the kind of place where metasociology assumes the categories of late modernity, including the ideal categories of individualism and individualization (e.g. Beck and Beck-Gernsheim 2001), as emerging properties which can be used to explain current trends. On the other end of social science—and following the ethnographic tradition in Spain—many would also assume that here 'family', even if redefined, remains the dominant unit for social analysis (e.g. De Miguel 2002). What the case of Manuel reveals is that neither of these alone is sufficient to account for what is going on with Manuel's sense of himself, his interests, dreams and fears.

As I have suggested here Manuel is individualistic in the way the concept is understood and lived in classic Spanish characterizations of individualism, i.e. as independent and lacking the need of others' favours or commitment. In other words, he embodies the exact opposite to the values attributed to individualism in other settings such as the American associative society (e.g. Putnam 2000) and theories of networked individualism on which the world of, for example, online social networking as presented by Horst in this volume, rely on. Yet Manuel does rely on the support and structure given by his nuclear family, as well as a wide range of rules, which at first sight could seem contradictory to individualism itself. Creativity seems

94 • *Anthropology and the Individual*

Figure 6.2 Innocent boy in a bar.

rather to emerge from a permitted terrain that is delineated by familial constraints. Yet it would also be misleading to suggest that Manuel prioritizes present or potential family or that his life is constituted as family-oriented, as is clear in his avoidance of the normative trajectory towards getting married and becoming a father. Instead we need to focus on the specific relationship between conformity and creativity and the notion of individual in practice that seems to be at stake in Madrid. This contradiction is taken to its extreme if the assumption exists that there should be a certain creativity that emerges from the 'inner' self.

There are two core characteristics to Manuel's individualism. On the one hand it manifests as a kind of independence from other people, be these friends or people to rely on. Yet this is a strange kind of independence. Manuel does not express his self-reliance and self-sufficiency from other people by keeping himself in the private sphere. Rather, in order to feel and achieve this independence Manuel has to constantly return to the street, bars, cinemas; corners of the city, and these days also his strolls with his girlfriend whom he actually found in the heart of the city. It is more properly an independence from people's intentions and good will. Yet he deeply depends on them for the achievement of that independence. The creation of this independence is crafted, it is performative and requires the approval of an audience, even if an imagined one, as in the case for the blog. This is a theatrical performance of self-reliance in which Manuel is at the same time accomplishing on behalf of the city the cultivation of a particular character—the individual—that is an established aspect of Madrid itself. Similarly Manuel's personal sense of taste as expressed in his hobbies and now in his blog is acceptable, because it rests upon an unquestioned conformity to the larger duties, rituals and routines of Madrid, both within the flat with his family and in his hanging out in the public sphere.

So Manuel's individualism is not in opposition to Madrid as a site of conformity; it is in its own way equally expressive of this dominant cosmology, which includes and incorporates the individual as one of its stock characters. This element of theatricality and public appearances is certainly reminiscent of the traditions of a court society; there is a history behind what we observe in the contemporary figure of Manuel. Madrid, through its 'invention' as a capital and the very centre of the Spanish empire, created a very specific theatre state of civility, with some similarities but many differences from that described by Elias (1978) for Paris, or London. Being in the street, founding and conforming to the norms of family, or even putting a blog out into cyberspace are about the development of certain appearances—appearances which depend upon rather than avoid creativity.

Indeed it is in this second characteristic of Manuel's individualism, its creative side, that we find the lack of contradiction between his inner self and Madrid. Manuel is very committed to his clothes and spends a great deal of effort in being original and tasteful. This follows directly from what we have just described in terms of the need for reassurance and fulfilment of one's individuality in the streets. This sense of being inventive and assured in himself is not opposed to his public presence. So the evidence for Manuel is entirely different from that general presentation of modernity in which it is assumed that the growth of a devotion to intimacy leads to an entire disconnection from the public sphere.

Manuel's sense of individualism and what he really likes doing and feels he wants to express is of a specific kind: Manuel is an artist of Madrid, and for Madrid. This is not only about the expected need for people to see and accept his photos or visit his blog, i.e. the possibility for self-expression. Manuel's sense of expression and creativity rely on the capturing, appropriating and crafting what he finds in his surroundings. Manuel's pictures of the city sunsets, its flowers, its bats, its people and fiestas are what he then works on at home in order to bring them out again. The blog is about his view and evaluation of what he sees around: what he likes and what he dislikes. Manuel's inner self and way of fulfilment is one that can only take place through his life in the city. His bedroom is the place where he works on these creatively, thoughtfully; never the starting point. His individual creativity is an expression of his relationship to rather than his distancing from the civilization that is Madrid.

Notes

1. In 2006 Spain and Norway led the percentage of inter-country adoptions in the world with 12.6 per 100,000 inhabitants, followed by Sweden (12) and Denmark (10.8). The United Kingdom adopted (0.6) per 100,000 inhabitants (Selman 2008: 10).
2. The extensive critique on these concepts and then of the understanding of the Mediterranean as a 'cultural area' (e.g. Herzfeld 1987; Pina Cabral 1989) led to its virtual disappearance within anthropological work in the last decades. For my aim here I only highlight the notion of honour as an aspect to consider for the understanding of Manuel's individualism.
3. Kenny (1960) observed in the 1950s that this gendered division of values applied less to Madrid than to the people of the *pueblos* in the case of Spain.

References

Beck, U. and Beck-Gernsheim, E. (2001), *Individualization: Institutionalized Individualism and Its Social and Political Consequences,* London: Sage.

Béteille, A. (1986), 'Individualism and Equality', *Current Anthropology,* 27: 121–34.

Chevalier, S. (1998), 'From Woollen Carpet to Grass Carpet: Bridging House and Garden in an English Suburb', in D. Miller (ed.), *Material Cultures: Why Some Things Matter,* London: University College London Press, 47–72.

De Miguel, A. (2002), *Las Transformaciones de la Vida Cotidiana en el Umbral del Siglo XXI,* Madrid: Centro de Investigaciones Sociológicas.

Dumont, L. (1986), *Essays on Individualism,* Chicago: Chicago University Press.

Elias, N. (1978), *The Civilizing Process,* Oxford: Blackwell.

Herzfeld, M. (1987), '"As in Your House": Hospitality, Ethnography, and the Stereotype of Mediterranean Society', in D. Gilmore (ed.), *Honor and Shame and the Unity of the Mediterranean,* Washington, DC: American Anthropological Association, 75–89.

Kenny, M. (1960), *A Spanish Tapestry: Town and Country in Castile,* New York: Harper & Row.

Menendez-Pidal, R. (1966), *The Spaniards in Their History,* New York: W. W. Norton.

Peristiany, J. G. E. (ed.) (1966), *The Values of Mediterranean Society,* Chicago: Chicago University Press.

Pina Cabral, J. (1989), 'The Mediterranean as a Category of Regional Comparison: A Critical View', *Current Anthropology,* 30: 399–406.

Putnam, R. (2000), *Bowling Alone: The Collapse and Revival of American Community,* New York: Simon & Schuster.

Selman, P. (2008), 'Inter-country Adoption in Europe 1998–2006: Patterns, Trends and Issues', Annual Conference of the Social Policy Association, Edinburgh.

Strathern, M. (1992), *After Nature: English Kinship in the Late Twentieth Century,* Cambridge: Cambridge University Press.

Unamuno, M. D. (2005), *En Torno al Casticismo,* Madrid: Catedra.

Warner, M. (1985), *Alone of All Her Sex: The Myth and the Cult of the Virgin Mary,* London: Picador.

Weiger, J. G. (1979), *The Individuated Self: Cervantes and the Emergence of the Individual,* Athens: Ohio University Press.

Williams, G. L. (1929), 'Energy and Individualism in the Spanish Character', *Hispania,* 12: 545–62.

Wright, R. (1957), *Pagan Spain,* London: The Bodley Head.

–7–

Aesthetics of the Self: Digital Mediations

Heather A. Horst

From theories of the 'network society' to networked individualism, one of the fundamental questions of the digital age revolves around the extent to which new media and technology contributes to increasing connectedness, or to the fragmentation and atomization of society. On the one hand, new media and technology enhance the level and degree of communication, leading individuals to communicate in an increasing number of ways and with greater frequency using mediums that enable connectivity across time and space (Horst and Miller 2005; Ling 2008; Matsuda 2005a,b; Miller and Slater 2000). Yet, these interactions may not fully compensate for a broader shift in society that is characterized by physical isolation and separation, as defined in relation to 'traditional' conceptions of communities, societies, neighbourhoods and other notions of place-based belonging (Low 2003; Castells 2000; Putnam 2000; Wellman 2001). This chapter explores the relationship between individuals, networks and places through a detailed case study of Ann, an eighteen-year-old high school student living in Silicon Valley, California, and her engagement with two popular social network sites, MySpace and Facebook.[1] As with other social network sites, MySpace and Facebook enable account holders to establish personalized profiles with links to friends and interests and provide a forum, or space, within which 'friends' can interact and 'hang out'. In this chapter I explore how youth construct a sense of order in and through these spaces and the interplay between these new media and their relationships with places, persons and objects. I further reveal the ways in which these media spaces suggest an act of self-construction that is highly social, but also constrained whereby individuality emerges through the ordering and configuring of space in relation to peers and parents. As in the other chapters in this volume, what is significant is not the degree of individualism Ann exhibits, but the ways in which individuals exist in alignment with highly socialized media of expression. This is perhaps even more evident with social network sites,[2] that enable youth to make public the bedroom, a space often viewed as a highly privatized and personal domain.

American Youth, Media and Networked Public Culture

Before turning to Ann's engagement with social network sites in more detail, I want to briefly contextualize this particular case study within the experience of coming of age in the United States. Whereas earlier work in childhood and youth culture focused upon the processes of socialization which shape the transmission of knowledge and information (Parsons and Bales 1955), recent work on the anthropology and sociology of childhood stresses the role of youth in 'shaping, sharing and transforming their own lives' (Livingstone and Drotner 2008: 7; James, Jencks and Prout 1998; Cosaro 1994). Within this framework, children and youth are recognized as 'beings' rather than 'becomings' who are capable of, and quite proficient at, creating their own social and material worlds. As is commonly acknowledged in popular and academic discourse, the teenage years mark a time in youths' lives where establishing independence and a sense of autonomy from families and other institutions (such as schools) gives way to the influence of friends and peer groups.[3]

In light of the tensions over independence and autonomy during the teenage years, the bedroom holds a special place in the imaginations of many youth. Within the United States, the importance of separate and distinctive bedrooms for siblings emerged in the eighteenth century (Aries 1962; Calvert 1992). As Karen Calvert (1992) observes, 'experts and parents believed that children given their own rooms would study better without interruptions, take greater pride in their room since it was really their own and so keep it clean and neat, and appreciate a private place to entertain their friends' (135–6). Perhaps more important, bedrooms emerged as a key space in the home because they represented a space of containment, a place where middle-class parents could keep their children, and especially their daughters, protected from the outside world (Gutman and de Connick-Smith 2008). Contemporary work on girls' identity development also reveals the salience of bedrooms in middle-class girls' lives. Re-appropriating the spaces of their historical containment, girls use their bedroom to express and develop their sense of self through the organization and decoration of walls and surfaces (Clarke 2008; Kearney 2006; Mazzarella 2005; McRobbie and Garber 2000; Steele and Brown 1995). As a location that tends to be 'private' (or at least is ideally associated with privacy), the bedroom represents an important space for exploration, experimentation and play (Bloustein 2003; Bovill and Livingstone 2001).

The presence of a host of new media in bedrooms—ranging from televisions, radios, telephones, mobile phones and computers—challenges the bedroom's status as a space of containment and privacy. Nothing has brought this tension to the fore more than teenagers' use of social network sites and other 'social media'. The creation of a MySpace or Facebook profile and page with pictures, personal details and other information is designed to connect and enhance communication between classmates, friends, family, co-workers and other acquaintances. Russell, Ito, Richmond and Tuters (2008) use the term 'networked public culture' to characterize the ways in which 'those cultural artifacts associated with "personal" culture (like home movies, snapshots, diaries, and scrapbooks) have now entered the arena of "public" culture (like newspapers, cinema, and television)'. Although the connections and interactions between participants qualitatively varies with particular Web sites, interests and activities, it is clear that a broad spectrum of kids and adults now participate in creating, maintaining and negotiating expanded range of connections using these sites. Indeed, much of the research on youth and the Internet have focused upon the public nature of these Web sites, particularly the role of an imagined and unimagined audience. Excited by the possibility of 'hanging out' with their friends in social spaces which are largely (though not exclusively) outside the purview of adults and parents (Horst, Herr-Stephenson and Robinson forthcoming), youth view social network sites as important tools and spaces develop relationships with their friends and peers. In the following sections, I turn to the ways in which American youth like Ann create order in and through the construction, alteration and appropriation of their interconnected media worlds.

Ann: An Introduction

I first met Ann during her senior year located in high school in a suburban neighbourhood between San Jose and San Francisco. A 'typical' American teenager, Ann's primary concerns revolved around clothes, her new car, her upcoming prom and spending as much time as possible with her friends. At the time of our first interview, she was living at home with her mom, dad and younger sister Becca in their recently remodeled ranch-style home. Like other middle-class homes in the area, the house includes a formal living and dining room which overlook their landscaped backyard and garden as well as 'the shed', a wooden rectangular-shaped building with a wireless connection which houses Ann's father while he works at home as a consultant. Their mother uses one of the four bedrooms for her home office. Ann and her sister each have their own bedroom which is outfitted with a twin-sized bed and dresser as well as an ample desk and chair. Each daughter also has her own computer, a second-hand machine from their parents or parent's co-workers, and they have broadband throughout the house. Although the house is wired, the age of these second-hand machines means that certain programs only run on the newer machine which belongs to Becca. For this reason, Becca's computer stores their iTunes collection and some of Ann's photographs of friends, scenery and volunteer work in Latin America during the summer. Although they may borrow each other's computers for particular programs, they do not share each other's usernames and passwords.

Looking at the layout of each daughter's room, the sense of order and balance immediately comes to the fore. As noted previously, each daughter's bedroom is outfitted with the same basic infrastructure—a bed with headboard, dresser, chair, desk, computer as well as a bulletin board which is placed on the wall over each daughter's desk—and in rooms which are virtually identical in size and shape. Although the arrangement of the furniture in the room(s) varies slightly, the walls have been painted in a two-toned matte color scheme which is 'unique' to each daughter. Becca's room is painted lilac with cream trim. The cream trim in the room is coordinated with the cream-colored desk, headboard, dresser and pinboard filled with pictures of friends, movie ticket stubs and mementoes from her soccer activities. Her bed linens are also lilac and cream. Ann's bedroom consists of cream-colored furniture, the furniture offset by pink walls, pink and brown striped curtains, a brown rug, pink bed linens and a chocolate brown comforter. Ann's color coordination continues in the range of pink and brown accessories, such as pink pen holders, brown file folders and a slightly lighter pink bulletin board which is filled with pictures of Ann and her friends attending dances, sports team awards, sports calendars, ticket stubs from a recent Britney Spears concert as well as two acceptance letters to college (see Figures 7.1 and 7.2).

Order and Disorder on MySpace

Throughout her junior and senior year of high school, Ann was an active MySpace user, uploading pictures and commenting on friend's comments on a daily

Figure 7.1 Ann's desk and bulletin board.

Aesthetics of the Self: Digital Mediations • **103**

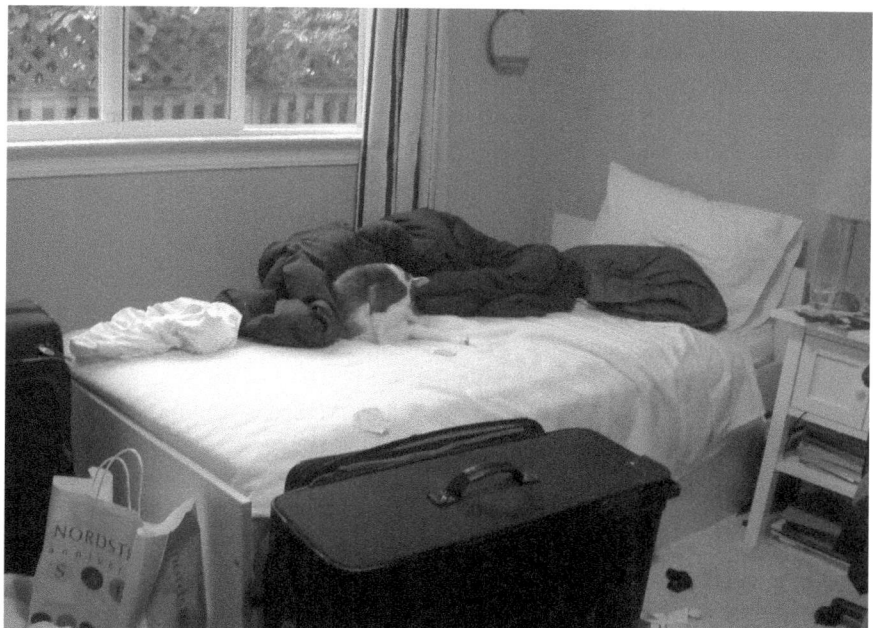

Figure 7.2 Ann's bedroom, one week before leaving for college.

basis. Beginning in the summer of her junior year, Ann also participated in what she called 'MySpace parties' which involved dressing up and taking photographs individually and with friends to post on their respective MySpace pages. In these 'parties', which were often provocative in nature, Ann and her friends enjoyed trying on different clothing, exploring their burgeoning aesthetic sensibilities and sexuality by donning short skirts, bra tops, fishnet stockings or other 'sexy' clothes (Woodward 2005). This space was particularly appealing for Ann who used MySpace to talk to 'guys' whom she was interested in; because she attended an all-girls religious school Ann felt she possessed precious little time for meeting and interacting with guys. With the incorporation of video on MySpace, Ann also viewed videos her friends crafted of 'funny stuff', such as her friends dancing or doing other 'random' things.

While the pictures, songs, personality, quizzes and other content on her MySpace page changed on an intermittent basis, Ann's favourite part of her page, and the most consistent feature of her MySpace page and profile, involved the incorporation of Ann's signature colors, brown and pink. Describing her MySpace page, Ann notes that '... it's actually the colors of my room so it's like brown and pink. And then I don't know. I had... a default pink so it's like what everyone sees when they see a comment.' As Ann suggests, her personal page mirrors the private space of her bedroom at home. The walls of her room are painted in a matte-based chocolate brown as are the main features of her room, such as her twin-sized comforter, her large desk and a large French bulletin board. Other mauve and chocolate brown accents, such throw pillows on the bed, the ribbon on her bulletin board, the cushion on her desk chair and picture frames, have been carefully selected and arranged throughout her bedroom.

For Ann, brown and pink constitute the backdrop to her daily life in 'online' and 'offline' spaces. However, after a myriad of media reports condemning MySpace, Ann's parents decided to ban MySpace from their daughters' lives. When I first arranged to interview Ann and Becca, their mother called my cell phone to inquire about interviewing her daughters. During our initial conversation, their mother stated somewhat defensively that 'the girls will probably tell you that they are mad at me' because she recently made them take down their MySpace profiles after all of the major controversy about girls running away or being abducted by strange older men lurking on MySpace (see Cassell and Cramer 2008; Buckingham 2000). She continued to explain that she did not think the girls fully understood that the site is not private and for this reason she decided to take a hard line, forbidding them from creating profiles on MySpace.

Indeed, when I arrived at the interview Ann was quick to tell me that her parents had banned MySpace multiple times and how difficult this regulation had been for her since she used MySpace (and Instant Messaging) to communicate with her friends outside of school. This also curtailed her ability to get to know and 'talk to' boyfriends before they officially become boyfriends, a practice she felt was an improvement upon the serial dating she would have engaged in without MySpace (Pascoe forthcoming). The first time her parents banned MySpace, Ann decided to change a few things to conceal her usage. A few weeks later her mother discovered she still had a MySpace profile and forced Ann to 'cancel it, delete it from there' just because 'they're like "oh, you're gonna get raped or something and someone's gonna find you."' Ann 'tried to live without it', but in a few weeks she broke down and created yet another new profile so that she could be 'in' on the gossip and news, one of the only ways that she could hang out with her friends outside of school. Given her identification with brown and pink, the color scheme was the first aspect of the page she decided to resurrect.

Shortly thereafter, yet another media frenzy made headlines, a teenage girl who had gone missing after meeting with a man she met on MySpace. The same day, Ann received a call from her sister Becca on her mobile phone while she was babysitting to say that she overheard their parents talking about confronting the girls about their MySpace profiles. Not wanting to get in trouble for still having a MySpace account, Becca immediately logged onto the site and deleted her own profile. Because she did not have Ann's password, Becca called Ann so she could change and delete Ann's account, thus avoiding a conflict at home.

While Ann's parents placed a great deal of pressure on their daughters to stay off MySpace, outside of her family, the pressure to have a MySpace profile was immense. One week later, a few of Ann's friends decided to establish a new MySpace page on Ann's behalf. Although her friends attempted to personalize her site by using a nickname, mentioning her favorite songs and uploading a few pictures, they failed to carry out one very critical dimension of Ann's aesthetic self, the mauve background and chocolate brown font. Between Ann's lack of identification with 'her' new MySpace page and the covert measures she needed to take to access the page (usually at a friend's house), Ann's interest in MySpace began to decline.

Imagining College Life on Facebook

Ann's dwindling participation in MySpace corresponded with a series of rites of passage associated with middle-class American teenage life: prom, graduation and, for the privileged, a post-graduation trip with friends to a resort in Mexico. Although Ann did not consider herself to be academically at the top of her class, she ultimately had the choice of a small, liberal arts college in Washington state or a school in the California State University system which offered Ann a small swimming scholarship. Her other friends, many of whom were accomplished athletes, opted for one of the large land grant schools in the University of California system, such as University of California, Irvine and University of California, Davis. Not long after she accepted her offer to a liberal arts college in Washington state, Ann received an invitation to participate in Facebook, a social networking site originally designed for the college community (see Figure 7.3).

By the time I interviewed Ann again in the summer of 2006, she was fully immersed in the transition into a new phase of her life and, in turn, a new set of social practices. Ann's formal introduction to Facebook came through her future dorm's RA (Resident Assistant). Ann's RA sent her an invite to be part of the 'Crystal Mountain' wing, part of a wider network of ninety dorm residents attending her new college. In the first two weeks after accepting the invitation and creating a page and profile, Ann spent hours at a time perusing different people's sites, looking for familiar names and faces and checking out friends of friends. Although unable to re-construct her page in brown and pink as she did on MySpace, Ann eventually added a picture of herself hiking in Mexico. As the summer progressed, she felt that she was becoming 'addicted' to Facebook, checking it anytime she has a free moment, typically for about ten minutes at a time. Ann checked her Facebook for status updates (e.g. if someone has changed his or her profile) an average of four to five times per day, in effect almost anytime she returned home. Through this brief, repetitive engagement, Ann started to meet the other students slated to live in her dorm, the most important

106 • *Anthropology and the Individual*

Figure 7.3 Ann checking her Facebook page.

and exciting of these new connections being her future roommate Sarah. Describing her Facebook page, Ann enthusiastically explains,

> And you can see everyone else's dorm room and I have groups. Like everyone in my dorm room is in this group. And you can see like all the others… and so like I can see who my RA is going to be and stuff and so it's like really cool. And then I have—I can show you my roommate! It's really exciting. So I can see her. And so it's, I don't know, I can just see a picture of her instead of having to wait and stuff.

Over the course of the summer, Ann and Sarah 'poked' each other, the digital equivalent of touching another person on the shoulder (indicated on the Facebook home page by an icon that says 'Sarah poked you') and wrote messages continuously.[4] Some of these conversations were pragmatic, such as when they planned to move, how much 'stuff' they had or what classes they thought they might take. But the substance of many of these conversations involved exploring how Sarah and

Ann would 'get along'. Just as Ann's sense of self materialized through the creation of a continuous aesthetic sensibility in her bedroom and on her MySpace page, she searched Sarah's Facebook page for insight into what she imagined would be a shared aesthetic. The first clues she detected involved Sarah's taste in music and media. As Ann describes,

> But actually her and I like a lot of the same music, I could tell from her Facebook. And so we were talking about concerts that we've been to this summer and stuff. So I'm sure—'cause she's bringing a TV 'cause she lives in a really, really rich area of Washington. And so I think she's bringing a really nice TV, so I'm like I should probably bring something kind of nice. So I think I'll bring this [iPod speakers] and then we can both hook our iPods up whenever we want...I'm supposed to bring a microwave but I don't think I'll bring a microwave.

As becomes evident in her discussion of what to bring to college, Ann was not just looking for shared interests or commonalities. She was also working to construct an aesthetic balance through consumer goods such as iPod speakers which she perceives as 'something kind of nice'. Purchasing new, trendy iPod speakers complemented a 'really nice TV' and created a space where they might share interests and, by extension, friendship. In addition to discerning each other's taste in music and media, Ann and Sarah also decided to upload a few pictures of their bedrooms at home onto their Facebook pages of things they planned to bring to their new dorm room (cf. Young 2004, 2005). Ann was thrilled when she looked at the photographs and saw Sarah's signature colors, 'I'm brown and pink stuff and she's brown and blue stuff!' Ann surmised that this aesthetic harmony would also signify a harmonious relationship.

Conclusion: Youth and the Aesthetics of the Self

Individuality is highly valued in the United States, particularly in a place like Silicon Valley where culture and competition are closely intertwined (English-Lueck 2002; Saxenian 2006). In American society, adolescence is segmented as a particularly important time for discovering and expressing a sense of self that seems 'uniquely' one's own, an identity which is separate and autonomous from given social relationships, such as families, neighborhoods and communities (although see Coontz 1992). The locations of self-making and, in the language of Erving Goffman (1959), the 'presentation of the self' have roughly corresponded with interplay between the front stage (public) and the back stage (private spaces).[5] In the age of networked public culture, the boundaries between the public and private presentations of the self are increasingly blurred.

Since Hugh Miller's (1995) application of Goffman's symbolic interactionist approach to homepages, the focus on 'face' and presentation have remained central to the study of the constitution of the self and individual identity on the Internet, especially the formal (and often static and textual) presentations on webpages and other online sites. However, the material properties of new media and social network sites like MySpace and Facebook not only shape the way that these are expressed but, increasingly, the very terms and definitions of self. In addition to maintaining a collection of 'friends' (boyd 2008, forthcoming), MySpace enabled Ann to customize the background color and font of her profile page in the same color palate as her bedroom. It was also possible to add favorite songs, videos and a range of other features. Indeed, MySpace makes it easy to 'copy and paste' html code from others' profile pages and Web sites so that one can customize and copy the style on one's Web page; this ability to customize ultimately undermined Ann's friends' attempts to re-create a profile after Ann's parents forced her to delete her profile out of fear of the 'scale' of MySpace (Perkel 2008). The ability to delete and re-create profiles thus structures a very different engagement with digital spaces.

In contrast to MySpace, Facebook's basic blue-and-white template occurs on all profiles, allowing members to upload pictures and customize their information. For this reason, Ann appropriated Facebook to develop a sense of her future roommate's interests through pictures and to discern decorative style from the pictures of her bedroom rather than the aesthetics of her Facebook profile. Ann's strategy of ordering via Facebook mirrored the processes of ordering space in her bedroom and family home; she felt compelled to maintain a balance in terms of the media which would be incorporated into their dorm room (a television and an iHome for their iPods). Ann also maintained the order of her future domestic life through the reconstitution of the two-toned color palette—brown and blue for her roommate Sarah and brown and pink for Ann—the brown working to merge Ann and Sarah's mutual sensibilities. Within the context of North American childhood, college also represents a time to assert independence and define and redefine one's own routines, habits and moralities. For most first- and second-year college students, dorm rooms represent a space over which they have full control without the input of their parents, siblings, cousins or grandparents, often for the first time in their lives.

One of the interesting aspects of Ann's use of MySpace and Facebook is the extent to which she sees her use of social network sites as intertwined with her everyday physical environment. This is a direct contrast to the ways in which Malcolm (see Daniel Miller's Introduction, this volume) comprehends the possibilities of aesthetic order between the relative materiality of the digital and physical spaces. For Malcolm, his engagements on his computer, over email and the 'digital' world are purposefully non-material and thus represent continuity between life and death and the spiritual world. By contrast, Ann views MySpace and Facebook as places where the physical and material—relationships, tastes and connections—are reaffirmed. Her engagement in the digital world is only significant in that it reinforces the same physical and material objects that Malcolm works to eschew (Strathern 2004). For Ann, MySpace and Facebook are tangible spaces where she establishes and asserts her sense of self. In a consumer culture like the United States, Ann essentially constructs herself as different configurations of pre-determined selections within the generally acceptable genres of her peers, a person who likes mauve and chocolate brown, someone who likes a particular kind of music and someone who maintains a balance and order in all of the 'environments' she inhabits. And like many American teenagers, her sense of self in the world hinges upon asserting a material presence in physical and digital worlds.

What this analysis suggests is that the literature on the self and self-formation is enhanced through a consideration of material culture precisely because the experience of what is being created here is not an isolated self based within the mind of the individual or a 'switchboard between ties and networks' that 'operates a separate community network, and switches rapidly among multiple sub-networks' (Wellman et al. 2003). Rather, it is an aesthetic based on the balance between and continuity between a variety of key relationships. These may be objects, persons or places. In many ways Ann uses her roommate as a critical background relationship for her Facebook profile, in much the same fashion she used her bedroom as the critical background relationship for her MySpace. The social network sites in which Ann chooses to participate extend the mirror in which she comes to see herself and gain a sense of who she might be. However, because the sites are used for these tasks, the virtual also must be fully grounded and compatible with offline relationships that are used to do much the same thing.

Just as the social network sites provide structures, and in turn, constraints upon the way the self is formed and re-formed online, ordering in homes and dorm rooms are also carried out within tight constraints. In the chapters by Julie Botticello, Gabrielle Hosein and Bodil Olesen in this volume, these constraints are the wider social norms or the state. In this chapter, it might appear as merely the private household and parents who embody such constraints. As becomes quite clear, Ann's parents' attitudes and anxieties concerning MySpace reflect the wider normative order being established by the public sphere and media concern with potential dangers to those who put themselves into the public domain. By the same token it is the normative order that provides for and facilities these zones of expression, from bedroom to college dorms to a social network site that encourages personalization, as in MySpace, or in some ways inhibits innovation as in Facebook. While there are particular distinctions in terms of content that are centred around the concerns of youth, the situation for these young adults is not particularly distinct from that of older adults. In many respects, Ann's attempts to order her world and her bedroom mimic an adult playing with the possibility of the house (Dimitris Dalakaglou, this volume) or a man finding himself in the mirror of commodities (Magdalena Crăciun, this volume). Juxtaposing this chapter with other chapters in this volume, it becomes clear that participation in social network sites and the motivations that underpin the ordering and negotiation of the self in these spaces are not fundamentally different from non-youth practices. The aesthetic of social network sites is based on a balance of constraint, normativity and innovation that Ann will very likely continue to be engaged with, using similar media and forms of expression, in common with groups of like-minded peers, for the rest of her life.

Acknowledgements

Research for this project was conducted in Silicon Valley, California, between January 2006 and June 2008 with the support of the John D. and Catherine T. Macarthur Foundation ('Kids' Informal Learning with Digital Media: An Ethnographic Investigation of Innovative Knowledge Cultures' project). I thank Danny Miller, C. J. Pascoe and Dan Perkel for their insights on this case study.

Notes

1. For an overview of MySpace (http://www.myspace.com/), Facebook (http://www.facebook.com/) and social network sites, see boyd and Ellison (2007); boyd (2009) and Perkel (2008).
2. There is some debate over the use of the term 'social networking sites' and 'social network sites' (see boyd and Ellison 2007). Although they are used interchangeably, I primarily use the term 'social network site' in this chapter in order to capture the sense that participants often discuss and understand them as 'places'.
3. These descriptions of childhood are particular to 'Western' and American constructions of childhood. For a review of recent work on childhood in a range of social and cultural contexts, see Gutman and de Connick-Smith (2008); Levine and New (2008); Stephens (1995) and Amit-Talal and Wulff (1995).
4. Facebook describes 'poking' as a way to interact with friends that is non-specific: 'A poke is a way to interact with your friends on Facebook. When we created the poke, we thought it would be cool to have a feature without any specific purpose. People interpret the poke in many different ways, and we encourage you to come up with your own meanings.' http://www.facebook.com/help.php?page=20, November 8 2008.
5. For Goffman (1959), the front is 'that part of the individual's performance which regularly functions in a general and fixed fashion to define the situation for those who observe the performance' (22), the space where one 'gives off' impressions to others. Although much of the interaction during the performance shapes the continued interaction, longer-term identity formation takes place in the back stage, the location where the individual internalizes what has been learned in the performance. As Robinson (2007) observes, 'the self internalizes the social world as part of the process of anticipating and interpreting the "generalized other"' (98). Admittedly Goffman used the dramaturgy of the stage (front stage

and back stage) as a metaphor rather than literal spaces. However, I would like to extend this conceptually to illustrate the shifts between private and public which are occurring here.

References

Amit-Talal, V. and Wulff, H. (eds) (1995), *Youth Cultures: A Cross-Cultural Comparison,* London: Routledge.

Aries, P. (1962), *Centuries of Childhood,* New York: Vintage Books.

Bloustein, G. (2003), *Girl Making: A Cross-Cultural Ethnography on the Processes of Growing Up Female,* Oxford: Berghahn Books.

Bovill, M. and Livingstone, S. (2001), 'Bedroom Culture and the Privatization of Media Use', in S. Livingstone and M. Bovill (eds), *Children and Their Changing Media Environment: A European Comparative Study,* Mahwah, NJ: Lawrence Erlbaum Associates, 179–200.

boyd, d. (2008), 'Why Youth (Heart) Social Network Sites: The Role of Networked Publics in Teenage Social Life', in D. Buckingham (ed.), *Youth, Identity, and Digital Media,* The John D. and Catherine T. MacArthur Foundation Series on Digital Media and Learning, Cambridge, MA: The MIT Press, 119–42.

boyd, d. (forthcoming), 'Friendship', in *Hanging Out, Messing Around, Geeking Out: Living and Learning with New Media,* Cambridge, MA: The MIT Press.

boyd, d. m. and Ellison, N. B. (2007), 'Social Network Sites: Definition, History, and Scholarship', *Journal of Computer-Mediated Communication,* 13(1), article 11, http://jcmc.indiana.edu/vol13/issue1/boyd.ellison.html (accessed 8 January 2008).

Buckingham, D. (2000), *After the Death of Childhood: Growing Up in the Age of Electronic Media,* Cambridge: Polity Press.

Calvert, K. (1992), *Children in the House: The Material Culture of Early Childhood, 1600–1900,* Boston: Northeastern University Press.

Cassell, J. and Cramer, M. (2008), 'High Tech or High Risk: Moral Panics about Girls Online', in T. McPherson (ed.), *Digital Youth, Innovation, and the Unexpected,* The John D. and Catherine T. MacArthur Foundation Series on Digital Media and Learning, Cambridge, MA: The MIT Press, 53–76.

Castells, M. (2000), *The Rise of the Network Society, The Information Age: Economy, Society and Culture,* vol. I, 2nd edn, Oxford: Blackwell.

Clarke, A. J. (2008), 'Coming of Age in Suburbia: Gifting the Consumer Child', in M. Gutman and N. de Coninck-Smith (eds), *Designing Modern Childhoods,* New Brunswick, NJ: Rutgers University Press, 253–68.

Coontz, S. (1992), *The Way We Never Were: American Families and the Nostalgia Trap,* New York: Basic Books.

Cosaro, W. (1994), *The Sociology of Childhood,* Thousand Oaks, CA: Pine Forge Press.

English-Lueck, J. (2002), *SiliconValley@Cultures*, Stanford, CA: Stanford University Press.

Gutman, M. and N. de Connick-Smith (eds) (2008), *Designing Modern Childhoods*, New Brunswick, NJ: Rutgers University Press.

Goffman, E. (1959), *The Presentation of Self in Everyday Life*, New York: Anchor Books.

Horst, H., Herr-Stephenson, B. and Robinson, L. (forthcoming), 'Media Ecologies', in *Hanging Out, Messing Around, Geeking Out: Living and Learning with New Media*, Cambridge, MA: The MIT Press.

Horst, H. and Miller, D. (2005), 'From Kinship to Link-up: Cell Phones and Social Networking in Jamaica', *Current Anthropology*, 46(5): 755–78.

James, A., Jencks, C. and Prout, A. (1998), *Theorizing Childhood*, Cambridge: Cambridge University Press.

Kearney, M. C. (2006), *Girls Make Media*, London: Routledge.

Levine, Robert and Rebecca New (eds) (2008), *Anthropology and Child Development: A Cross-Cultural Reader*, Oxford: Blackwell.

Ling, R. (2008), *New Tech, New Ties: How Mobile Communication Is Reshaping Social Cohesion*, Cambridge, MA: The MIT Press.

Livingstone, S. and Drotner, K. (2008), 'Introduction', in K. Drotner and S. Livingstone (eds), *The International Handbook of Children, Media and Culture*, Los Angeles: Sage Publications, 1–16.

Low, S. (2003), *Behind the Gates: Life, Security, and the Pursuit of Happiness in Fortress America*, London: Routledge.

Matsuda, M. (2005a), 'The Social Construction of Technological Systems: Discourses of Keitai in Japan', in M. Ito, D. Okabe and M. Matsuda (eds), *Personal, Portable, Pedestrian: Mobile Phones in Japanese Life*, Cambridge, MA: The MIT Press, 19–40.

Matsuda, M. (2005b), 'Mobile Communication and Selective Sociality', in M. Ito, D. Okabe and M. Matsuda (eds), *Personal, Portable, Pedestrian: Mobile Phones in Japanese Life*, Cambridge, MA: The MIT Press, 123–42.

Mazzarella, S. R. (2005), 'Claiming a Space', in S. R. Mazzarella (ed.), *Girl Wide Web*, New York: Peter Lang Publishing, 141–60.

McRobbie, A. and Garber, J. (2000 [1978]), 'Girls and Subcultures', in A. McRobbie (ed.), *Feminism and Youth Subcultures*, 2nd edn, London: Routledge, 12–25.

Miller, D. and Slater, D. (2000), *The Internet: An Ethnographic Approach*, Oxford: Berg.

Miller, H. W. (1995), 'Goffman on the Internet: The Presentation of Self in Electronic Life', Paper presented at the Embodied Knowledge and Virtual Space Conference, http://www.ntu.ac.uk/soc/psych/miller/goffman.htm (accessed 15 September 2005).

Parsons, T. and Bales, R. F. (1955), *Family, Socialization and Interaction Processes*, New York: The Free Press.

Pascoe, C. J. (forthcoming), 'Intimacy', in *Hanging Out, Messing Around, Geeking Out: Living and Learning with New Media,* Cambridge, MA: The MIT Press.

Perkel, D. (2008), 'Copy and Paste Literacy? Literacy Practices in the Production of a MySpace Profile', in K. Drotner, H. S. Jensen and K. Schroeder (eds), *Informal Learning and Digital Media: Constructions, Contexts, Consequences,* Newcastle: Cambridge Scholars Press, 203–24.

Putnam, R. (2000), *Bowling Alone,* New York: Simon and Schuster.

Robinson, L. (2007), 'The Cyberself: The Self-ing Project Goes Online, Symbolic Interaction in the Digital Age', *New Media and Society,* 9(1): 93–110.

Russell, A., Ito, M., Richmond, T. and Tuters, M. (2008), 'Culture: Networked Public Culture', in K. Varnelis (ed.), *Networked Public Culture,* http://www.networked publics.org/ (accessed 25 June 2008).

Saxenian, A. (2006), *The New Argonauts: Regional Advantage in a Global Economy,* Cambridge, MA: Harvard University Press.

Steele, J. R. and Brown, J. D. (1995), 'Adolescent Room Culture: Studying Media in the Context of Everyday Life', *Journal of Youth and Adolescence,* 24(5): 551–76.

Stephens, Sharon (ed) (1995), *Children and the Politics of Culture,* Princeton, Princeton University Press.

Strathern, M. (2004), 'The Whole Person and Its Artifacts', *Annual Review of Anthropology,* 33: 1–19.

Wellman, B. (2001), 'Physical Place and Cyber-place: The Rise of Networked Individualism', *International Journal for Urban and Regional Research,* 25: 227–52.

Wellman, B., Quan-Haase, A., Boase, J., Chen, W., Hampton, K., Isla de Diaz, I. and Miyata, K. (2003), 'The Social Affordances of the Internet for Networked Individualism', *Journal of Computer Mediated Communication,* 8(3), http://jcmc.indiana.edu/vol8/issue3/wellman.html (accessed 28 June 2008).

Woodward, S. (2005), 'Looking Good, Feeling Right: Aesthetics of the Self', in S. Kuechler and D. Miller (eds), *Clothing as Material Culture,* Oxford: Berg, 21–40.

Young, D. (2004), 'The Material Value of Colour: The Estate Agent's Tale', *Home Cultures,* 1(1): 5–22.

Young, D. (2005), 'The Colours of Things', in P. Spyer, C. Tilley, S. Kuechler and W. Keane (eds), *Handbook of Material Culture,* Thousand Oaks, CA: Sage Publications, 173–85.

–8–

Unmaking Family Relationships: Belgrade Mothers and Their Migrant Children

Ivana Bajić-Hajduković

This chapter is based on an ethnographic study of the material culture of post-Yugoslav migration from Belgrade, conducted in the period 2005–2006 in London and Belgrade.[1] London-based stories of Serbian migration were 'classic' accounts of struggles for continuity in one's narrative identity (Ricoeur 1992) ruptured temporarily by the loss of citizenship,[2] ethnic conflicts and genocide, the rise of nationalism and dictatorship in Serbia. Those were stories about ruptures, but also about new beginnings, new homes, about their new families and their future. Immigrants from ex-Yugoslavia whom I met in London belonged to the cosmopolitan city as much as they carried in themselves a part of an imagined Yugoslav community (Anderson 1983) which withered away fifteen years ago with the break-up of Yugoslavia. Most of my London-based informants were aged between twenty-five and forty-five; some of them had started a family in their new country, few were divorced or single; all of them, however, were settled down in London. They are not temporary guest workers in the United Kingdom and they do not have a family to feed in Belgrade. In contrast to the chapter by Dalakoglou they do not build homes in Belgrade because they have a mortgage to pay in London.[3] Most of the migrants had no intentions of moving back to Belgrade because of the children, as they wanted them to have a better future.

There is now a considerable amount of research on these trajectories of migrants and their stories,[4] but by comparison there is a much neglected other story which is rarely told. What happened to those left behind in Belgrade? What about the ageing parents, brothers, sisters, nephews and nieces? How are they affected by the migration of their loved ones? Do they see them merely as a source of income to top-up their pensions? What happens to a parent-child relationship in a specific context of immigrants' families in Belgrade for whom it is almost impossible to get a visa for any country, and who see their children once a year or once in five, ten or fifteen years? For those left behind in the homeland, I would argue, migration of their loved ones is often the end of what had been a sustained and significant relationship. The relationship does not necessarily cease but it certainly is transformed as a result of migration.

Unlike English kinship which is characterized by the individuality of persons (Strathern 1992: 14), the first fact of Serbian kinship is shared normativity. Thus, as the results of my ethnographic research with post-1990 emigrants from Belgrade have demonstrated, relationship between parents and migrant children transforms because practices (Bourdieu 1977) of migrant children change compared to those of sons and daughters who stayed in the country of origin. My research has shown that migrant children are more likely than their non-migrant siblings in Belgrade to betray normative expectations in favour of a more, in their view, practical, experiential relationship. Through clashes between normative expectations and negotiated experience in the relationship between Belgrade parents and their migrant children becomes apparent an objectification of tensions inherent in different conceptualizations of kinship relationships.

As Miller argues in the 'Introduction' to this volume, instead of juxtaposing individuals to society, we look at how the individuals appropriate the world through relationships to things and to others. These relationships, according to Miller, constitute what he terms an 'aesthetic'. This chapter is an attempt to sketch out nuances of the aesthetics of a mother-child relationship, as it manifests itself in the context of post-1990 Serbian migration from Belgrade. What makes this example particularly interesting is a sense of tragedy that transpires from a relationship based on two opposing outcomes, that of a migrant son-cum-Londoner who repudiates prior expectations, and his mother living in Serbia where kinship relations are still dominated by strong normative expectations. Both a mother and a son make sense of their lives according to certain normative rules, but when it comes to their relationship, the difference between those becomes painfully and irreconcilably apparent. Only one event has the power to bridge the gap between the son's and the mother's sense of normative, and that is death.

Mrs Anka[5] is a retired teacher of mathematics and physics in her early seventies. She lives in a small town near Belgrade; her son Vladimir has been living in London for the last fifteen years. Vladimir was in his late twenties in 1992 when he left Belgrade. The theatre he worked for went on a world tour in 1992; instead of returning to Belgrade, Vladimir decided to leave his job in the theatre and go to London. Since then Vladimir has never been back to Belgrade.

The case of Mrs Anka and her son Vladimir is a bit extreme in a sense that Serbian society is still dominantly patriarchal and family ties play a very important role (see for example Milić 1994; Blagojević 1997; Tomanović 2004), and Vladimir's behaviour, though not an exception among my London informants, was not common. On the other hand, however, Vladimir's case is typical in a sense that he managed to blend into London's diverse social landscape, and similarly to my other Serbian informants, he was free to contextualize his existence between a cosmopolitan Londoner and a 'stateless' person.[6] In other words, there is nothing unusual about Vladimir within a London context and in this respect he could easily fit in within the framework of Miller's study of people living in a randomly chosen street in South

London (see Miller 2008). His case reads as extreme only when placed in a context of a parent-child relationship in Serbia.

In the first part of this chapter I will present the son's and mother's narratives, which richly illustrate strategies of making sense of one's life in a post-communist and a post-conflict Serbian society; one of the consequences of this turmoil was a massive emigration from Serbia, with hundreds of thousands of young and skilled Belgraders seeking their fortunes in London, New York, Toronto and elsewhere. In the second part of the chapter I will discuss the objectification of a mother-son relation in this context of Serbian migration. Following Strathern's distinction between mediated and unmediated relationships (Strathern 1988: 178–9), I will discuss tensions arising from this particular mother-son relationship as an example of unmediated relations which creates asymmetry between the two parties. Finally in the concluding part of this chapter I will tie the previous discussion to the concept of aesthetics as used by Strathern (1988) and by Miller in the 'Introduction' to this volume.

The Son

Vladimir came to London in December 1992. He left behind a job in a theatre, his flat in central Belgrade, unfinished studies of architecture, and a girlfriend who was pregnant with his child at that time. He also left behind a country that was at war in which he did not want to take part. He had subsequently never returned to visit Serbia. Vladimir is in his mid-forties now; for the last ten years he has been living in the same house in east London, sharing with nine or ten other people. He is not married but has a son with his ex-girlfriend from Belgrade. We first met in October 2005 for an interview; soon after that Vladimir asked to stop seeing me in person and instead offered to answer the rest of my questions via email. It was not before March 2006 that he let me visit him in his home. Before going there I went through my notes and email correspondence and came across an interesting passage about the connection between his London life and events in the former Yugoslavia in the 1990s:

> [...] It was even worse in 1995 when Krajina fell... I was at that time working in some office, designing a sports hall for a college in Dublin, a fire staircase for a Turkish restaurant, a canteen for a textile factory, counting windows in some warehouse... and in this finally won deep ignorance, I didn't read newspapers nor watched television, nor was I interested in anything going on there. I remember my cold answer and switching to another subject when my boss one morning all worried showed me the front page of 'The Independent' with Serbian refugees fleeing on tractors from Croatia to Serbia. Man, he was more distressed than I was and I didn't even understand what was going on! Only much later did I understand and feel what actually happened in that dirtiest 'Storm' in the West.

I remember in 1997 when Belgrade was for three months clogged with protestants against Milošević one of our lecturers told me dead serious while we were on a study trip in Crete: 'You should be there!' I wanted to hit that infantile spoilt idiot for whom protests were something romantic and exotic, a man who never participated in any protest, who was never beaten up by police, who hasn't lived a single day in exile nor frequented refugee courts which I, thank goodness, had visited all. I didn't have a country, a people, a nation, only what at that moment and time I was working on.

I think you are right, my life doesn't correspond to anything that goes on there [in Serbia] nor to what was going on in the 1990s; the thought about travelling to Serbia is like a thought about travelling in a time-machine back to childhood, time not present. I don't exist there now. Once the relationship with a homogenous national surrounding was broken, new horizons had opened in front of me and I now live in a world, without a country, without a nation, as a migrant at one place, as a citizen of the world, a nomad with a garden.

Greetings from a room of trees.

V
CV
G.

Vladimir's house is distinctly separated between the communal and the private space. The kitchen which he shares with other flat-mates is crammed with things such as jars with spices, mugs, glasses, pots hanging all over, plants and pebbles thrown randomly on the floor, among which a kitchen table and chairs disappear visually even though they hold a central position in the room (see Figure 8.1). In contrast to the kitchen his living room looks like everything but a space in which someone has been living for more than ten years. It is a huge white space of around twenty square metres, with a high ceiling and no furniture apart from an architect's desk and chair. In one of the corners there is a bare piece of wall with the bricks exposed; Vladimir explains that originally there had been a massive built-in cupboard fitted by hinges onto the wall; as he did not want any solid furniture to take up space in the room, he pulled the cupboard out. Behind the drawing desk there is a pot with a banana tree, to the left of it a lemon tree; in the left part of the room there is a linden tree and in the left corner stands a fig tree. A hammock hangs between the linden tree and the fig tree. In the corner next to the brick wall there is a rolled-up mat, which, Vladimir explains, serves as a bed. In the left corner there are two smallish piles of clothes and several toiletry items (see Figure 8.2). There is a newly fitted wooden floor in the room and several small rugs and scarves thrown on it. Behind the lemon tree, next to the outer wall facing the street, there are several books, mostly reference books—dictionaries, astrology books and one or two on architecture. The architect's drawing desk, which does not have any drawers, is higher than normal desks, as is the chair. There is a laptop on the desk, a stack of papers and a desk lamp. Along the wall on the right there are dried flowers, some pebbles and shells and dried banana

Unmaking Family Relationships • 119

Figure 8.1 Kitchen in Vladimir's house (photo: I. Bajić-Hajduković).

Figure 8.2 A detail from Vladimir's room (photo: I. Bajić-Hajduković).

leaves. There is not a single piece of furniture or a box for storing anything in that room. Everything that is contained in the room is on display, and everything on display is transient. The sleeping mat is rolled up and placed in the corner during the day, clothes can be moved from the left corner and placed anywhere else, the trees can be shuffled around the room or put outside in the garden, the small scarves and rugs are slippery and not fixed in one place on the floor. The only object with any storing facilities in the room is a computer. However, not even the computer is used to store memories as Vladimir deletes all emails he receives, taking care that there is no clutter or memories stored anywhere. This deliberate emptiness strikes me as most unusual (although it obviously builds upon a certain minimalist aesthetic that is associated with designers and architects) and I try to find out if there is by any chance another room or space in which he actually keeps things, photographs, anything:

> 'Well, you see, there is no other stuff,' replies Vladimir. 'This is all. What you see in front of you, that's my life. This room was completely bare until a couple of months ago when I fitted the new wooden floor and put these trees in pots. Until then there was literally nothing inside but the drawing desk. I simply don't like to remember the person I was yesterday or at any time in the past. Sometimes I would buy a t-shirt, wear it only once and then take it to a charity shop. I lost a country, I lost my mother tongue, I don't belong to any nation any more... I am like Corto Maltese,[7] a sailor without a ship... I reject things, people, relationships, I move on very easily and I don't want to remember the years gone by and the different lives I've had in which I was someone I now wish I hadn't been... If you really insist to know, there is one thing which I kept throughout all these years—a battery charger that I brought with me from Belgrade.'

Vladimir is very systematic in clearing out anything that he thinks belongs to the past. This includes documents related to his studies in Belgrade, as well as a hefty file with his asylum application:

> The day I got 'Indefinite Leave to Remain' (in the United Kingdom), I burnt, literally burnt, all the documents, and trust me after years and years spent fighting with the Home Office in courts and repeating the same story of being a citizen of a country which ceased to exist in 1991 dozens of times in front of various officials, I had a huge amount of papers. I just wanted to forget what I'd been through, the humiliation, the despair, and a never-ending fight to prove I had no country to return to. It was such a relief getting rid of those papers. Now I'm officially recognized as a stateless person who doesn't belong anywhere. There is no continuity; I don't want to have continuity between the various Vladimirs I've been so far.

The Mother

Vladimir was one of the few London informants who agreed to put me in touch with their families in Serbia. His mother arranged to meet me in Vladimir's flat in the centre of Belgrade, where his sister has been living since Vladimir went away. Mrs Anka greets me outside the flat, at the lift door, smiles and takes a good look at me as if I am someone she has not seen in a while. As I prepare for the interview and put my notebook and pencil on the table, I suddenly hear Mrs Anka weeping. Her daughter

Mirjana bows her head and I sit there feeling very uncomfortable and unsure of what to say or do to ease this unpleasant situation. Mrs Anka stutters through the tears: 'What can I tell you about my Vladimir...I haven't seen him for fifteen years ...' We sit in the absent son's flat, we have gathered to talk about him, the absent son, and yet, during those endless minutes of crying his absence is more present and more tangible than anything else. His present absence is what makes his mother break down in tears in front of a stranger who has come to interview her, what makes his sister voiceless and still as a grave, as if he were an invisible conductor standing in the room and orchestrating the pool of emotions.

> 'I believe that he works so hard there just for sheer existence that he can't afford to come and visit us ...' begins Mrs Anka's story. 'I didn't want to be a burden to him and I said "Vladimir, I will come with a tourist agency to London and you will have no obligations towards me, I will arrange everything through the agency and we will only meet at a specific time, whenever you say, and this is how we will see each other." "No mother, I will come" [he would say to me]...and it's been like this for fifteen years. God knows how many times I've said I would go to see him, regardless of whether he wants it or not. And then again I think what's the point in going there against his will, what if he would get angry and say—"Mother, why did you come here, we haven't agreed to this"...It was much harder in the beginning; it is still hard, of course, but now this wish to see my son has become a dream...I imagine the door would open and Vladimir would come in. This is my dream now...and I would still like it to happen, but it will be as God says. It is all God's will. I am seventy, I approach the end of the life and I have witnessed that [it is all God's will]...I didn't give birth to my son to be separated from him for so many years. I thought he would live in our country and that everything would be alright. But it wasn't. That wretched war and everything else that was going on here in 1990s...horror. And the bombardments in 1999...as if it were a dream.'

Mrs Anka goes silent for a moment and then continues:

> He became estranged. I am not sure that it is only because he works a lot that he can't visit us. It seems that he accepted that world of alienation and that he doesn't need us any longer. The only thing left is when I tell him at the end of our conversation 'your mother kisses you' and he replies 'I kiss you too, mother.' We write to each other on the Internet, and every time I try to say some gentle words, he would make fun of it; I guess that's his way of pushing nostalgia away and of letting me know that he is not so sad about not being with us. He used to be very sensitive, very emotional. I think that severity of tense and difficult life over there has made him stronger and tougher. But I also think that he is a coward and that he is not so much afraid of the meeting as much as of the separation, how he will survive that...There is something else there as well. You know, Vladimir was pretty handsome and beautiful and I fear that maybe now that he got older his hair has become grey and maybe he is bald and that's why he wouldn't send any photos of himself to us. When I ask him to send us a photo, he only sends some where you can

see his profile or something like that. So either something happened with him or he is so vain that he doesn't want us to see what he looks like nowadays. Well, he is forty-three, you know.

Mrs Anka stops talking and gives me a long silent look. Even though she does not say it aloud, I feel the heaviness of her question hanging in the air. As I sit there listening and watching a mother dreaming to see her son, wondering why she was rejected as a mother and struggling to find excuses for his rejection, I find myself in an awkward position. I become like Hermes, a messenger carrying news from the underworld. I know what her son looks like, where he lives, what he eats, I know his girlfriend, some of his friends, I know what he does for a living, and I know why he will not go back to Serbia. I even have a photo of Vladimir and his house on my digital camera in a rucksack on the floor next to me. One part of me is urging me to take my camera out of a bag and shower this desperate woman with photos of her son, tell her everything that I know about him. And yet I have an equal amount of responsibility to protect her son's privacy. The pressure of the mother's unasked question feels heavier with every minute. Finally I resolve to answer this question and tell the mother what she hopes to hear about her son: that he is very busy, that he works really hard which is probably why he cannot visit them, that he did finish his studies in architecture and that he looks very youthful. I do not know if this has made me a lesser anthropologist, but it seemed the only right thing to do in that situation.

That was one of my last days in Belgrade and I was soon leaving for London. I offered Mrs Anka to send something to her son with me. I offered the same to Vladimir before going to Belgrade; he thanked me and said there was nothing he wanted to send and that he also did not need anything from there. His mother asked if I could take two or three litres of šljivovica.[8] I accepted to take one litre with me, and offered to take something else as well—photographs, books, or some food. She shrugged saying:

> He doesn't eat our food any more, not even sausages; his taste has changed. I know that he doesn't drink šljivovica either but his friends like it and I want him to have something from home to share with them. He always liked to have friends around, to cook, to bake cakes...he was still in primary school when he would bring a bunch of school friends home and make pancakes for them...I would only see the smoke coming out of the kitchen...then they would go to Mirjana's room and make a mess in there...Yes, he always liked to cook...It was nothing for him to make a rice pudding and bring a bunch of friends over to share it with them. He was a very social boy, he liked to play football, to hang around with his friends...Though I think in love he was very emotional and vulnerable and he would get really hurt after a break-up. He had that long-term girlfriend, he fell out with her, Yugoslavia fell apart, the war started, and he went on a tour with his theatre...that was the last time we saw him...

The Relationship

During the course of writing this chapter I learned about the death of Vladimir's sister. She died of cancer in her early forties. Vladimir went to Serbia for the first time since leaving the country in 1992, to bury his sister. A couple of months later, he went again to Serbia to visit his parents. When I asked him how come he was going there for the second time after such a long period, Vladimir replied: 'I went to a funeral; it was too short, too emotional... One minute mother was crying because of my sister, and the next she was smiling because of me... I had to go there again... my parents are old, and now that my sister is dead they have no one left.'

What this epilogue adds is an insight into how differently parents and children conceive of their relationship. Leaving Yugoslavia in early 1990s was a must for Vladimir; it was a refusal to fight in a war in which he did not want to take part, and a refusal to live as a refugee in his own country. After the first multiparty elections in Serbia in which Milošević's party won, Vladimir made a list of all the people he knew; he realized that he and his friends lived in a delusion because their impression had been that democrats would easily win the elections, and that now with Milošević as the leader of the country, Serbia was no longer the place for him to live. For Vladimir leaving Yugoslavia was also a refusal to be forced into a marriage that he did not want, and an attempt to start a new life without the burden of expectations from the family and his girlfriend.

Objects, according to Rowlands, 'are culturally constructed to connote and consolidate the possession of past events associated with their use of ownership' (1993: 144). Rowlands argues that the link between past, present and future is made through materiality of objects kept (1993). I have argued elsewhere (see Bajić-Hajduković 2008) that not objects alone but relationships as well are the embodiments of memories and as such they can also create links between past, present and future. Thus by rejecting both objects and people that may bring memories of his past, Vladimir not only repudiates the past, but rather the link between his past, present and future. He wants to live his life in London free from expectations from his family in Serbia, free from a burden of a contested Yugoslav identity, free to choose to work as an architect and/or a bicycle courier, and free to create his future as he wishes.

As much as Vladimir was concerned about his present life and trying to get rid of burdensome traces of the past, his mother was constantly slipping back into the past throughout our encounter. For Mrs Anka, her son is a reified memory of the boy she raised. While her daughter was alive, Mrs Anka could enact a mother-child relationship characteristical of the Serbian patriarchal society in which a child is expected to act as a child as long as the parents are alive. Thus to be rejected as a mother in a mother-child relationship by one child, while being able to maintain such relations with another child, was even more hurtful since she could compare the two relationships. She laments that she had not given birth to her son merely to be separated from him for so long, and she blames the war for this misfortune. In a mother-child relation where a son refuses to enact his part, the absence of a son implies an absence of a mother as well. To mourn the missing son is to mourn the missing mother as well. The grave atmosphere which characterized most of my encounters with mothers of emigrant children from Belgrade was thus not only caused by grief felt for a child who had gone away for good; it is as much a lament over one's own loss of 'mother' in herself.

In a study of shopping in North London, Daniel Miller (2001) argues that anxieties and tensions that arise from a mother-child relationship stem from clashes between a mother's idealized image of her child with that of her real child. Mothers in Miller's study would go shopping for food thinking about what would be best for their child to eat; however, when confronted with a fact that a child does not necessarily want to eat what is good and healthy and prefers the taste of what mothers often considered 'unhealthy', the mothers would then try to find a compromising solution that would hopefully satisfy at least to some extent, both child and mother. Miller's argument is that relationships and kinship are not relational and processual as Strathern and other social scientists have argued (see for example Finch and Mason 2000; Carsten 1995, 2004), but that they are instead a result of negotiating relationships within a strongly normative framework (Miller 2007).

Following on from these debates I would argue that my material lends support to a third view on parent-child relationship different from both Strathern's and Miller's. While Serbian kinship is still dominated by normative expectations from both parents and children, in the context of migration it is not uncommon to find that adult children often evade these norms in relation to their parents, thus creating serious cleavages and misbalances in kinship ties. In effect the mothers maintain a view of kinship that is close to that of Miller, while the children are striving for something closer to Strathern's model. This, however, does not preclude the possibility of migrant children imposing normativity onto their relationship with their own children as things stabilize around a new order.[9]

Relations between mothers and children are characterized by Strathern as 'unmediated' because both mother and child have a direct impact on one another. 'The capacity to have an unmediated effect', argues Strathern, 'creates a distinguishing asymmetry between the parties' (Strathern 1988: 178). The way this relation manifests itself, or in other words, the way that a relation between 'mother-as-term' and 'child-as-term' becomes apparent, Strathern calls 'objectification' (Strathern 1988: 181). According to Gell, Strathern refers to objectification as an 'aesthetic', 'that is a system of social conventions within which appearances indicate which relations between which terms' (Gell 1999: 37). Gell warns us that Strathern does not use the term 'aesthetics' in its literal meaning, i.e. in relation to sensory appeal, but rather as 'the metaphysical project of deriving the world of appearances from, or at any rate, via, the Idea' (Gell 1999: 38). In the 'Chapter One' to this volume Miller uses the term 'aesthetic' to connote the balance and form according to which people make sense of their lives and create order (see Miller, page 6–8). The concept of 'aesthetic' in both

Strathern's and Miller's terms is used to describe how human relationships both with others and with objects manifest themselves in the world. Miller's use of the term 'aesthetic' relates to a wider holism that implicates both the individual and the wider society. But often that which links the two is the kind of aesthetic that is the subject of Strathern's use of this term, as a means to understand the nature of relationships. So there is a considerably greater compatibility between Miller and Strathern in their theory of the aesthetic than in their approach to kinship.

When 'aesthetics' is taken from these academic debates and recast through the exploration of migration and its consequences, other implications emerge. The detailed presentation of a single mother-child relationship that occupies most of this chapter brings out the poignancy, and maybe even a sense of tragedy, that is contained in this term 'aesthetics', when we think in terms of actual individuals. If the academic analysis has credibility it is partly because their arguments over incompatible perspectives has at another level become the extreme difficulty that a mother and son have in reconciling their own perspectives. As an academic dispute between different contemporary theories about kinship this is not particularly tragic, but as an incommensurable perspective within a family, it reaches the heights of tragedy, with many wounded survivors coming out of the battle between kinship expectations and individual interests.

Notes

1. The fall of Yugoslavia in 1991 and the ensuing ethnic wars in Croatia and Bosnia and Herzegovina had as a consequence massive migration movements both within the region of the former Yugoslavia and outbound towards Western Europe, North America and Australia. Numbers of refugees and internally displaced people have risen even higher after the NATO bombardments of Serbia and Montenegro in 1999. In addition to involuntary migrants, another half a million of young people have emigrated from Serbia since 1991, fleeing the political regime of Slobodan Milošević and raging nationalism, army conscription and poverty. According to estimations of the Serbian Ministry for Diaspora, there are more than three million Serbian immigrants abroad, which is more than one-third of the current population of Serbia, estimated to be seven and a half million (Maletić 2006, Serbian Ministry for Diaspora, personal communication).
2. The Socialist Federal Republic of Yugoslavia, country of immigrants' origin, disintegrated in 1991.
3. Other research (see International Organization for Migration 2006) about migrant-sending households in rural Serbia to which Serbian guest-workers in Switzerland send regular remittances concurs with Dalakoglou's findings in Southern Albania. Similarly to Albanian migrants in Greece who build Greek-style houses and furnish them with luxury furniture only to leave them empty, as described

by Dalakoglou, Serbian guest-workers in Switzerland build enormous houses of ten rooms or more in their villages in Serbia with building materials sent from Switzerland, furnish them with Jacuzzi bathtubs even though there are no running water hook-ups, and often leave them empty, with the idea of moving into them upon retirement (IOM 2006: 42–3). I have argued elsewhere (Bajić 2007) that this difference in sending practices among migrants from rural as opposed to urban parts of Serbia serves as a class signifier to distinguish between 'peasants' on the one side, who are expected to financially support their extended families (such was the case in '*zadruga*', a collective household, before the Second World War, in which resources were pooled and children were valued primarily for their usefulness to the collective), and on the other side 'modern urbanites', who treated children as luxuries and did not expect them to provide for the family.

4. For ethnographic monographs about immigrants in the United Kingdom see, for example Bhachu 1985; Foner 1979; Gmelch 1992; Hall 2002; Werbner 1990; for immigrants in France see Beriss 2004; Brettell 1995; Silverstein 2004; for examples from the United States see Chavez 1992; Freeman 1995; Gold 1995; Grasmuck and Pessar 1991; Guest 2003; Holtzman 2000; Koltyk 1998; Lessinger 1995; Mahler 1995; Margolis 1994; Nash and Nguyen 1995; Stepick 1998; Stoller 2002 (cited in Brettell 2008: 114). Literature about post-1990 immigrants from the former Yugoslavia focuses mostly on Bosnian and Croatian refugees and their experiences in host societies; see, for example Al-Ali 2002a,b; Čolić-Peisker 2003; Eastmond 1998, 2006; Franz 2003a,b; Jansen 2008; Kelly 2003; Korać 2003a,b; Marković and Manderson 2000a,b; Owens-Manley and Coughlan 2000; Povrzanović-Frykman 2002; Waxman 2001; Wight 2000 (cited in Jansen 2008: 186).
5. Names of informants in this chapter are pseudonyms.
6. Vladimir belongs to generations born and raised in Tito's Yugoslavia and for whom Yugoslavia was their homeland; with the fall of Yugoslavia in 1991, Vladimir and many more from those generations lost their homeland; they became '*apatridi*'. '*Apatrid*' in Serbian translates as 'stateless person' in English.
7. Corto Maltese is a character from an Italian-French graphic novel written and drawn by Hugo Pratt, one of the most famous Italian graphic novel artists of the twentieth century.
8. Plum brandy, in this case home-made by Vladimir's father.
9. For further analysis of this issue see Bajić-Hajdukovic 2008.

References

Al-Ali, N. (2002a), 'Gender Relations, Transnational Ties and Rituals among Bosnian Refugees', *Global Networks,* 2(3): 249–62.

Al-Ali, N. (2002b), 'Trans- or A-National? Bosnian Refugees in the UK and the Netherlands', in N. Al-Ali and K. Koser (eds), *New Approaches to Migration: Transnational Communities and the Transformation of Home,* London: Routledge, 96–117.
Anderson, B. (1983), *Imagined Communities: Reflections on the Origin and Spread of Nationalism,* London: Verso.
Bajić, I. (2007), 'Serbian Remittances: From Development Myths to Ethnographic Reality', Paper presented at workshop Remittances and Transnational Livelihoods, 31 October–3 November 2007, PRIO (Oslo) Norway.
Bajić- Hajduković, I. (2008), 'Belgrade Parents and Their Migrant Children', PhD thesis, University College London, London.
Beriss, D. (2004), 'Scarves, Schools and Segregation: The Foulard Affair', *French Politics and Society,* 8: 1–13.
Bhachu, P. (1985), *Twice Migrants: East African Sikh Settlers in Britain,* London: Tavistock.
Blagojević, M. (1997), *Roditeljstvo i fertilitet: Srbija devedesetih,* Beograd: Institut za sociološka istraživanja Filozofskog fakulteta u Beogradu.
Bourdieu, P. (1977), *Outline of a Theory of Practice,* Cambridge: Cambridge University Press.
Brettell, C. (1995), *We Have Already Cried Many Tears: The Stories of Three Portuguese Migrant Women,* Prospect Heights, IL: Waveland Press.
Brettell, C. (2008), 'Theorizing Migration in Anthropology: The Social Construction of Networks, Identities, Communities, and Globalscapes', in C. Brettell and J. Hollifield (eds), *Migration Theory: Talking across Disciplines,* London: Routledge, 113–59.
Carsten, J. (1995), 'The Substance of Kinship and the Heat of the Hearth: Feeding, Personhood and Relatedness among Malays in Pulau Langkawi', *American Ethnologist,* 12(2): 223–41.
Carsten, J. (2004), *After Kinship,* Cambridge: Cambridge University Press.
Chavez, L. (1992), *Shadowed Lives: Undocumented Immigrants in American Society,* Fort Worth, TX: Holt, Rinehart and Winston.
Čolić-Peisker, V. (2003), *Bosnian Refugees in Australia,* New Issues in Refugee Research Working Paper 97, Geneva: UN High Commissioner for Refugees.
Eastmond, M. (1998), 'Nationalist Discourse and the Construction of Difference: Bosnian Muslim Refugees in Sweden', *Journal of Refugee Studies,* 11(2): 161–81.
Eastmond, M. (2006), 'Transnational Returns and Reconstruction in Post-War Bosnia-Herzegovina', *International Migration,* 44(3): 141–64.
Finch, J. and Mason, J. (2000), *Passing On: Kinship and Inheritance in England,* London: Routledge.
Foner, N. (1979), *Jamaica Farewell,* London: Routledge and Kegan Paul.
Franz, B. (2003a), 'Bosnian Refugee Women in (Re)Settlement: Gender Relations and Social Mobility', *Feminist Review,* 73: 86–103.

Franz, B. (2003b), 'Transplanted or Uprooted? Integration Efforts of Bosnian Refugees Based Upon Gender, Class and Ethnic Differences in New York City and Vienna', *European Journal of Women's Studies,* 10(2): 135–57.

Freeman, J. (1995), *Changing Identities: Vietnamese Americans 1975–1995,* Boston: Allyn and Bacon.

Gell, A. (1999), *The Art of Anthropology: Essays and Diagrams,* London: Athlone Press.

Gmelch, G. (1992), *Double Passage: The Lives of Carribean Migrants Abroad and Back Home,* Ann Arbor: University of Michigan Press.

Gold, S. (1995), *From the Workers State to the Gold State: Jews from the Former Soviet Union in California,* Boston: Allyn and Bacon.

Grasmuck, S. and Pessar, P. (1991), *Between Two Islands: Dominican International Migration,* Berkeley: University of California Press.

Guest, K. (2003), *God in Chinatown: Religion and Survival in New York's Evolving Immigrant Community,* New York: New York University Press.

Hall, K. (2002), *Lives in Translation: Sikh Youth as British Citizens,* Philadelphia: University of Pennsylvania Press.

Holtzman, J. (2000), *Nuer Journeys, Nuer Lives: Sudanese Refugees in Minnesota,* Boston: Allyn and Bacon.

International Organization for Migration. (2006), 'A Study of Migrant Sending Households in Serbia-Montenegro Receiving Remittances from Switzerland', Geneva: IOM/SECO.

Jansen, S. (2008), 'Misplaced Masculinities: Status Loss and the Location of Gendered Subjectivities amongst "Non-transnational" Bosnian Refugees', *Anthropological Theory,* 8(2): 181–200.

Kelly, L. (2003), 'Bosnian Refugees in Britain: Questioning Community', *Sociology,* 37(1): 35–49.

Koltyk, J. (1998), *New Pioneers in the Heartland: Hmong Lives in Wisconsin,* Boston: Allyn and Bacon.

Korać, M. (2003a), 'Integration and How We Facilitate It: A Comparative Study of the Settlement Experiences of Refugees in Italy and the Netherlands', *Sociology,* 37(1): 51–68.

Korać, M. (2003b), 'The Lack of Integration Policy and Experience of Settlement: A Case Study of Refugees in Rome', *Journal of Refugee Studies,* 16(4): 398–421.

Lessinger, J. (1995), *From the Ganges to the Hudson: Indian Immigrants in New York City,* Boston: Allyn and Bacon.

Mahler, S. (1995), *American Dreaming: Immigrant Life on the Margins,* Princeton, NJ: Princeton University Press.

Maletić, N. (2006), Serbian Ministry for Diaspora, personal communication, 6 July.

Margolis, M. (1994), *Little Brazil: An Ethnography of Brazilian Immigrants in New York City*, Princeton, NJ: Princeton University Press.

Marković, M. and Manderson, L. (2000a), 'European Immigrants and the Australian Labour Market: A Case Study of Women from Former Yugoslavia', *Journal of Ethnic and Migration Studies*, 26(1): 127–36.

Marković, M. and Manderson, L. (2000b), '"Nowhere Is as at Home": Adjustment Strategies of Recent Immigrant Women from the Former Yugoslav Republics in Southeast Queensland', *Journal of Sociology*, 36(3): 315–28.

Milić, A. (1994), *Žene, politika, porodica*, Beograd: Institut za političke studije.

Miller, D. (2001), *The Dialectics of Shopping*, Chicago: University of Chicago Press.

Miller, D. (2007), 'What Is a Relationship? Is Kinship Negotiated Experience?', *Ethnos*, 72(4): 535–54.

Miller, D. (2008), *The Comfort of Things*, London: Polity Press.

Nash, J. and Nguyen, E. (1995), *Romance, Gender, and Religion in a Vietnamese-American Community: Tales of God and Beautiful Women*, Lewiston, NY: The Edward Mellen Press.

Owens-Manley, J. and Coughlan, R. (2000), *Adaptation of Refugees during Cross-Cultural Transitions: Bosnian Refugees in Upstate New York*, Levitt Report, Clinton, NY: Hamilton University.

Povrzanović-Frykman, M. (2002), 'Homeland Lost and Regained: Croatian Diaspora and Refugees in Sweden', in N. Al-Ali and K. Koser (eds), *New Approaches to Migration: Transnational Communities and the Transformation of Home*, London: Routledge, 118–37.

Ricoeur, P. (1992), *Oneself as Another*, Chicago: University of Chicago Press.

Rowlands, M. (1993), 'The Role of Memory in the Transmission of Culture', *World Archaeology*, Conception of Time and Ancient Society [Special issue], 25(2): 141–51.

Silverstein, P. (2004), *Algeria in France: Transpolitics, Race and Nation*, Bloomington: Indiana University Press.

Stepick, A. (1998), *Pride against Prejudice: Haitians in the United States*, Boston: Allyn and Bacon.

Stoller, P. (2002), *Money Has No Smell: The Africanization of New York City*, Chicago: University of Chicago Press.

Strathern, M. (1988), *The Gender of the Gift*, Berkeley: University of California Press.

Strathern, M. (1992), *After Nature: English Kinship in the Late Twentieth Century*, Cambridge: Cambridge University Press.

Tomanović, S. (2004), 'Roditeljstvo u transformaciji: kapitali, problemi, strategije', in A. Milić (ed.), *Društvena transformacija i strategije društvenih grupa: svakodnevica Srbije na početku trećeg milenijuma*, Beograd: Institut za sociološka istraživanja Filozofskog fakulteta u Beogradu, 347–73.

Waxman, P. (2001), 'The Economic Adjustment of Recently Arrived Bosnian, Afghan and Iraqi Refugees in Sydney', *International Migration Review,* 35(2): 472–505.

Werbner, P. (1990), *The Migration Process: Capital, Gifts, and Offerings among British Pakistanis,* New York/Oxford: Berg.

Wight, E. (2000), *Bosnians in Chicago,* Sussex Migration Working Paper No. 2, Brighton: Sussex Centre for Migration Research, University of Sussex.

–9–

Fashioning Individuality and Social Connectivity among Yoruba Women in London

Julie Botticello

In contrast to most discussions of dress and Diaspora, the focus of this chapter is not on clothing as an expression of political or ethnic identity, but on how clothing mediates the relationship between an individual and her community. Dress, as Oyetade notes, is one of the more prevalent forms of explicit identification among Yoruba people in London, with many dressing in Yoruba textiles and clothing designs in the warmer weather, but especially for ceremonial life, such as naming ceremonies, house warmings and weddings (Oyetade 1993: 74). As clothing 'speak[s] socially' (Sennett 1986: 165), this dressing is not only of personal importance but also public because, as Hendrickson argues, the surface of the body has implications for both individual and social identities; 'being personal, it is susceptible to individual manipulation. Being public, it has social import' (Hendrickson 1996b: 2). For African women, Dogbe argues that dress is the means by which women 'construct meaning in their lives and publish their presence in the community' (Dogbe 2003: 391). Clothing and body coverings express ideas to the wearer about herself, to those outside her looking on, and to the connections or disparities between these.

For a people living in the land of their former colonizer the issue of dress could be a highly political expression of identification, as Dogbe sees it, constructed in 'the interstices of multiple cultural and socioeconomic grammars—colonial, local, global, and neocolonial' (Dogbe 2003: 382). In this arena, how one dresses can express as much individual identification, internal cohesion within a group, incorporation of new ideas, as it can resistance to oppressive schemes of control and subordination. This 'polyvalency' (Durham 1999) is one of the key points about dress, of its ability to embody multiple meanings dependent not only on context, but also on the perspective from which it is viewed, rendering dress able to be 'read in many ways' (Maynard 2001: 190). Even in the context of living in the seat of former colonial power, what dress means and to whom is similarly multiply inflected.

While some of the discourses on dress address macro-political issues, with particular reference to identification in the context of Westernization (Allman 2004;

Dogbe 2003; Friedman 1994; Hendrickson 1996a; Maynard 2001; Okpokunu et al. 2005; Rabine 1997, 1998; Ruether 2002; Schneider 2006), as James notes, others are 'perceptible no more widely than within local communities themselves' (James 1996: 34). Harris states that among the Yoruba involved in an Aladura church in London, a low political profile was the aspiration, and that these church members 'preferred public invisibility to a political presence' (Harris 2006: 37) to protect their interests and status as guests in the United Kingdom. This is not to say that anonymity prevails, but overtly active opposition to the host country and its ways were not the methods employed for identity expression. By maintaining a focus on the macro-politics of dressing, one tends to lose the nuances of individual identification implicated in dress as addressed to the collective. As James shows, on the micro scale, there is much to understand about how dress is acutely implicated in individual women's lives in relation to her parents, her husband, her education and her work. Through an exploration of the dress practices of an individual as these occur in the context of daily life, one can see the divergent connections which are expressed between the self and the social, and glean a picture of the logic which underpins these materialized relations.

This is the context for the chapter that follows. It focuses on dress practices in London among Yoruba women connected to a local street market and how these relate to the notion of the individual and to her social standing within the wider group. Research undertaken on a London street market during the period 2005 to 2006 particularly focussed on the life of one stall holder, and this chapter reflects that concentration. Highlighted here will be dress and its relation to other materializations of self and social identity at significant rite-of-passage birthday celebrations. Along with the events listed by Oyetade above, significant birthday parties are also something celebrated with splendour among the Yoruba. As Guyer notes, 'the party has become a major institution in Yoruba areas. Graduations of social importance—of occasions, of families, of individuals—are all given material meaning in the context of the party' (Guyer 1994: 243). A glance through *Ovation, The Entertainer, High Life*, or *GEMS International* magazines reveals a profusion of such celebrations, taking place both in Nigeria and abroad. These reveal not only the significance of parties, but also the importance of dress as a prime constituent of their materialization. Although the presentation of parties in these magazines concentrates upon a rich minority within Nigeria and the Diaspora, these events are generally celebrated by Yoruba people in London, where both throwing and attending parties is an important part of their lives here.

Oyewumi argues that among the Yoruba, 'as social relations derive their legitimacy from social facts... how persons were situated in relationships shifted depending upon those involved and the particular situation' (Oyewumi 2005: 13–14). As will be seen in this chapter, the individual and her clothing stand at a pivotal point in the making both of herself and of the group, such that one is dependent upon the other for recognition and support. Attaining these two divergent aspirations is not without conflict, however, as the individual strives to find the necessary social balance between autonomy and association.

Autonomous Assertions

Jo is a respected and active member of the Yoruba community in London. In her early forties, she has been living in London for nearly two decades. Although divorced from the father of her two teenage sons, she has since remarried and given birth to another child, also a boy. She runs a market stall in a south London street market from which she sells a variety of herbal remedies for health care, body maintenance and restoration and gives advice on health issues. Her customers range from those seeking to shed a few pounds to others looking to leave their hypertension drugs behind through the taking of an alternative herbal treatment. People travel from all zones of London to visit her stall and seek her advice; in exchange for their custom and their continued purchasing of her goods, she gives to them her time and her knowledge. Jo prides herself both on the value of her goods and on her ability to sell, stating that what brings customers to her stall is the singularity of her wares, 'It is uniqueness that sells in any market. Uniqueness. If you are unique in what you do [people will come to you].' This uniqueness is not just evident in her goods. It is also evident in herself. If the singularity of her goods entices custom, it is her expertise which seals the deal. According to Jo, her customers 'are not just buying my things, [they] are buying my knowledge'.

Before taking on a stall, Jo used to have a shop, also local to her home, where she sold homemade oils and body creams. During the few years she has been selling in the market and in her shop, Jo has built up a network of clients, some of whom have become close friends. These she speaks to regularly in person when they pass down the market, or by telephone, should someone not appear for a while. In the workaday situation, practical exchanges take place between herself and her fellow female Yoruba stall holders, such as sharing child care, lending money or simply minding a stall for another having a break. Other less intimate exchanges also take place between Jo and the English stall holders, mostly for giving change, but also to share the odd joke and pass the time. When leaving the market for the day, Jo stops to greet and exchange news with a number of traders, making her departure from the market a slow one. Should Jo decide to take in some shopping on the high street after closing her stall, or later, when traveling back home on the bus, these events too are punctuated with further dialogues with those she counts among her acquaintances.

On the occasion of her fortieth birthday, Jo decided to have a big celebration. Having built up a network of association among fellow stall holders, customers and local shop keepers in the area, as well as other members of her faith, Jo had the potential to throw a reasonably large party for herself from these diverse connections. To this end, she rented a hall not far from the market. She engaged the cooks, organized and sent out the invitations, bought token presents to give to the guests, arranged for a DJ, got in supplies of alcohol and drink. She worked out a colour scheme—green and yellow—for the party, on the night decorating the hall in matching balloons and tablecloths. In short, she organized, planned and implemented to make sure that everything would work out at the party as she envisioned, relying on exchanges with different of her associations to make it happen.

Eager to be included in this event, I also offered my services in a capacity I felt I could fulfil, and became engaged in designing and printing the invitations to her specifications. She wanted an image of herself on it, with a pink, yellow and green colour scheme, and some information about what the party was for and where it would take place. As she wanted it to be a 'world party', this theme was put across on the invitations, with the words '40th birthday cocktail party', 'world music', 'healthy food', and 'an 8 o'clock start' clearly stated on the cards. In all, 150 invitations were printed and distributed, as after the first printing of 100 invites ran out, a further 50 were run to include more people. She stressed that many people asked for an invitation in hand and would not come without the material formal request, as a verbal invite would not suffice. It seems that to be invited was a privilege, which needed concrete materialization as a card, tangibly confirming one's social status with Jo.

Running out of invitations was one of her concerns as this meant not being able to extend an initiation to those in her vast social network. Moreover, these fears were not unfounded, for after the party, she was chastised by some of her Yoruba and Nigerian acquaintances who had not been given invitations. Having heard of her party from mutual associations, these non-guests were upset at their social exclusion, thereby not being allowed to enter into the flow of social circulation. 'Attendance itself [to parties]—just being there—offers a stepping stone, a minimal common ground for the creation of stronger ties between people' (Guyer 1994: 244). An invitation was an opportunity to manifest or stretch one's own social prowess and connectivity. Its absence could imply a lesser social status than those included.

Others were not only invited, they were active participants in the creation of the event. Regarding the food and service, Jo engaged a few Yoruba women friends to do the catering and food service preparations. Of these, one was a fellow stall holder on the market; another, the tailor who made both of the outfits Jo wore that night. More were involved in the food preparations, including Diana, the host of a sixtieth birthday party to take place the following year, and Ayo, a young woman who sometimes baby sat Jo's youngest son while she worked. Not entirely visible during the party's preparations, these helpers dressed in their normal clothes while working, and then changed into fine Yoruba dress once their set-up work had been completed. After the party and back on the market, Jo introduced some of these women to me as those who 'did the food' for her party. Her network of debt association was essential for this aspect of her party to be a success and was something she seemed happy to engage in.

This involvement of others in this process, however, is not always welcome. Another woman, Toyin, connected not to the market but someone I met at a Yoruba cultural association in London, had battles with her friends over the food preparations at the forthcoming wedding for her daughter. Because she wanted things run with absolute precision, Toyin announced to those who wanted to 'do the food' that they could do so only if they were not also guests at the event. 'To take part, people want to help when it suits them... The lady who says she is going to do the cooking, she is harassing me in the hall, and then she said something and I pretend I didn't hear it. And I hear that she wants to be in the hall dressed up and celebrating! And when we got home, I asked her, "Tell me what your programme is on that day, because I think I heard you say you want to come and sit at the table. If you are going to sit at the table, you are not going to be in charge of the food, I cannot leave that to chance."' Durham notes that for women in Botswana, 'to be able to act autonomously and to command the labour of others are compelling aspirations' (Durham 1999: 394). Here Toyin wished to command the labour of the woman solely on her own terms, with no social returns to the helper, who also wanted to socialize as an invited guest, 'crossing thresholds' (Barber 2007) between back stage cook and front of house guest, so that she could be valued for her individuality as a guest as well as a contributor to the party's overall success. The identities of those 'helping out' are multiply enmeshed, as are the clothes they wear to undertake these, where their own dress embodies the different roles they play in the production of the event.

Although Jo did not contest the back stage versus front of house identity of her helpers-cum-guests, she did have her own crisis when friends forced the issue about her own dress for the night. On the market before the event, Jo said that she was being hassled by her friends to wear the 'right' clothes—'traditional' dress and shoes and bag—to her party. She complained that she didn't like the material offered by Gladys, her home sewing tailor friend, food preparer and guest, and wanted to assert herself by defiantly wearing clothes of her own choosing—a short skirt and boots. She even suggested we go shopping in Harrods to buy these, provisionally planning a shopping trip in town for the following week, though, this was never followed up.

On the night of her party, when Jo presented herself to her guests, she did so in two outfits. She made her first appearance in a two-piece fitted outfit, a skirt and blouse, peach in colour and African in design. This was complete with matching shoes and bag, and a necklace and earring set made by Helen, a Yoruba woman who designs jewellery and is a customer from the market. Later in the evening, when Jo presented herself again, it was in an even more grand manner, as she wore a 'traditional' Yoruba outfit consisting of a green and gold *buba* (blouse) and *iro* (wrapper), *gele* (head-wrapper) and *ipele* (sash), with another necklace and earring ensemble made by Helen, together with green shoes and matching bag. Jo never appeared in 'her own clothes'. Rather, she was dressed in items which literally embodied her social connections. These were those close friends who were responsible for the success of the party, not just in Jo's appearance, but as in the case of Gladys, for the food as well. Jo's dress was an objectification of these connections with others, without which she could not have manifested a successful event.

Discourses on dress and bodily coverings, Durham argues, are not confined to dualist, reductionist narratives, nor are the conflicts purely societal. 'Heteroglossia... is also a condition of human consciousness; even "inner thought" enters into discourse with different potential meanings' (Durham 1999: 391). Jo battled within herself and with her friends over how she should present herself on the night of her own birthday, with conflicts between what she would have liked to do and what she must. Although Jo wished to deviate from the expectations and demands of her friends for their own expression of their social reach, perhaps even, like Toyin, to command labour and at the same time remain autonomous, she found that in the overall running of the party, from food preparation to her dress, she could not.

Rather, it was made essential that she conform to a 'moral aesthetic' (Durham 1999: 392). This, as Miller argues in the introduction, is not necessarily one of visual harmony, but one which objectifies a sense of 'internal consistency and order' (Miller, this volume). Whereas Jo did not struggle with maintaining that aesthetic for the food service, she did when these social relations impinged upon her own physical appearance. By protesting and attempting to be dressed just 'as herself', Jo wished to avoid these robes of association, those garments and adornments which objectified her social support networks. In the wearing of these vestments, the status of these supporters becomes objectified through Jo's clothes attesting their own significance. Through the dress Jo's friends insisted she wear, it was revealed who she was—a respectful Yoruba woman completing a landmark rite of passage, with enough financial and social resources to dress well (twice over)—as well as to whom she was connected, namely her market women colleagues and friends without whom she would not have been able to reveal the former in this public context. As Byfield states, for the Yoruba, one's dress indicates 'one's gender, identity, character, wealth and status', it also 'determine[s] and negotiate[s] social relationships' (Byfield 2004: 31). To reveal the former, that is Jo's individual identity, it was necessary that she also reveal the latter, the connection to and support from her friends.

This emplacement of the individual within a social support network can also be seen to work in the reverse. Whereas in the previous example, Jo was unwilling to wear the clothes which revealed her connections, in the following example, Jo actively adorns the dress of others to gain their support. Deviating momentarily from ceremonial life, we move back to the street market, and forward to July 2006, when the England football team was playing in the World Cup. On the market during this season, many of the English stall holders adorned their stalls with red-and-white England flags or wore the football shirt of their nation's team. On one visit down to the market, one of the English stall holders told me that Jo also supports the England team, coming to the market dressed in the country's signature red and white on the days of England's matches. He'd even got someone to snap a photo of himself and Jo in this dress, on his mobile phone, which he then went on to show me. The next time

Fashioning Individuality and Social Connectivity among Yoruba Women • 137

England were scheduled to play a match, as anticipated, Jo appeared on the market in her 'I support England' gear: a white top and a red skirt, with a mini flag of the cross of St. George tied around her head (Figure 9.1). Although Nigeria were not playing in the World Cup as they hadn't qualified, Jo said that her demonstrations of support for the England team earned her much flack from her fellow compatriots for being a traitor. As related above, her English colleagues, however, were incredibly pleased with this expression of her affinity.

Jo's dress and her intentions on the occasions of her birthday party and the football matches differ significantly; in the end, however, these are guided by a similar logic or aesthetic and cause a similar result. In the former, although at first unwilling, her dress was a literal and material embodiment of her social relations which, in the widest sense, made the honouring of herself in the form of her birthday party possible. The social connections involved enabled both herself and other Yoruba women

Figure 9.1 An England flag worn as a head scarf during the 2006 World Cup.

to assert their individualities through their emplacement in the wider collective. In the latter, through her choice of dress, Jo sought to insert herself into the popular culture of the host country. Although wearing only one specifically purchased object, the England flag, through her choice of red and white clothing, Jo nevertheless communicated her willingness to be allied with this nation. At the same time, by wearing the flag tied as a head scarf, she also retained her own identification as an African, Nigerian or Yoruba woman, asserting her individual character in this extended identification. Far from expressing the depth of a 'pathological colonial psychology of self-hatred' (Schneider 2006: 212), Jo's dress suggests instead a logic of dress as a materialization of social connectivity, this time transposed into a new potential circle of association. As a regular trader on the market, she also needs the goodwill and support of her fellow English stall holders to make her work environment pleasant and to get support from them should she need it. Although her self-constructed dress did not objectify present relationships with significant others upon whom her social standing rested, Jo's embodiment of England colours from her own clothes suggested instead a willingness for potential involvement. Whereas the desire to wear her own clothes at her birthday party represented autonomy, in this case Jo used her own clothes to physically construct alliance. This lends credence to the polyvalency of clothing and the many levels on which it can be read. Recalling Harris's statement earlier on political anonymity, Jo's dress here seeks to overtly bridge political divides in a gesture of inclusion, even to the consternation of her fellow nationals.

Divergent Association

These ambivalences and nuances were clarified by another occasion. At Jo's request, I was a guest at the sixtieth birthday party of her friend, Diana, one of the Yoruba women who had helped with the food at Jo's own birthday. This was an altogether bigger event, held in the larger hall of Millwall Football club, with more than 300 people in attendance. For this celebration, Jo had the privilege of inviting her own selection of guests, which is how I got to attend a birthday party for a woman I did not know. Furthermore, as I was entertaining a visitor from Nigeria at the time, I asked Jo if I could bring my own guest along as well. Given that this guest knew neither Jo nor Diana, I had created a circuitous connection through which both Diana's and Jo's social reach could potentially be further extended.

On the night, when my guest and I arrived, other guests were sparse and distributed around the large hall. As Jo had not yet arrived, we seated ourselves at an empty table at the back, so as not to be too conspicuous. Shiny red helium balloons decorated the football club space, white tablecloths covered the tables, with glittery coloured sequins cut into '60' scattered across. When Jo arrived and saw us sitting at the back, she beckoned us forward to 'her table'—the place for the guests she had invited. The guests at her table were her responsibility to look after, providing extra food, extra seating and extra gifts. All of them had something to do with the market and Jo, as vendors, helpers, customers or were their friends and relations.

When Jo first made her appearance, she was still busy with the preparations, and not quite fully dressed herself. Although wearing the red quilted and sequinned *buba* (blouse) and *iro* (wrapper) she would wear for the duration of the night, she was without any head dress. This was later corrected when she reappeared in a crisp red damask *gele,* one of the *aso-ebi* or 'like dressings' for the party. The head scarf or *gele* colour for Jo's allegiances was red. Gold and white *gele* marked two other *aso-ebi* for different guests and their sub-hosts. Most, but not all, of those sitting at the market table wore red *gele;* certainly those important fellow Yoruba women traders who work with her on the market did. As Jo had told me in advance that the colour of the *aso-ebi* was going to be red, I wore a red dress in my attempt to fit in. As I did not buy a *gele* from Jo, however, I could not be counted among those who were 'dressed alike'. The *aso-ebi* must all come from the same cloth and be bought from the host of the event. It is a dress practice heavily laden with financial and social investment, beyond the desire to wear the same things. Those women who work with Jo on the market demonstrate their social connection to her and their willingness to perpetuate this into the future through buying and wearing Jo's red *gele.* Their vestments embody that relationship to Jo, and at the same time, reveal their connections to each other as market women, as all these are 'dressed alike'. Byfield comments that 'a diverse group of women' can thus be rendered 'into visual equals' (Byfield 2004: 42) through like dressing practices. Those such as myself, who dressed themselves in the right colour acquired from the wrong source, lacked the social relevance to be counted as one among the group. In the case of *aso-ebi,* while association is one aim, there is equally an accent on differentiation from those not taking part. For me and those others at the market table not wearing red *gele,* this social exclusion was connoted materially and visually by our disconnected dress. The exclusivity of the *aso-ebi* does not end with the dress; as mentioned earlier it extends into other forms which materialize levels of social connection.

One of these further materializations occurs in the practice of spraying. This is when the party's host gets covered in money, literally through the laying on of bills (often US dollars) onto her face and upper body by her close connections. At spontaneous moments throughout the party, groups will gather around the celebrant and adorn her with single dollar bills, sticking them to her face, neck and upper body. Like the material clothing, spraying with money to create a cloth of currency is another way of demonstrating rank and connectivity for public view. In the words of one informant, it is 'supposed to be a sign of honour, honouring you'. The act of spraying is an honouring of the recipient by dressing her in the ultimate finery: money. It is also a further way to invest in another, through this symbolic and literal repayment. At Diana's party, it was not only Diana who received spray sessions from her close alliances, but also those other women, like Jo, who were already carrying much of the financial and social burdens for the party. When Diana did have her spray session, no one from the market table took part in this, not even Jo, as she was already repaying Diana by helping to make the party bigger through the invitation of her own guests and catering for them. Rather, Jo was later treated to her *own* spray session. Before this occurrence, there was a bustle at the market table between the money changers working at the party[1] and those wanting to take part in the spraying, to exchange pounds for dollars. Like the red *gele* wearing, not all at the table did take part, but those who did were women from the market, and fellow traders at that (Figure 9.2). Not a 'like dressing', but a performance nevertheless of social connectivity involving bodily adornment wherein individuals taking part stand to gain their own recognition by being included.

The public placement of money upon the body of another does not just benefit the status of the recipient, but can also demonstrate the capacity of guests to bestow material and social recognition onto others. The acquired status is possible only with the help of others. It is, in other words, a practice which is 'inherently social' (Barber 1995: 207). These transactions not only express relationships, but also become the precondition for being recognized as an individual, on the one hand by being able to take part, and on the other by being able to command a following willing to do so.

Figure 9.2 Fellow market workers, adorned in red *gele*, assemble their dollars to engage in the spraying.

Before the party's end, Jo in her turn acknowledged the social regard given by her market colleagues, through gifts given back to them. For those at the market table, there were two sets of gifts forthcoming: presents for Jo's guests who took part in the *aso-ebi* and the spraying, and smaller items for those who did not. Whereas the former received boxed china dinner sets, irons, and bathroom rug sets, the gifts for the latter were less significant: a bag of rice and a bottle of washing up liquid. The gifts returned were representative of the financial investments Jo's guests made to her. Those who made larger investments—economic and social—were given more durable objects than those who did not. The conspicuous exchanges between Jo and her market women at this birthday party demonstrate their connectedness to one another within the public realm of the Yoruba 'community' in London. At this birthday celebration, what can be seen are the rankings of individuals, enacted through a conspicuous differentiation from the whole. This is achieved through separate grouping at tables, through selective participation in the 'like dress' practice, in the spraying of immediately significant alliances, and in the disparities between the gifts returned to invested friends and those more distant guests.

Through material and monetary investment in these ceremonial activities, the hosts and her guests are recognized at once as members of a group, and as individual players within it able to make more significant gains than others through their own degree of outlay and involvement. Dress and bodily coverings, whether this be fabric of cloth or clothes of money, are significant markers in the status of individuals, showing that these are not rigidly static entities, but shifting and ephemeral productions of identification, allegiance and status. Dress and its implication for individuality, recognition, identity and community cannot be viewed as separate from other materializations of social alliances objectified through food production, spraying practices, additional invited guests or improved international co-worker relations.

Conclusions

It can be seen through the examples in this paper that by 'manipulating' (Hendrickson 1996b: 2) sartorial presence, assertions of autonomy or stratifications of relation are actively constructed by individuals. Dress and bodily appearance objectify individual investments and contestations in ongoing social exchange networks between Jo and her fellow Yoruba market women and projected associations (and distinctions) between Jo and her English market co-workers. Jo uses dress to 'publish [her] presence' (Dogbe 2003: 391) in these two distinct 'communities', expressing both alliance and differentiation at the same time. Her failure to wear 'her own' clothes to her birthday party assured the party's success, as this latter was dependent on the contribution of others, which Jo's imposed 'acceptable' dress objectified. In wearing this fashion, she also conformed to cultural expectations about how she ought to present herself at such an event. During the World Cup football season, Jo's wearing of red and white to express her support for things English and to gain support from her English colleagues risked the alienation of her fellow nationals and colleagues. This expression of English alliance, however, was tempered through the way she fashioned her dress, constructed through her own clothes and worn in an 'African' style. The public demonstration of alliances through 'like dress' practices and money spraying at the birthday party Jo supported simultaneously differentiated and ranked Jo's group of associates, where even amongst the invited, greater and lesser degrees of social connectivity were revealed materially.

In these examples, clothing speaks a 'language capable of unifying, differentiating, challenging, contesting and dominating' (Allman 2004: 1). This takes place between distinct groups as well as between the individuals who constitute a given group. The clothing practices of just one individual demonstrates the nuanced and multivalent nature of not only dress and its meanings, but the social connections it objectifies. These practices also map in material form how an individual continually pivots between autonomy and allegiances. Through the use of bodily adornments, individuals both express themselves and make claims on others. Within this Yoruba community the only way that individual recognition can become manifest is through these systems of social significance.

As noted earlier, there is plenty of work already published that focuses on dress in terms of politics and identity (Allman 2004; Dogbe 2003; Friedman 1994; Hendrickson 1996a; Okpokunu et al. 2005; Rabine 1997, 1998; Ruether 2002); on both the issues of a Diaspora in a post-colonial context and the degree to which the selection of African fashion situates people and their identities in relation to that wider politics. This has not been the focus of the chapter presented here. Instead I have tried to show how the encounter with an individual as expressed in her dress and appearance is deeply embedded in much wider forms of social exchange and social connectivity that involves not just the matter of dress as appearance, but also the selection and construction and performance that goes with appearance. I cannot argue that this particular case can stand for the whole experience of Yoruba women in London. In choosing to focus on an individual member of that group, however, insight into how such a group is constituted, maintained and contested can be seen, not as a collective force, but as the result of the actions and assertions of individuals such as Jo. Furthermore, these many negotiations and contestations involved ultimately lead to one person becoming more successful or less agile in securing a particular outcome. In this way dress doesn't just express a social collectivity and its rules of convention and expectation: as a practice it also secures the individualization and differentiation of the persons involved.

Acknowledgements

This research has been funded by the Arts and Humanities Research Council (AHRC).

Note

1. In addition to the support provided by Diana's women friends, several entrepreneurs were also engaged in making the party a success. These included money changers, chair dealers and portrait photographers. Through the trade of their goods, the entrepreneurs enabled the social relationships between the hosts and guests to be more clearly materialized.

References

Allman, J. (ed.) (2004), *Fashioning Africa, Power and the Politics of Dress,* Bloomington: Indiana University Press.

Barber, K. (1995), 'Money, Self-realisation and the Person in Yoruba Texts', in J. Guyer (ed.), *Money Matters: Instability, Values and Social Payments in the Modern History of West African Communities,* Portsmouth, NH: Heinemann, 205–24.

Barber, K. (2007), 'When People Cross Thresholds', *African Studies Review,* 50(2): 111–23.

Byfield, J. (2004), 'Dress and Politics in Post–World War II Abeokuta (Western Nigeria)', in J. Allman (ed.), *Fashioning Africa, Power and the Politics of Dress,* Bloomington: Indiana University Press, 31–49.

Dogbe, E. (2003), 'Unraveled Yarns: Dress, Consumption and Women's Bodies in Ghanaian Culture', *Fashion Theory,* 7(3/4): 377–96.

Durham, D. (1999), 'The Predicament of Dress: Polyvalency and the Ironies of Cultural Identity', *American Ethnologist,* 26(2): 389–411.

Friedman, J. (1994), 'The Political Economy of Elegance: An African Cult of Beauty', in J. Friedman (ed.), *Consumption and Identity,* Chur, Switzerland: Harwood Academic Publishers, 167–87.

Guyer, J. I. (1994), 'Lineal Identities and Lateral Networks: The Logic of Polyandrous Motherhood', in C. Bledsoe and G. Pison (eds), *Nuptiality in Sub-Saharan Africa, Contemporary Anthropological and Demographic Perspectives,* Oxford: Clarendon Press, 231–52.

Harris, H. (2006), *Yoruba in Diaspora, An African Church in London,* New York: Palgrave Macmillan.

Hendrickson, H. (ed.) (1996a), *Clothing and Difference, Embodied Identities in Colonial and Post-colonial Africa,* Durham, NC: Duke University Press.

Hendrickson, H. (1996b), 'Introduction', in H. Hendrickson (ed.), *Clothing and Difference, Embodied Identities in Colonial and Post-colonial Africa,* Durham, NC: Duke University Press, 1–16.

James, D. (1996), '"I Dress in This Fashion": Transformations in Sotho Dress and Women's Lives in a Sekhukhuneland Village, South Africa', in H. Hendrickson (ed.), *Clothing and Difference, Embodied Identities in Colonial and Post-colonial Africa,* Durham, NC: Duke University Press, 34–65.

Maynard, M. (2001), 'Blankets: The Visible Politics of Indigenous Clothing', in W. Parkins (ed.), *Fashioning the Body: Dress, Gender and Citizenship,* Oxford: Berg, 189–204.

Okpokunu, E., Agbontaen-Eghafona, K. and Ojo, P. (2005), 'Benin Dressing in Contemporary Nigeria: Social Change and the Crisis of Cultural Identity', *African Identities,* 3(2): 155–70.

Oyetade, A. (1993), 'The Yoruba Community in London', *Journal of African Languages and Cultures,* 6(1): 69–92.

Oyewumi, O. (2005), 'Visualizing the Body: Western Theories and African Subjects', in O. Oyewumi (ed.), *African Gender Studies, A Reader,* New York: Palgrave Macmillan, 3–21.

Rabine, L. (1997), 'Not a Mere Ornament: Tradition, Modernity and Colonialism in Kenyan and Western Clothing', *Fashion Theory,* 1(2): 145–68.

Rabine, L. (1998), 'Scraps of Culture: African Style in the African American Community of Los Angeles', in E. Barkan and M. Shelton (eds), *Borders, Exiles and Diasporas,* Stanford, CA: Stanford University Press, 58–80.

Ruether, K. (2002), 'Heated Debates over Crinolines: European Clothing on Nineteenth-century Lutheran Mission Stations in the Transvaal', *Journal of Southern African Studies,* 28(2): 359–78.

Schneider, J. (2006), 'Cloth and Clothing', in C. Tilley, W. Keane, S. Küchler-Fogden, M. Rowlands and P. Spyer (eds), *Handbook of Material Culture,* London: Sage Publications, 203–20.

Sennett, R. (1986 [1977]), *The Fall of Public Man,* London: Faber and Faber.

–10–

Creating Order through Struggle in Revolutionary Cuba

Anna Pertierra

In carrying out fieldwork in urban Cuba, it is quite evident that this is a society in which the sorts of individuals Daniel Miller has described in his introduction simply do not exist: contemporary Cuban life precludes both the heterogeneity and the individualism of London. Indeed, the temptation in writing about individuals in socialist Cuba is to focus exclusively upon the restrictions that seem to exist upon individualistic activities and aesthetics. Yet, as with the other chapters in this volume, the issue of the degree of individualism should not preclude another discussion that is just as important in Cuba as anywhere else. Although Cuba may not be individualistic, I was still studying individuals, and I am equally concerned to document how individuals can create their own narratives and make sense of their own experiences within a context of homogenous social structures and an ethos of communitarianism.

There are ways of ordering the world within a highly normative society such as Cuba which still allow individuals to account for their varied life trajectories. One example of this is the ordering concept encapsulated by the term *luchar,* the Spanish word for struggle. Within the context of Cuban socialism individuals tend not to understand their own life trajectories through valorizing individualism or choice as is common within the liberal tradition. Rather, the capacity for individuals to affect and direct their own lives is largely represented by Cubans through focussing on the philosophy and the practices subsumed by this work *luchar.* To briefly illustrate this argument, this chapter describes my encounters with two women in the city of Santiago de Cuba whose lives, while very different, show the capacity of individuals to appropriate discourses of struggle usually associated with Cuban socialism to order their own experiences and practices to amount to what Miller has referred to in the introduction as an 'aesthetic'.

The first clue for an outsider to understand the importance of struggle as a theme shaping life can be found in everyday conversations, which frequently draw from a set of recurring themes summarized in the very popular Cuban phrase 'It's not easy' (*no es facil*). The objective of these conversations is usually to demonstrate the features of each person's character that enable him or her to endure or overcome difficulties in his or her life. Within such conversations, Cubans typically include stories of how their everyday tasks are complicated by the obstacles of poverty and scarcity. Such poverty and scarcity has been seen as definitive of life in the post-Soviet era,[1] and the burden of the resolving everyday economic and household problems has fallen particularly heavily upon Cuban women, as they are traditionally responsible for the management of the domestic economy.

I have developed a broader discussion of the history, politics and practices of a worldview in which *luchar* forms a central philosophy elsewhere (Pertierra 2006); here there is space sufficient only to note in passing two salient features. Firstly, it is clear that suffering is a central motif to the life narratives of Cuban women, and this emphasis upon suffering has a long and deeply gendered history across the Latin American region as seen, for example in discussions of female *marianismo* as an alternative code to male *machismo* (Melhuus and Stølen 1996, but for a complementary analysis of male struggle see Lancaster 1994). The resonance of struggle as an ordering notion is not therefore restricted to women in Cuba. Secondly, despite the broader regional history of struggle (and evidence around the world of suffering and struggle as being frequently invoked as motifs of womanhood), in Cuba women's understanding of life as struggle has clearly been informed by the particular political and economic events of the post-Soviet crisis. This dramatically reduced the capacity of many women to maintain the material standards of living to which they were accustomed, while increasing the polarization of wealth within communities. Elsewhere I explore how the everyday events that shape women's discussions of life as being a struggle point to an underlying preoccupation with material scarcity as the defining feature of contemporary Cuban society (Pertierra 2006). But here the focus is on how this concept is differentially appropriated by two individual women: Fernanda and Reina both understood their lives as a struggle, but used this seemingly shared notion of life as struggle to order very different life trajectories. To appreciate why this may be the case, it is important to understand some of the ways in which contemporary Cuba presents very different opportunities for the individual shaping of practices and philosophies, as contrasted with most other social contexts represented within this volume, although normative pressure is also central to the chapters by Olesen, Murray and as contested in Botticello.

Isolation and Monoculture in a 'Somewhat Big Society'

In recent work Miller has argued that, by virtue of their exposure to diversity and globalization, the fast-moving populations of London have become 'very small societies' (Miller 2006). In contrast, Cuba's political and social isolation since the decline of the Soviet coalition has made it a relatively 'big' society, in which approximately eleven million people experience a largely shared structure that underlies their everyday practices. The development of mass migration and the globalization of capitalist economies has radically increased the mobility of populations in both metropolitan centres like London and small populations on the margins of world economic development, like Jamaica; for people moving in, out and between such places, the intimate networks of personal relationships that anthropologists have traditionally seen as definitive of a community are simply no longer bound by a shared geographical space (Appadurai 1996). In many cases such relationships are now maintained across geographical space through the use of media and communications technologies (Horst 2008; Morley 2000).

However, the impact that globalization has had upon most Cubans has been very different. Since the Soviet networks of trade and development upon which Cuba's economy depended crumbled in the early 1990s, Cuban policymakers did make significant openings to the global economy, by inviting some foreign investment, legalizing the use of US dollars, and developing a tourist industry. However, such reforms remained heavily structured by the creation of state enterprises rather than a private sector. Although money began to flow into Cuba from industry, emigrant remittances and a flourishing black market, many aspects of everyday life for Cuban citizens remain organized through state institutions that limit the sorts of individual diversity that are frequently observed by anthropologists elsewhere in the contemporary world. Cuba is one place that has not become more cosmopolitan through the impact of globalization. If anything, the structures that organize Cubans' lives have become more isolated from more common experiences of globalization found elsewhere in the Caribbean. Although emigration rates are high, unlike most other Caribbean nations, return visits from emigrants are rare, as bureaucratic processes and political difficulties for US-based migrants make travelling both in and out of Cuba complicated (US Department of State 2008). The development of tourism in Cuba can similarly be seen as something which, while bringing more foreigners into Cuba, purposely maintains a distance between visiting tourists and local populations through policies that have often been described as 'tourist apartheid' (Roland 2006). Thus, the policies the Cuban government has developed since the 1990s have been specifically calculated to maximize income from global economic developments but minimize the direct interaction of individual Cubans with the global economy in their daily lives (Eckstein 2003).

There is evidence to suggest that before the revolution Cubans were affected by other, equally important normative systems, which may provide more continuity with how people order their lives in the socialist era than would be imagined or officially admitted. Speculatively, a broader history of normative systems in Cuba might consider such sources as the highly segregated categories of class and race articulated through nineteenth-century plantation economies and marriage laws, the influence of West African and consequently Afro-Cuban spiritual worldviews, and the political, gendered and theological teachings of the Roman Catholic Church (Kirk 1989; Martinez-Alier 1989; Palmie 2002). The historical development of spirituality, kinship and notions of gender, class and race clearly all contribute to the development of Cuban conceptions of individualism and individuals. But the political economy of Cuba in the early twenty-first century, while not isolated from these factors, is an important framework which creates the conditions for *luchar* or struggle to be seen as definitive of the contemporary Cuban aesthetic.

There are countless ways in which this formal structuring of Cuba's politics and economy impacts upon individuals in a consistent form. As I discuss below, key forms of consumption, including shopping for staple foods, rely upon a limited number of stores that are all state-owned. Every student attends state schools, and every visit to a doctor or hospital is undertaken within a state-structured system. Many of the highlights of people's social calendars remain sponsored by government organizations, such as annual *Carnavales,* street fairs and public concerts. In these and many other ways, people in Cuba really do share a common set of activities, institutions and cultural resources that create a common base of experience among residents in a manner that is usually more associated with small remote communities than with urbanized or nationalized populations.

Although individuals in Cuba may interpret and negotiate their everyday experiences in an infinite number of ways, the activities that constitute the everyday in Cuba are limited in number and form. Even the most banal examples of domestic life can illustrate this point: in urban households, most commonly used goods depend upon processes of manufacturing and distribution that are beyond the control of an individual consumer (a feature of consumption by no means particular to socialist societies). Vegetable oil, sugar, soap and toothpaste are all mass-produced products Cubans regard as basic necessities that hold together the very practices of everyday life. Until the mid 1990s, the socialist economy delivered only one kind of each of these products, as manufacturing and distributed systems prioritized reaching the entire population over providing variety. When economic crisis in the early 1990s halted the regular production and delivery of consumer goods, the Cuban government introduced the use of US dollars in specific stores to purchase consumer goods at unsubsidized prices, but only in rare cases were multiple brands of the same good introduced. As I have discussed elsewhere, Cuban consumers developed a myriad of responses to overcoming such challenges to consumption. But the myriad of responses still only result in a narrow number of material goods people can acquire. What is more, all Cuban consumers, even those with money available to buy unsubsidized goods, share common experiences of queues, shortages and visiting the same limited number of consumer spaces. It is through these common experiences of consumption that women most often evoke the importance of *luchar* as the definitive process of their everyday lives.

Clearly, the contents of Cuban pantries are more homogenous than in Miller's London, and the practices through which consumers acquire their goods do not result in as wide a gap between the most and least affluent residents, even with the partial opening of the economy since the 1990s. The involvement of the state in directly shaping most economic, leisure and labour activities creates a hegemony of everyday practices in Cuba to a degree that is impossible in most other industrialized mass populations. But in struggling for consumer goods, people do engage in a wide range of strategies to achieve their goals. They have individual problems and victories and strategies and relationships, although all of this diversity tends to be similarly explained as endless permutations of struggle. Although this does not make Cuban culture entirely homogenous, cultural diversities do spring from specific sets of experiences that almost all Cubans share. In emphasizing the degree to which individuals' lives in contemporary Cuba exist under shared institutions that are mostly state-organized, I do not want to be misconstrued as arguing that Cuban life denies any capacity for individual agency. I by no means want to replicate a stereotypical neoliberal image of life in Communist societies that suggests there is no space for individual freedoms at all. At times this cliché about the homogeneity and anti-individualism of Communist societies is also perpetuated by people who themselves live within socialist or post-socialist nations. In contrast, my own research experience in Cuba suggests that, as in capitalist societies, many people interpret and negotiate the institutions that organize their lives in varying (and often quite subversive) ways. Anthropologists across the socialist and post-socialist world have made similar observations (Berdahl 1999; Fehérváry 2002; Humphrey 2002). But one of the particular characteristics of the concept of struggle which makes it so powerful in a communitarian society is that it offers individuals the possibility of struggling for themselves or their loved ones while also positioning themselves as part of a broader collective movement. Two brief case studies of women living in an urban neighbourhood of Santiago de Cuba can illustrate how ordering one's life through the concept of struggle makes space for individual trajectories while accepting a communitarian ethos.

Two Women Who Have Struggled: Fernanda and Reina

Fernanda and Reina are neighbours[2] who get along well, but the two women have had very different relationships to Cuban politics; accordingly, the state has very different impacts upon not only the ideas or interests they hold, but also on the material conditions of their lives. Although both Fernanda and Reina come from backgrounds of significant poverty, Fernanda's household today is considerably better off economically than Reina's, which is one of the poorer households in their neighbourhood. For decades, Fernanda has been very actively involved in community organizations and remains very committed to the Cuban Communist Party, while Reina has never had any interest or involvement in political or community organizations. To some degree, the generational difference between the two women might account for their differing political outlooks, as Fernanda, in her sixties, was raised in the era of high revolutionary fervour, while Reina, in her thirties, was more immediately faced with the challenges of caring for small children through the economic crisis of the 1990s.

But in reality, there are many other neighbours of Fernanda's age who are largely apathetic towards community and political activism, while a few people of Reina's generation continue an active involvement in state and community activism.

Despite the considerable differences in Fernanda's and Reina's experiences and attitudes, their conversations as told to me over several months (whether as casual parts of our daily encounters or in a more formal interview setting) consistently centred upon the theme of women's need to overcome adversity through personal strength and ability to continue with the struggles of everyday life through being resourceful and inventive. It is this theme that I identify as *luchar,* and which is also materialized through the practices of economic management, housekeeping and consumption that make up the daily lives of most Cuban women.

Fernanda

Fernanda's life story is the stuff of revolutionary folklore; from my first meeting with her soon after arriving in the Tivolí, I felt that her life narrative had been consciously shaped around the goals and gains of the revolution. Fernanda grew up with her poor white family in the rural Sierra Maestra mountains outside the city of Santiago— the same mountains which had sheltered the revolutionary guerrillas in the earliest years of her life—and she personally experienced the transformations that the early years of the revolution brought even to the most remote areas of Cuba. Fernanda's father supported his wife and four daughters on an unreliable agricultural worker's salary of a couple of pesos a day and had no sons to gain additional family income. Fernanda's village had no electricity, school or medical services; as the revolution established itself her own childhood changed, such that she could complete most of her primary schooling in her own village and then stayed in another village with relatives to complete sixth and seventh grades. Fernanda would proudly tell me that although she had only reached seventh grade in her education, that it was the seventh grade 'of those times', which counted for a lot more than it does today. Fernanda is certainly literate and highly numerate, and enthusiastically attended the *Universidad de Adultos Mayores* (University of Older Adults), a community college general education course held on Saturdays for local residents more than sixty years old. Thus, in her late sixties, Fernanda relished becoming a University graduate, and attended a formal graduation ceremony with her neighbours in August 2005 in the Provincial theatre.

In addition to her own stories of the poverty of her childhood, Fernanda was always keen to emphasize the extreme isolation and rough conditions of rural life in pre-revolutionary Cuba. Fernanda's parents were both illiterate, the children of nineteenth-century immigrants from Spain. In her early twenties, Fernanda met her husband; also a white man of humble origins, but one who lived in the city of Santiago de Cuba. Around twenty-five years ago Fernanda moved into his family home and together they built their own house above Fernanda's parents-in-law, which is where Fernanda now lives with her husband, two adult children and her teenage granddaughter.

In conversing with Fernanda about a wide range of topics, she would frequently return to examples of how she has lived her life with a cheerful resilience and capacity for hard work. Fernanda is on the executive committee of her block's Committee for the Defence of the Revolution and also the Federation of Cuban Women, and is always writing documents or attending meetings or reporting to delegates from higher branches of official organizations. She is proud of the struggles that she has successfully waged to overcome poverty and consciously embraces the discourse of the revolution to describe her own activities and priorities in life. But Fernanda's enterprise and energy is not only restricted to community work; she is equally committed to running her household and creating a comfortable, convenient and functional family home. Most of Fernanda's prized objects, such as the television, the two refrigerators and some of the furniture had been earned by her husband by gaining merit points in his workplace, or were recognitions of Fernanda's own community work and revolutionary activity. The contents of Fernanda's living room effectively traces a biography of her family's involvement in labour and community activities under the auspices of the socialist revolution. Her interest in acquiring material comforts such as furniture and domestic appliances is not antithetical to her socialism, and in many ways it is precisely her qualities as an enthusiastic (and also enterprising) socialist that have enabled her family's capacity to exist relatively comfortably. Although her household is not enviably well-off, and they do not have any close relatives abroad, the family is never short of food and has always met their basic needs. Above the house, on the flat concrete roof, Fernanda raises pigs and chickens, slaughtering them periodically and selling some of the meat to neighbours, but also retaining substantial amounts for the family. She also makes juice or soft drinks, either from fresh fruit and sugar or from packets of powdered flavouring bought in dollar shops, and sells the drinks at a peso a glass to neighbours. Sometimes she sells cigarettes as well, unused from family rations, and occasionally coffee, which is similarly obtained. Although they do not have access to dollars, the vast majority of the family's costs are in Cuban pesos, of which they have a steady supply. Through industriousness and 'humility' Fernanda provides for her family with a sense of satisfaction. Partly due to the low expectations with which she was raised, partly in loyalty to the revolution, and partly from a genuine contentment with her life, Fernanda never expressed to me a dissatisfaction with her material conditions. Her positive attitude was a true testament to the revolutionary ideal of the humble worker's loyalty and generosity, and is, perhaps, a snapshot of a life and perspective which is fast fading (but which, importantly, was at one time dominant) in Cuban society.

When I asked Fernanda what she wanted in life, and what she thinks is important in life, she emphasized particular qualities which had helped her to succeed and which resonate very strongly with Cuban socialist imagery of the noble *guajiro* or rural poor:

> There are people in this world who don't have anything, but they are very dignified. You have to have dignity and also to fight (*struggle*) to make your life, even when things can be difficult. I am someone who has always cared about my family, my neighbours, and they also help me. In this neighbourhood the people all know one another and we help one another...But I am from the country originally and country people are very humble but very hardworking.

Reina

Reina is a slim white woman; quite softly spoken but articulate. When I first met Reina, her household comprised herself (housewife), her eleven-year-old son (student), her common-law husband (unemployed), her father (pensioner) and her grandmother (pensioner). In later months, Reina was working on a contract basis in a local government initiative, which improved her domestic economy but also increased her stress levels considerably as no-one was at home to care for her sick and demented grandmother. Reina has two other children; a teenage daughter, who lives with Reina's mother, and another son, who lives with the father's family—Reina is simply unable to support these two older children, although she assists in their maintenance whenever possible. For example at the beginning of the school year Reina was very worried about finding a backpack for her daughter; it fell to her to pay for these larger items.

Reina gave me many examples of strategies she had developed to find money to support herself and her family, and says she has never been afraid to work or to do whatever is necessary. When her first child was born, Reina was a teenager and had left high school, so she made *cremita de leche* (milk caramels) to sell to neighbours. In the early 1990s when the economic crisis hit Cuba, soaps and detergents suddenly disappeared, and in Santiago people resorted to using particular leaves from plants that grew in the countryside surrounding the city which, when mixed with water, had an antiseptic and stain-removing effect. However the water and the plants were unpleasant to touch, many people had allergic reactions or rashes and the water would leave women's hands stained. Reina took in the laundry of better-off neighbours for a fee, and this formed her major access to income during the most difficult economic period of modern Cuban history.

More recently, Reina has also sold some food products acquired by her boyfriend to neighbours (for example cooking oil, which is a major domestic expense). But when necessary Reina has also supplemented her income with sex work; as she explained 'If I need to find money then I will dress up and go out on the streets to find it', or 'If I have to open my legs to feed my children, I do it without a problem.' She does not have a clientele, nor does she identify as a prostitute, but rather, will accept opportunities to earn money through using her body sexually if they arise, and categorizes this as simply a marginally less publicly acceptable way of using her body than washing laundry or making sweets. In 2003, Reina met an Italian tourist who spent several weeks in Santiago over two visits. They developed a relationship and Reina was his girlfriend for the duration of his stays; in addition to enjoying the activities they could share such as eating in restaurants and visiting tourist sites, Reina acquired several sets of clothing and shoes bought in dollar shops in Cuba, certain items for her children and cash as a result of this relationship. Reina is very careful in caring for the clothes dating from this time, as they are her only 'good' clothes which she uses both for going out and for working in her local government job. At the time of the visits by this Italian tourist, Reina had not yet met her current partner, and whilst she said to me that she hopes the Italian returns to Santiago soon, because she needed the material help he can give her, she also indicated that as she is in a relationship now she cannot or does not have sex with people other than her partner, not even for money. She once told me that 'a woman really has to be in love' to put up with having a husband, because he is a lot of extra work and stops you from being able to have other opportunities—at first I had thought she was joking but in fact she made the statement without any intended irony.

Reina's conversations with me emphasized how excluded she has always been from material comfort and how hard she has to struggle to acquire even the money and goods she sees as basic necessities:

> The boy's shoes cost me 300 pesos. You don't know how many things I had to do for those 300 pesos. Listen, I went out night after night to be able to find the shoes for my son. Because where will it come from if I'm already working? And I resolved it... This problem of the backpack, that has my blood pressure high, I've had headaches, from the pressure and the tension I have. Where to acquire the backpack. With the number of books she takes in the morning. All the kids with their backpacks, except mine. And so, what happens, I've got two pairs of trousers. I thought of selling one to solve this problem, but in any case, I'm not going to do anything. Honestly, I'm not going to do anything. Getting rid of something I can use for work, and anyway when I get paid, we'll see what we can resolve, what we'll do. I don't know... I live from the invention.
>
> What do I want to achieve in life? What I'd like to have in life is health. Because with health, everything else can be achieved. Which is what I don't have... for my children to have health. And to have a house where I can have all three of them. That, yes, I wish for. Because the girl and boy are separated from me, and it hurts me not to have them with me because of the conditions I have... They're three totally different characters. I would really like—if God or Nature allows it, I don't know—to have them in my house. Which I can't have. Them with their space; each one with their own room so that each lives in their own space... Because my parents have given me nothing, and you see how we live? To have my own house, I have to wait for my grandmother to pass away, and then for my

father to pass away, to then therefore be able to have my own house. And this is why it's gotten lodged in my head to fight (*luchar*), but hard! To buy myself even a little house. But for problems of sickness, it can't be. Because you can't exchange money for health. It's not easy, you know?

Fernanda and Reina, while having quite opposite experiences of life success, both invoke the rhetoric of *luchar*; Fernanda defines her ability to succeed in life through the need to struggle, while Reina complains that she needs to struggle as a result of her poverty. We can see how Fernanda sees herself as having engaged in lifelong struggle as part of the broader revolutionary movement to improve herself, her family and her community. In contrast, Reina spoke of political institutions only insofar as they let her down, such as when government rations and benefits are insufficient. But in both cases, images of sacrifice and struggle that are often part of the Cuban state rhetoric are closely connected to the very personal experiences of individuals like Fernanda and Reina when they think about their lives, their desires and their conceptions of self.

As the concept of *luchar* is so closely associated with the language and policies of the Cuban state, it can be invoked by people who are apathetic or even hostile towards socialism in general, without inviting critique. Indeed, for many people talking about life as a struggle in the post-Soviet era involves a heavy dose of irony, as the language of revolution is subverted to describe the struggles of individuals to overcome the conditions they feel are largely a result of negligent or hostile governmental policies. However, even in Cuba there is no simple division between people who are 'for' the revolution and understand *luchar* as a revolutionary concept and people who are 'against' the revolution and use *luchar* as an entirely ironic or subversive critique. On the one hand, people can embrace a communitarian emphasis of Cuban socialism in ways that further their individual interests. And on the other hand, people can feel generally marginalized by the institutions that are so constitutive of Cuban life while still employing the ideals and rhetoric of those institutions to express their very marginalization.

The Cuban example suggests that while individuals may not be encouraged to adopt an explicit philosophy of individualism in socialist societies, they are very capable of incorporating revolutionary narratives and discourse to make sense of their individual personal trajectories. Even a largely anti-individualistic ideology can inspire citizens in conceptions of themselves that emphasize a strong capacity for agency. Brian Morris makes a similar argument in considering the dialectical relationship between the social and the individual across many world cultures when he points out that 'a sociocentric conception of the person in no way excludes an equal emphasis on the idiosyncratic self or on the individuality of the human subject' (1994: 193). Even within the most community-oriented of societies individuals are perfectly autonomous beings who do not particularly sacrifice their own interests or needs on behalf of their group (Morris 1994).

There is a tendency in research on socialist societies to focus on the defining features of life under a Communist or socialist regime that can be found in oppression of individuals through policies that limit rights to free speech, travel, economic activities or other well-documented activities that are generally associated with life in the public or civic sphere. Anthropologists, while preferring to examine the grass roots effects of socialist regimes in diverse communities, have been as likely as any other set of researchers to examine the nature of social life in socialist societies as being largely shaped by the institutions and policies of the socialist state. However, a lack of emphasis on individualism as a philosophy does not mean that the individual as a category is unimportant. Clearly, although revolutionary ideology emphasizes community over the individual, Cubans at a ground level do actually use these same revolutionary ideologies and discourses (such as *luchar*) as a metaphor or model for their own individual lives and experiences. While being enthusiastic about the Cuban state (as Fernanda generally is) may allow for the conscious embracing of the rhetoric of revolutionary struggle, people like Reina who are entirely apathetic about state ideology are just as likely to espouse the importance of communitarian spirit, or emphasize the need to make sacrifices for the family. The Cuban revolution, both as the symbol of a set of values, and as a series of institutions that regulate the practical conditions of citizens' lives, is extremely intertwined with how Cuban individuals understand their own life trajectories and life philosophies. Further, as is shown with the example of Reina, many individuals may invoke discourses and images associated with socialism that are neither supporting or opposing ideological positions such as communitarian socialism or individualist capitalism, but are serving entirely less polarized purposes. As anthropologist Alexei Yurchak has argued with reference to the late years of the Soviet Union, when trying to understand the diversity of individual responses to authoritarian state ideologies, it is problematic to assume a simple binary between believing in or opposing state practices (Yurchak 2005). Yurchak's work demonstrates why associating agency with a resistance to social norms is an error, as individuals can often exert agency by being entirely in keeping with social norms, which is clear in the case of Fernanda.

While people continue to forge their own divergent, sometimes contesting or conflicting, paths in life within societies that emphasize the well-being of a community over the preferences of an individual, the communitarian emphasis of such societies does seem to create a different starting point for people's understanding of self. Claudio Lomnitz-Adler's discussion of communitarian ideologies, which draws from Weiner's discussions of exchange, speaks directly to the relationship between state ideologies and ideas of individualism as expressed through individual and group practices:

> The totalizing visions that underlie communitarian relationships are always based on definitions of goods or rights that are common and inalienable to all. The relationships of differentiation that are later constructed within and between communities are defined

with reference to the series of goods that are inalienable to the group. (Lomnitz-Adler 2001: 36)

The assumption of particular rights and goods as 'common and inalienable to all' is indeed central to Cuban invocations of *luchar;* when people describe themselves as struggling to achieve a better life, the understanding is that they are working to maintain a quality of life to which they have an incontrovertible right. Such rights as education and health care are obvious examples of how Cuban socialist society has been defined with reference to particular goods and services being inalienable. But the examples of inalienable rights Fernanda and Reina focus on are somewhat less tangible; both women take for granted their right to raise children in a healthy and comfortable environment, and their right to actively seek economic improvement on behalf of their families. Given the poverty-stricken backgrounds of both Fernanda and Reina, it is relevant to note that for the most vulnerable Cubans the very communitarian ethos of the revolution has often enabled them to emphasize their agency and individual worth more effectively, with a reduced (but never erased) dependence upon family or class-based networks. Yunxiang Yan's excellent study of private life in rural China makes a similar point; young men and women in China have increasingly been able to reject longstanding norms of filial piety to create lives that are largely independent from parental and grandparental obligation (Yan 2003). An apparently authoritarian state, in a society deeply committed to mutual support, has nevertheless offered new opportunities for individualism.

What the divergent uses of *luchar* have in common is that they make reference to a shared Cuban conception of a 'good life', which includes not only educational or health services but also a range of important material goods which are seen as intrinsic to emotional well-being. Individuals are understood to struggle to attain or maintain a 'good life', and this is not seen as antithetical to the communitarian emphasis of Cuban socialism. On the contrary, this very struggle for intellectual, emotional and material upliftment lies symbolically (if not always in practice) at the heart of Cuban state ideology. Such an ideology is clearly very different from the Protestant-inspired ideology of individualism famously identified by Weber. Yet the Cuban use of *luchar* to order one's life and make sense of one's fate can be seen to fulfil a comparable role in providing individuals with a capacity for affecting their own destiny. Women like Fernanda and Reina use their understanding of *luchar* to explain how their particular actions in particular circumstances have led them to become who they are, as opposed to someone or something different. Struggle in this context is an expression of agency to become one kind of person or claim some particular virtue. The relative inability to become a 'pure' individual in contemporary Cuba in no way curtails the capacity for individual Cubans to engage in ordering their sense of self; on the contrary, these very communitarian ideologies and discourses provide fertile ground for individuals to order and understand their life trajectories.

Notes

1. The term 'post-Soviet' has become increasing used by anthropologists to describe the period of Cuban society from approximately 1991 until today.
2. These case studies were part of a broader ethnography conducted with women living in the city of Santiago de Cuba in southeastern Cuba. I conducted thirteen months of participant observation in 2003/2004, with follow-up visits in 2006 and 2008.

References

Appadurai, A. (1996), *Modernity at Large: Cultural Dimensions of Globalization,* Minneapolis: University of Minnesota Press.
Berdahl, D. (1999), *Where the World Ended: Re-unification and Identity in the German Borderland,* Berkeley: University of California Press.
Eckstein, S. (2003), *Back from the Future: Cuba under Castro,* London: Routledge.
Fehérváry, K. (2002), 'American Kitchens, Luxury Bathrooms, and the Search for a "Normal" Life in Postsocialist Hungary', *Ethnos,* 67: 369–400.
Horst, H. A. (2008), 'The Blessings and Burdens of Communication: Cell Phones in Jamaican Transnational Social Fields', *Global Networks,* 6: 143–59.
Humphrey, C. (2002), *The Unmaking of Soviet Life: Everyday Economies after Socialism,* Ithaca, NY: Cornell University Press.
Kirk, J. (1989), *Between God and the Party: Religion and Politics in Revolutionary Cuba,* Tampa: University of South Florida Press.
Lancaster, R. (1994), *Life Is Hard: Machismo, Danger, and the Intimacy of Power in Nicaragua,* Berkeley: University of California Press.
Lomnitz-Adler, C. (2001), *Deep Mexico, Silent Mexico: An Anthropology of Nationalism,* Minneapolis: University of Minnesota Press.
Martinez-Alier, V. (1989), *Marriage, Class and Colour in Nineteenth-Century Cuba,* Ann Arbor: University of Michigan Press.
Melhuus, M. and Stølen, K. A. (1996), 'Introduction', in M. Melhuus and K. A. Stølen (eds), *Machos, Mistresses, Madonnas: Contesting the Power of Latin American Gender Imagery,* London: Verso, 1–33.
Miller, D. (2006), 'The Eighth Annual Annette B. Weiner Memorial Lecture: Beyond Social Science: Social Reproduction in South London', New York: New York University Department of Anthropology.
Morley, D. (2000), *Home Territories: Media, Mobility and Identity,* London: Routledge.
Morris, B. (1994), *Anthropology of the Self: The Individual in Cultural Perspective,* London: Pluto Press.
Palmie, S. (2002), *Wizards and Scientists: Explorations in Afro-Cuban Modernity and Tradition,* Durham, NC: Duke University Press.

Pertierra, A. (2006), 'Battles, Inventions and Acquisitions: The Struggle for Consumption in Urban Cuba', PhD thesis, University College London.

Roland, L. K. (2006), 'Tourism and the Negrificación of Cuban Identity', *Transforming Anthropology*, 14: 151–62.

US Department of State. (2008), 'Cuba Travel Information', http://travel.state.gov/travel/cis_pa_tw/cis/cis_1097.html (accessed 15 June 2008).

Yan, Y. (2003), *Private Life under Socialism: Love, Intimacy, and Family Change in a Chinese Village,* Stanford, CA: Stanford University Press.

Yurchak, A. (2005), *Everything Was Forever, Until It Was No More: The Last Soviet Generation,* Princeton, NJ: Princeton University Press.

–11–

Food, Family, Art and God: Aesthetic Authority in Public Life in Trinidad

Gabrielle Hosein

This is a departure from understanding Caribbean societies and cultures in terms of their institutions... It searches for other essences beside ethnicity, national identity, pluralism, classes, gender, cultural resistance etc. and instead delves into internal dynamics, cultural creativity, aesthetic, emotions, experiences and the different ways these expose particularities, personalities and unique ways of creating and understanding order. (Johnson 2002: 21)

In the small city of San Fernando in Trinidad,[1] market vendors' needs and illegal squatters' aspirations illuminate the significance of relationships and practices that most matter to ordinary women and men. Equally, Muslim women's piety and Carnival mas makers' artistry provide sources for understanding how people order their lives and judge each other. Together, these also explain the workings of macro structures such as bureaucracies and the law, and macro-practices such as national elections and state patronage. As women and men privately and individually make sense of their experiences, beliefs, desires and identities, they deeply define politics in public life.

Ethnographic research, in the Central Market,[2] on the Railway Line section of the King's Wharf,[3] in an Anjuman Sunnat Ul Jamaat Association (ASJA) *Masjid* (mosque),[4] and at the Lionel Jagessar and Associates Mas Camp,[5] enabled me to explore the kinds of authority women and men mobilized as they participated in public life (Navaro-Yashin 2002: 2). As I waited for taxis, bought vegetables, listened to business transactions, attended women's meetings or just sat with fishermen at the waterfront in San Fernando, the surprising ways ordinary people governed normative order stood out. As a case study, the city provided a setting for interrogating how dispositions, circulating within individuals' lives, define informal, formal and even state-centred kinds of power and meaning.

As Merlene, Sandy, Ruqaya and Lionel's stories below show, order-making practices rest on what most matters to women and men, and their capacity to legitimize aesthetic authority. Through the examples that follow, I define what I mean by 'aesthetic' in this chapter. I also show how an aesthetic is lived and becomes the basis for authority. Finally, I illustrate how conceptualizations of individual aesthetic can be expanded to the study of public life, and can show the macro significance of individual order-making practices.

Theorizing Aesthetic Authority

Let me first review a set of premises, regarding individuals, aesthetic and authority, engaged by this collection of essays. Authority, for Miller, is grounded in forging, maintaining and conducting relationships. It emerges from the ways that women and men, amidst great social heterogeneity,[6] make 'highly integrated meaningful worlds, carefully crafted lives, with considerable consistency or clearly worked through contradictions' (2006: 3). People's relationships may be to their bodies, others, things, practices and ideals. These shape and are shaped by what matters to them, and the narratives they reproduce to make sense of their past and present.

Following Bourdieu (1977), Miller argues that early parental influences, later relationships and the wider cultural order build on each other. They create meanings that people work out daily. Past and present influences may be widely divergent and completely contradictory. Women and men, therefore, choose to sometimes emphasize some influences more than others. The sense that they seek to make through their practices and relationships creates an overall, totalizing order in their lives. Miller calls this 'cosmological architecture' (2006: 23), an 'aesthetic'. This aesthetic is, in essence, a habitus. It expresses ideals of order and balance, and the centrality of practice. But while habitus derives from the normative social order, Miller is concerned with the order individuals or households partly create for themselves within a modern de-centred and relatively apolitical space, such as within the private home.

As Miller writes, 'At any given point of time the aesthetic is distributed through a series of relationships to different material genres or aspects of one's life' (2006: 15). In the context of this chapter, the norms and meanings created through family, village and agricultural life may influence market vendors' relationships to money, police and public space while current economic demands and difficulties, religious conversion or change in legislation may shift these relationships or reproduce them in new ways. I argue that influences such as these are the basis for vendors', squatters', Muslim women's and mas makers' *aesthetic authority*.

In this chapter, I take ideas that Miller claims to have located in the private sphere and cast them back into the public domain, the effect of which is to highlight their role in adjudicating authority. The two contexts are themselves connected. Unrelated vendors can behave like family members. Community Environmental Protection and Enhancement Programme (CEPEP) workers who, in their heads, constantly add to and shuffle the list of party activists they can turn to for help behave much like a man constantly re-organizing his email as he affirms his place in his world or a woman who collects and moves around her furniture to feel she has some means of controlling her life.

Desire for and practice of relationship marks those experiences, values, people and things that are considered inalienable. This is because, notwithstanding their relations to wider social norms up to and including the state, much of women and men's emotional and personal concerns are centred on a few primary relationships with things, familiar places, people they love and even God. This is what Yael Navaro-Yashin (2002) and Lisa Douglass (1992) refer to when they discuss affect or emotions and sentiments as 'forms of both power *and* meaning' (Douglass 1992: 3).[7]

In the connection between these close relationships and the wider public sphere, women and men's decisions about what really matters to them, and what they feel makes sense highlight the ideals and practices that order their lives. Together, their practices create and express an aesthetic that they use to legitimate what they do in the present and to mediate different forms of power and meaning. This is what I call *aesthetic authority*.

What Matters?

Aesthetic authority is, therefore, the basis for the legitimacy that Trinidadians feel when they make decisions regarding their own lives and their relationships with others, things, spaces, institutions and practices. It is based on the importance that they give to what most matters to them and their feeling that, based on what matters, they have an authority that does not need the legitimacy of legislation, rules, office or other formal bases of power. It is an authority based on what feels right and reasonable, and what provides a sense of balance and order. In this sense, an aesthetic is normative, shaping how public space and public life are privatized and poeticized.[8] It shows individuals as far from simply lawless, indisciplined, disorderly or immoral.

Fittingly, I first show how Merlene's aesthetic, as a market vendor, makes illegality legitimate. Her aesthetic expresses the idea that everyone should be able to make 'an honest dollar' so that they can feed their families. It competes for moral authority with state legislation and business people's ideals regarding use of public space. On the Railway Line, a similar desire to participate in banal aspects of nationalism (Billing 1995) legitimizes the fact that, in this instance, not everyone will get employment or be able to access money or food. Sandy uses her connections to make sense of, order and fulfil her own aspirations for family life. Her aesthetic competes with bureaucratic ideals, and election platform promises regarding state spending and welfare provision.

At the nearby mosque, Ruqaya's aesthetic expresses an ideal that worldly practices should be guided by spiritual correctness. Her cosmology guides how she makes sense of and advocates for gender justice, as she believes God would have wanted it, among women and men. It gives her authority to challenge male leadership's decisions and definitions of democracy in the politics of her mosque, on the basis of what seems right and reasonable. Elsewhere in San Fernando, Lionel's aesthetic idealizes identification with the materials, characters and artistic skills associated with making (North American) Indian Carnival costumes. It enables him to challenge bureaucratic officials' views regarding participation, and patronage obligations, on the basis of his family's needs and aspirations, and his own notions of spiritually correct leadership. The following stories highlight areas of authority and governance that are in practice only made legitimate and effective when they align with a normativity derived from women's and men's experiences and ideals regarding family, spirituality, livelihood, community, culture and leadership. We need to pay much more attention to this underlying aesthetic authority which connects daily life to the institutions which claim dominance and power.

Merlene

Usually, in the afternoons before the market closed, I went to visit Merlene. Often, she had already cleared her stall in the market, and carried her peppers and seasonings out to the street where they were displayed on boxes or crocus bags for passers-by to see. A no-nonsense, Indo-Trinidadian grandmother, she would be sitting behind her goods and calling out her prices to potential customers while keeping a stern eye on the street's activities. Merlene would also make space for other vendors when they arrived, share scales and small change, and even help sell friends' goods.

The ideal that 'everybody have to eat' or has a right to secure a livelihood underscored her decisions regarding conflict, competition and cooperation with other vendors, and the ways she negotiated with police and government policy regarding sidewalk vending. Merlene was proud of the strong reciprocal relations that characterize market life because 'all ah we come here to get some food to carry home'. This ideal shaped relationships between spouses, as well as those between extended family and between neighbhours in her village, neighbours at the market or on the road, and even with police. Business was not simply about being competitive, but about balancing 'making a dollar' with not taking away someone else's. While small quarrels sometimes arose on the road as they hustled to make a brisk trade, vendors were also quick to point out that 'the road is for everybody'.

As Figure 11.1 shows, police ritually arrived on the road each afternoon. When they began to tell vendors to move, Merlene would pack up her goods, or pretend to, or even hustle a quick last sale while the police walked up and down ensuring vendors' compliance. She would throw a 'cut eye' (a bad look) at unfriendly or rough police and chat with those she considered 'genuine' while moving to the pavement to wait for the police to leave so she could begin to sell again. For her, it was fair to sell on the road, despite its illegality, because she needed to sell any remaining perishable goods and make enough profit to pay her debts to wholesalers. More important, she felt that making an honest living to support her family was more important than

Food, Family, Art and God • 163

Figure 11.1 The line of legitimacy.

supporting the law. Yet, not only could she not openly defy police, Merlene also felt that vendors needed to respect that police were doing their job and their duty. She would therefore also throw 'cut eye' to vendors who gave police too much trouble.

While some police would 'advantage' vendors (treat them unreasonably) by talking to them 'like hogs', vendors felt police often gave them a chance because they knew them from years of selling on the road or knew they were trying to earn an honest livelihood. Also, police may have had family selling on the road, known sales were hard that day or planned to sell in the market after retiring. As a law-abiding matriarch, Merlene expected police to understand her decision to sell on the road because she understood their job was to move her from selling there. She saw police as vendors—as women and men just doing the job they have to. Conversely, she expected police to see her like themselves—as if there were reasonable grounds for what she was doing, as long as she didn't attempt to 'advantage' them, the law and public space.

In addition to legal regulations, police and local politicians highlighted 'moral' concerns related to hygiene, safety and security as reasons to discontinue street vending. Their empathy was limited by their perception that the 'market is real profit' and vendors were not simply 'making a dollar'. Business people also argued that vendors didn't pay taxes and blocked their storefronts. In the eyes of these authorities, vendors should not be on the road. Yet, to some extent, police empathized with vendors' attempts to earn a livelihood and they recognized the demand for roadside sales. Illegality was considered reasonable and legitimate by vendors and state officials to different degrees.[9]

Merlene's aesthetic, her sense of the proper moral order of the world, determined whether the use of power was legitimate or not. It was based on her family's needs, her livelihood options, her long-held aspirations for economic independence, the practices of her village neighbours and values she learned growing up in an agricultural family. Yet, shared aesthetic explains why vendors were able to negotiate with police, why they were patronized by other citizens, and why even politicians were aware of depriving them of their 'dollar'. In this sense, this aesthetic enabled vendors, politicians and police to mutually legitimize a variety of kinds of power.

On the roadside, the spectrum of forms of power at play included hustling, legislation, pretence, bribes, 'sweet talk' and friendship. This public politics reflected individual normative practices that continually intersected formal and state-centred bases for social order. It showed the significance of Merlene's aesthetic, that the law should be lived in ways that enabled her to make 'an honest dollar', and the legitimacy that aesthetic offered to illegality in public life.

Sandy

When I first met Sandy, she was living with her common-law partner Boscoe. They had informally adopted Brendon, their neighbour's baby. Sandy and Boscoe didn't feel they could have children together, and their neighbour's drug addiction was affecting her son's health. Brendon didn't only alter Sandy and Boscoe's relationship but created a new experience of parenting. This young couple wanted to 'build up' their one-room house on the Railway Line and get regular income because they now had a 'son'.

They were able to survive before on temporary employment and hustling some fish from friends on the Wharf. Boscoe often got jobs with the Unemployment Relief Programme (URP) because his uncle worked there. Sandy was able to access relief employment less regularly, but sometimes worked informally with Community Environmental Protection and Enhancement Programme (CEPEP) when her aunt or sister, who were employed with the programme, fell ill. However, with Brendon in their care, CEPEP, URP and the contacts they had with these programmes now became crucial. The couple's relations with neighbours, and Sandy's sister, mother and aunt on the Railway Line, were also deepened as everyone often helped to feed or look after Brendon. He became infused with their connection to extended family and neighbours, fishermen on the Wharf, political activists, elections and state programmes providing work and welfare.

Sandy's aspirations for family life meant that, even more than before, she had to turn to her 'contacts', those women and men she knew who could advise and help because of their status, knowledge or networks. Sandy's own efforts to make sense of her realities and hopes showed a desire to access those aspects of saving, consumption and helping others that many take for granted, and to create a more permanent home on the Railway Line, though its illegality would mean that she couldn't access pipe-borne water or electricity. She imagined herself as a part of everyday normative life, including the exemplary red beans, macaroni pie, chicken, iced drinks and radio music (here playing from a recharged car battery) typical of Trinidadian 'Sunday lunch', though unusual for this neighbourhood of low-income families. For Railway Line residents like Sandy (Figure 11.2), it was precisely concerns grounded in family life that were the basis for the exchange of votes and jobs so central to patronage. Democracy, coupled with patronage, secured the chance of *feeling* Trinidadian, a part of wider publics of parents with children in government schools or families that could afford groceries at the supermarket.

As Sandy sorted through the people who could help her access family, income, food and welfare, she created a sense of order that affirmed a world order in which not everyone gets to eat. Her aspirations made her participation as a voter in national elections significant, not just in terms of politics, but also in relation to ideas of family, community and work. It also legitimized her expectations for the kinds of reciprocity that accompany patronage obligations. Despite party activists' and politicians' exhortations that CEPEP and URP were administered without political bias, here too shared aesthetic explained partisan allocation of scarce resources.

When I last visited Sandy, she and Brendon were by her mother who was talking about getting him to participate in Kiddie's Carnival just as her other grandchildren did, often in costumes paid for with CEPEP and URP wages. Boscoe and Sandy had broken up and so their different degrees of engagement with family, neighbours, politics and the state had shifted once again. Amidst these new circumstances, Sandy

Figure 11.2 One woman, one vote.

166 • *Anthropology and the Individual*

was trying to make ends meet and still dreamed of expanding her single room overlooking the sea.

Forming and mobilizing many contacts who were willing to help was an aesthetic that enabled Sandy to participate in aspects of Trinidadian family life, to use her vote as a form and meaning of power, to successfully make claims on political party activists' patronage obligations, and to make sense of the reality that not everyone gets food or money to take home. For Sandy, like so many others, political participation was not necessarily different from the ways she created a sense of order out of her aspirations, family experiences, economic opportunities, intimate relationships and neighbourhood friendships. The overall configuration of values and relationships came through fortuitous connections and, with Sandy, was the by-product of her continuing willingness to single-handedly adopt and love Brendon.

Ruqaya

One October morning, Ruqaya, a motherly looking woman wearing a *hijab*, met me and drove us to the site of the ASJA election, an Islamic girls' school. I had seen her petition against women's disenfranchisement circulating the San Fernando *Jama Masjid* (Figure 11.3). A short paragraph, at the top of the page of the petition, had asserted that the ASJA constitution did not bar women from voting and sought signatures of support below. I could not have gone alone to the election. Comfortably, neither could she. When we arrived, there were about 150, mainly Indo-Trinidadian, men milling around. Many wore *kurta* shirts and headwear. Fewer wore Western clothes. This signalled that this event was both an administrative and sacred space and exercise.

We sat in chairs closest to the door. The Chairman of the Electoral Committee soon came to tell us to leave. Ruqaya said there was nothing in the constitution to

Figure 11.3 Higher authority.

make her leave. He said it was 'custom'. She asked, 'Am I doing anything wrong? Am I offending anybody?' He asked where she was from. She told him she was from the San Fernando *Jaamat* (community) and that she paid her $10 to the women's group. He responded that they didn't recognize those payments. She quietly reassured me that they could not (physically) move us. He seemed to give in. She said, 'Well, I am glad you understand.' Vexed, he responded that he did not understand our point and didn't support us being there.

He went away and sent a hesitant young security guard to tell us to leave. She again said to tell her why and who said so and that she wasn't leaving. Grumbling about 'all these men who want to decide my life', she explained to me, 'I am here because if my God asked me what I did when the ASJA was in this state, what can I say, I was home cooking?' She said she asked three other women to come but they were afraid of censure, afraid of the President General and 'afraid of the men'. Constitutional rules did not prevent women from attending, but the habitual practice and pressure women felt did.

The event began with a *dua* (prayer), but the atmosphere was tense. The election officials stood next to us looking displeased. At one point, the President said, 'Sisters were not allowed and I don't know who invited them, but they are here.' He didn't publicly tell us to leave. Ruqaya declared, 'I guess the President accepts us' and was pleased that his opening address began 'Brothers and Sisters'. Later, on the podium to announce the election, the man who first tried to make us leave also addressed the assembly as 'My beloved Sisters and Brothers'. Ruqaya noted this ironically.

After the election, men we knew from various *masjids* came up to joke about our temerity and how 'they wanted to throw all yuh out'. Many were supportive of us staying. The community is small so women and men generally know each other well. Women didn't fear individual men's responses and, in fact, would have been surrounded by male neighbours, family, co-workers and friends. The election moment highlighted more generalized, gendered fears of social shame, community leaders' censure and gossip amongst men. In this instance, Ruqaya invoked the ASJA constitution to challenge norms regarding gender segregation. She also invoked the higher authority of God, over the traditional authority of religious and administrative leaders, to justify women's participation in Islamic public life.

Ruqaya's aesthetic, idealizing a relationship between gender, democracy, leadership and community as God intended, was her personal version of issues that were shared by other members of the *Masjid*. So not everyone would have reached exactly the same conclusions as to what was reasonable. While some women and men felt that women did not need to participate in 'men's activities' such as the election, others thought that women's family roles provided decision-making knowledge and power they could bring to community governance. Some advocated complete equality in ASJA governance and democracy and others desired simply more recognition for the women's group and the right to vote for all levels of leadership.

Ruqaya's personal sense of meaning and power, however, came not only from the mosque and her readings from the Koran and the life of the Prophet Mohammed, but also from her family experiences, occupation, political participation in national government, educational attainment and conceptions of fairness. She agreed that the leader of the community and *Jamaat* should be male. Yet, she felt that, when men were not behaving according to the *Sunnah*[10] or the ASJA constitution, when a *kutbah* (sermon) was chauvinistic or when women were reduced to their domesticity, in their role as moral guardians, women had a right to discipline the men. Her challenge was based on a sense of authority, grounded in her relationship to God, regarding the beauty and justice of 'correct' Islamic order and gender balance.

Lionel

Tagging along with Lionel as he went to a San Fernando Carnival Committee meeting one evening, I listened as bandleaders complained about prizes, parade routes and lack of respect while politicians and bureaucrats cajoled them to cooperate, to support the Committee's framing of Carnival as a 'product', and to be 'patriotic' to San Fernando. We had walked over from the Jagessars' mas camp where, for close to thirty years, Carnival costumes were made almost year-round by friends and family. Bandleaders Lionel and Rose produced 'Indian mas' costumes that stylized North American Native 'Indian' nations' dress, leadership, ancestry and cosmology. Their artistry continually re-imagined and revitalized a connection to a Native American identity and spirituality within Trinidad's Carnival.

The camp relied on friends' and family members' freely given time and skill to make costumes for the band. In exchange, they got food, and free or cheaper costumes. While the most skilled might be waged, the majority supported the band through late nights and long days of work because of a loyalty to Rose and Lionel, Carnival and mas, Indian mas, San Fernando and Trinidad. For the Jagessars, the band was a labour of love, or a medley of practice and emotion, that affirmed their authority and autonomy while providing an income.

Like bandleaders, the San Fernando Carnival Committee made yearly attempts to harness, define and direct this love. Aiming to appropriate ultimate leadership of the event, this local government branch flexed its own legal power in contested meetings about the management, development and purpose of Carnival. While debate and disagreement pivoted on routes, prizes and rules, it was really about the relationship between ideas of state and nation. On the one hand, Lionel's aesthetic nationalistically brought the two together. On the other, it provided the very reason he resisted state domination, and separated state from nation. It made the materials, characters and artistic skills that are associated with making North American Indian Carnival costumes forms of meaning and power that could contest authority based on patronage, legislation, bureaucratic power and facilitation of market imperatives.

At the meeting, disagreement ended with the Mayor telling the bandleaders to consider his position as a facilitator of many different stakeholders and as a politician. He told bandleaders they had to make a sacrifice. As he put it, 'This is not about you. This is about San Fernando's Carnival.' A bandleader grumbled that, 'We were here doing our thing for twenty years for only so much profit each year and plenty of family and friends' free work and here he is telling us how if we don't come into his project we are bad people not supporting San Fernando Carnival.' When another bandleader talked about one, famous for many years in San Fernando, who had played mas in Port of Spain that year, the Mayor responded, 'That is because he is not a patriot.' He went on, 'This is a give-and-take situation. Why don't you all work with me? All you want is money, money, money.' Ritually invoking ideas of sacrifice and duty to nation and state, Carnival participation was turned into an opportunity to validate the committee's authority and its assumption that Carnival's purpose was 'to make everyone happy'.

Carnival provides a livelihood and Lionel felt he had to negotiate prizes and penalties while repudiating obligations based on patronage. He welcomed state participation while denying legitimacy to state domination because, as artist and expert, he had moral authority based on what most mattered to him. Lionel (Figure 11.4) was King of the private space of the mas camp and the public space of the road, and his authority was already legitimized. For its power to be legitimate, the Carnival Committee had to, somehow, also become a King of the Road, capturing leadership of the spirit of Carnival and not just its bureaucratic organization. In this context, state actors had to resort to representing themselves as if they loved Carnival, San Fernando and Trinidadian national culture more than bandleaders, and then substituting state-centred versions to manage how these were brought together.

Lionel's aesthetic gave his own informal leadership a legitimacy transcending that of the politicians and state bureaucracy. For him, the authority associated with his skill in portraying aspects of Native American spirituality and cosmology had greater meaning and power than that associated with money, office or legislation. Even if he, like other bandleaders, gave in publicly to the Carnival Committee's rules and plans, he did not give up any sense of his own power. As his own experience shows, his aesthetic authority explains why points of disagreement may therefore remain unresolved over decades and successive governments.

Legitimacy in Public Life

These examples show how what matters to these individuals comes to determine the way they order their relationships and their sense of legitimacy in what they do. Aesthetic authority justifies Merlene, Sandy, Ruqaya and Lionel's interactions and decisions because it feels right and reasonable to them, grounding them in a particular

170 • *Anthropology and the Individual*

Figure 11.4 King of the Road.

moment and place. It is this rather than the formal authority claimed by laws, institutions or powerful persons that determines their decisions and actions. This is how everyday morality is articulated in and orders public life. It is not necessarily just, equitable or kind, and may in turn be experienced by others as arbitrary, unfair, self-interested, immoral or exploitative, and as 'advantage' (of others). Nonetheless, it is not simply individualistic, and also shows an engagement and claim on larger structures, institutions and norms.

This aesthetic is therefore about more than individuals' 'tactics' (de Certeau et al. 1998) or resistance (Scott 1990). It shows an order that makes sense and can be easily mobilized by women and men negotiating efficacy, leadership, legitimacy, reciprocity, belonging, common sense, personal style and 'correct' practice. It shapes how these women and men participate in public life, whether on roadsides or roads, in meetings in City Hall and constituency offices, in associational and national elections, or in neighbourhoods and on job sites. Each story depicts politics from 'the margins' where legitimacy is being constantly refounded as people secure political, economic and cultural survival (Das and Poole 2004: 8). Together, they show that authority springs from sources as diverse as emotions, personal style, bureaucracy, artistry and gender. It is cast and recast by women's and men's gender relations, survival needs, leaders' influence or beliefs in God. The things that matter most to women and men in one space are expressed through different relations in another, but circle constantly to return to the value of family, reciprocity, fairness and participation.

Drawing on the work of Yael Navaro-Yashin (2002) on Turkey and Lisa Douglass (1992) on Jamaica, I want to especially highlight affect or sentiment as 'forms of both power *and* meaning' (Douglass 1992: 3).[11] Writing of Jamaica, Douglass defines sentiment as 'historically derived and culturally meaningful embodied experience' (1992: 18). It has meaning in terms of love, loyalty, unity and distinction. It is related to power because of the ways it legitimizes social hierarchy. Yet, more fundamentally, it is both powerful and a source of power in its own right because of the cultural meanings invested in it. Douglass's approach is useful for moving beyond sentiment as simply sociological construct (Lutz and Abu-Lughod 1990), sphere of meaning (Rosaldo 1980), ideological practice (Lutz 1988), methodological lens (Rosaldo 1989) or instrumental tool for material gain (Medick and Sabean 1988). Like Navaro-Yashin, Douglass is concerned that an emphasis on ideas, consciously articulated discourses and ideologies misses why women and men really do things and misreads the frequent disjuncture between thought and action. As Douglass writes,

> Ideology, when considered only as a type of cognition or consciousness (or its lack), fails to detect the moral content, the emotional effects, and the appraisal of values involved in social life. In social processes, including ideological processes, thought, practice, *and* sentiment come into play...They do so in ways that may be either mutually reinforcing or contradictory. Sentiment may reinforce *or* disengage the hegemonic power of ideas and practices. (1992: 20)

Strikingly, both Navaro-Yashin and Douglass reach similar conclusions about what Douglass calls 'ruling sentiments' (1992: 20). Conscious deconstruction of material and ideological power 'may not be enough to change practices or to transcend the moral power of sentiment', writes Douglass (1992: 21). Rather, we should acknowledge that various forms of affect have hegemonic power because they are 'meaningful and of value in their own right' (1992: 21). This suggests that we should attend to the meaning and value that different groups of women and men attribute to various forms of sentiment. The emotions that they signal, such as love, empathy and feelings of togetherness as well as disappointment, frustration and fear, are seen as expressions of and ways of engaging moral and political power.

Like sentiment, sources of power such as need, God, culture, institutional clout or 'who you know' are hierarchically organized. Firstly, this is because women and men of various groups have differential and unequal access to them. Secondly, this hierarchy reflects the greater or lesser degree of authority associated with different kinds of power. In other words, like gender or class, these powers mark social stratification. These differences in access in turn influence the extent to which the legitimacies they offer are accepted or seen as reasonable. But while they are hierarchically ordered they cannot be reduced to a single dimension such as class. As Douglass puts it, 'A person's ideology is not determined by class position alone, for within every class there are other status differences and many varieties of experience' (1992: 18). The hierarchical register of authority itself is not stable.

Institutions may even have different amounts of legitimacy depending on the situation. For example, the Carnival Committee has to rely on the more democratized and general 'love for mas' to justify its authority. Females in the mosque may go up to the level of Quranic interpretation in order to challenge institutionalized male authority. Even the Prime Minister may have to be a 'true true Trini' (Eriksen 1992) in one instance, but not another. What can be done with this legitimacy, how it can be made to matter and even where it is on the hierarchy are all negotiated and shifting constantly. These stories show how individuals claim all forms of legitimacy, even those seen to belong properly to the state, regardless of their status or resources.

Conclusion

As single snapshots, these examples highlight different aesthetic orders in practice. They don't pursue when or how these same individuals might mobilize completely different aesthetics or engage their own aesthetics in completely diverging processes and the effect such shifting may have on legitimate authority, the state and public life. Lionel's aesthetic may be reshaped by his religion or fatherhood and Ruqaya's sense of moral balance may be changed by her participation in national politics. Yet, the aim here has been to show the homologous ways that a habitus may be lived across diverse circumstances, and its impact on order. It has also been to avoid an over-reliance on both individualistic and structural explanations, while leaving room for the varying influences that may adapt and alter what most matters.

Primarily, these four ethnographic examples of encounters between people and others, institutions, ideas and spaces show how women and men mobilize an aesthetic that gives them a sense of individual authority that can stand up to and mediate formal structures of authority. It further illustrates how their own individual cosmologies and order-making practices also shape and order state bureaucracies, gendered leadership, law enforcement, democracy and patronage. Ethnographic attention to particular and individual lives alerts one to the degree that a habitus coalesces around an individual's socialization and disposition, which is not quite the same as the larger social dispositions. This perspective enables us to navigate between claiming either a governing habitus or disorder and anomie, and to see the analogous ways that authority is deployed to order aspects of an individual's life, and between individuals and others, things and spaces.

The chapter therefore focuses on the significance of 'aesthetic authority' to how women and men make sense of and order their lives. From this angle, normativity or ideals of order and balance can also be seen as bases for governance. This is because aesthetic authority is lived in homologous ways by women and men situated all along the continuum between social life and the state. These dispositions may be lived in individually negotiated and meaningful ways, but they are also widely shared. As individuals make sense of their needs, ideals, experiences, expertise, feelings, leaders, art and identities, the relationships created, together, define 'political society'[12] (Chatterjee 2005).

Starting with individual cosmologies highlights the contradictions and homologies in how women and men both participate in widely shared aspects of normative life, and are constantly creating meaning, relationships and order in their own ways. The ethnographic examples show, whether in relation to individuals, leaders, bureaucracies or law, aesthetic authority shapes the way that public life is ordered and made meaningful. A lens on individuals and aesthetic can therefore be extended to help explain governance in social life and the state, and legitimate authority in public life in San Fernando, Trinidad.

Notes

1. Fifty-six kilometres from the capital Port of Spain, the 18 km sq city of San Fernando has its own pre-Columbian, colonial and post-colonial story lacing through the larger history of the southern Caribbean twin-island Republic of Trinidad and Tobago. Though first conquered by Spain, Trinidad and Tobago was ruled by Britain from 1797 until Independence in 1962. By the end of the nineteenth century, and following the abolition of African slavery in 1834, Indians, Chinese, Syrians, Portuguese and others had been brought to the colony as labourers or migrated as traders. Census data published in 2002 give the total population of Trinidad and Tobago as 1,262,400 and Trinidad as 1,208,282. San

Fernando's population is now 55,419 (28,325 women and 27,094 men), and is larger than Port of Spain's by just over 6,000 persons (Government of Trinidad and Tobago Central Statistical Office 2000). Nationally, the population is self-designated as 37.5 per cent African, 40 per cent Indian and 20.5 per cent 'mixed'. The city comprises about 4 per cent of the nation.

2. The Central Market was first established in the early 1900s. The market population of 300 to 400 vendors is highly heterogeneous. Among other distinctions such as ethnicity and religion, goods sold, relation to space and days spent selling there differentiate individuals and groups. Street vending in San Fernando in general has been noted since 1842 (Ottley 1971: 17).

3. The Wharf lies at the very base of the city, and directly faces the sea front. A Public Transport Service Corporation (PTSC) bus system replaced its once-famous railway. After the railway was discontinued, bus company workers and squatters replaced the railway workers who once lived in houses provided at the end of the Railway Line. By the 1970s, with the railway gone and the decline of the Wharf as a port, dereliction began to set in. After amenities were discontinued in the early 1980s, only squatters were left living along the Line. The Railway Line road extends away from the Wharf and ends in a cul-de-sac after a few hundred feet.

The nation-wide Unemployment Relief Programme (URP) aims to provide temporary employment to those finding it hard to secure paid employment. The Community Environmental Protection and Enhancement Programme (CEPEP), established in 2002, is intended to be more than short-term employment relief. It aims to 'clean and beautify the environment, provide employment for unskilled and semi-skilled workers and develop a cadre of micro-entrepreneurship and new business'. Both programmes are popularly associated with patronage and together, they employ the majority of the Railway Line residents.

4. The San Fernando *Jama Masjid* (central or main community mosque) is part of the national, Islamic, Anjuman Sunnat Ul Jamaat Association (ASJA). Although Islam first came to Trinidad with enslaved Africans (Campbell 1974), by the middle of the nineteenth century their community presence had disappeared (Samaroo 1988). Its resurgence came with indentured Indians' arrival in 1845. Of the 144,000 Indians brought to Trinidad and Tobago during the indentureship period, approximately 23,600 were Muslim (Ali 1995: 7). The ASJA represents the largest group of Muslims in the country. In San Fernando, where the ASJA *Jama Masjid* is located, there are 2,822 Muslims (1,401 females and 1,421 males). Census data suggests that 1,457 Muslims (734 females and 723 males) belong to the ASJA and 1,365 belong to other Islamic groups (CSO 2000: 37–9). Approximately 150 families currently belong to *Masjid*. This community is primarily Indo-Trinidadian and middle-strata.

5. Mas makers are women and men who spend about half a year preparing costumes for their Carnival 'band' or group of costumed masqueraders. There are hundreds of these 'mas' (masquerade) bands led by their own bandleaders who

'play' King and Queen of the Band. Mas bands may each consist of a dozen, hundreds or a few thousand women and men who will 'play mas' on the streets for the two days before the beginning of Lent, which starts on Ash Wednesday, each year.

In Trinidad, Indian mas was observed as early as the 1840s (Cowley 1996: 36). Red Indian mas emerged from the Warao, aboriginal natives of Venezuela who traded with Trinidad until the 1920s. Playing mas does not necessarily involve wearing a mask but is based on wearing a costume 'based on a theme from history, current events, films, Carnival tradition, from the imagination, or from a combination of these' (Crowley 1956: 194). Indian mas costumes reflect 'comic books, *National Geographic* and other magazine illustrations, and particularly cowboy-and-Indian movies' (Crowley 1956: 194). The Lionel Jagessar and Associates Fancy Indian Band and camp, where costumes are made, officially started in 1978. Rose and Lionel Jagessar head an Indo-Trinidadian, Hindu family from San Fernando with two sons and two daughters.

6. Miller would agree with Held (1989) that contemporary economic, political and social life, or modernity, creates heterogeneity, dispersion and diversity. However, his position is the opposite of Held's that theorizing about legitimate authority should be rooted in fragmentation and atomization.
7. Emphasis in original.
8. In the words of de Certeau et al., 'The city, in the strongest sense, is "poeticized" by the subject: the subject has refabricated it for his or her own use by undoing the constraints of the urban apparatus and, as a consumer of space, imposes his or her own law on the external order of the city... urban space becomes not only the object of knowledge, but *the place of recognition*' (1998: 13). Emphasis in original.
9. Lloyd-Evans and Potter (2002: 108) state that government regulation is not as stringent in lower-middle income housing or rural areas or where traders provide a much-needed service to local residents. Enforcement is stricter near or in areas of high-income housing.
10. The teachings and practices of the Prophet Mohammed.
11. Emphasis in original.
12. Chatterjee defines 'political society' as the sphere of direct encounter between the state and communities and individuals from 'popular' worlds (Hansen and Stepputat 2005: 24). These relations are constitutive of democratic politics as 'a constantly shifting compromise between the normative values of modernity and the moral assertion of popular demands' (Chatterjee 2005: 86). Within this 'pure politics', civil-social norms and constitutional proprieties are not certainties, sovereign power has ambiguous legitimacy, and rights and rules seem continuously negotiated afresh (Chatterjee 2005: 99). This concept usefully signals a way that irregular, illegal, informal and seemingly 'inappropriate' ways of participating in public life can be named and normalized. Trinidadians' claims on authority and

bases for legitimacy similarly suggest that 'proletarian conceptions' (Best 2001: 11) and concerns grounded in labour, need, dignity and relationship form bases for governance.

References

Ali, A. I. and Mansoor, I. (1995), *Islam in Trinidad and Tobago*. Port of Spain, Trinidad: Anjuman Sunnatul Jamaat Association.
Best, L. (2001), *Race, Class and Ethnicity: A Caribbean Interpretation*, The Third Annual Jagan Lecture presented at York University on March 3, 2001, Centre for Research on Latin America and the Caribbean Colloquia Paper.
Billing, M. (1995), *Banal Nationalism*, London: Sage.
Bourdieu, P. (1977 [1972]), *Outline of a Theory of Practice*, Cambridge: Cambridge University Press.
Campbell, C. (1974), 'Jonas Mohammed Bath and the Free Mandingo in Trinidad: The Question of Their Repatriation to Africa 1831–1838', *Pan African Journal*, 7(2): 129–52.
Chatterjee, P. (2005), 'Sovereign Violence and the Domain of the Political', in T. B. Hansen and F. Stepputat (eds), *Sovereign Bodies: Citizens, Migrants and States in the Postcolonial World*, Princeton, NJ: Princeton University Press, 82–102.
Cowley, J. (1996), *Carnival, Canboulay and Calypso: Traditions in the Making*, Cambridge: Cambridge University Press.
Crowley, D. (1956), 'The Traditional Masques of Carnival', *Caribbean Quarterly*, 4(3 and 4): 194–223.
Das, V. and Poole, D. (2004), 'State and Margins: Comparative Ethnographies', in V. Das and D. Poole (eds), *Anthropology in the Margins of the State*, Santa Fe: School of American Research Press and Oxford: James Curry, 3–34.
De Certeau, M., Giard, L. and Mayol, P. (1998), *The Practice of Everyday Life, Volume 2: Living and Cooking*, trans. T. J. Tomasik, Minneapolis: University of Minnesota Press.
Douglass, L. (1992), *The Power of Sentiment: Love, Hierarchy and the Jamaican Family Elite*, Boulder, CO: Westview Press.
Eriksen, T. H. (1992), *Us and Them in Modern Societies: Ethnicity and Nationalism in Mauritius, Trinidad and Beyond*, Oslo, Norway: Scandinavian University Press.
Government of Trinidad and Tobago Central Statistical Office. (2000), *Population Social and Vital Statistics*, Port of Spain, Trinidad: CSO.
Hansen, T. B. and Stepputat, F. (2005), 'Introduction', in T. B. Hansen and F. Stepputat (eds), *Sovereign Bodies: Citizens, Migrants and States in the Postcolonial World*, Princeton, NJ: Princeton University Press, 1–38.
Held, D. (1989), *Political Theory and the Modern State: Essays on State, Power and Democracy*, Cambridge: Polity Press.

Johnson, K. (2002), *The Soul in Iron: Origin and Development of the Steelband, 1939–1951,* PhD dissertation, The University of the West Indies, St. Augustine.

Lloyd-Evans, S. and Potter, R. (2002), *Gender, Ethnicity and the Informal Sector in Trinidad,* Aldershot: Ashgate.

Lutz, C. (1988), *Unnatural Emotions: Everyday Sentiments on a Micronesian Atoll and Their Challenge to Western Theory,* Chicago: University of Chicago Press.

Lutz, C. and Abu-Lughod, L. (eds) (1990), *Language and the Politics of Emotion,* Cambridge: Cambridge University Press.

Medick, H. and Sabean, D. W. (eds) (1988), *Interest and Emotion: Essays on the Study of Family and Kinship,* Cambridge: Cambridge University Press.

Miller, D. (2006), 'The Eighth Annual Annette B. Weiner Memorial Lecture: Beyond Social Science: Social Reproduction in South London', New York: New York University Department of Anthropology.

Navaro-Yashin, Y. (2002), *Faces of the State: Secularism and Public Life in Turkey,* Princeton, NJ: Princeton University Press.

Ottley, C. R. (1971), *The Story of San Fernando,* Laventille, Trinidad: International Print.

Rosaldo, M. (1980), *Knowledge and Passion: Ilongot Notions of Self and Social Life,* Cambridge: Cambridge University Press.

Rosaldo, R. (1989), *Culture and Truth: The Remaking of Social Analysis,* Boston: Beacon Press.

Samaroo, B. (1988), 'Early African and East Indian Muslims in Trinidad', Conference on Indo-Caribbean History and Culture, Centre for Caribbean Studies, University of Warwick, May 9–11.

Scott, J. (1990), *Domination and the Arts of Resistance: Hidden Transcripts,* New Haven, CT: Yale University Press.

Index

Adams, G. 46
adoption 84, 164
aesthetics 124–5
   aesthetic of order 3–6
   Greek house in Albania 14–15, 51, 52, 53–62
   public life in Trinidad 18–19, 159–73
Albania 51
   Albanian migration to Greece 52–3, 60–1, 64–5
   Greek house in Albania 14–15, 51, 52, 53–62
Annales school 5
Asad, T. 34
Austin-Broos, D. J. 79
Australian Aboriginal people 8

Bali 5
Bamama people 38, 47
bedrooms 100, 101–2
Belgrade, migration from 115–25
Béteille, A. 85
Bird, C. S. 47
blogging 92
Boas, Franz 64
body piercings and tattoos 9–10
bògòlan cloth 14, 37–48
Bourdieu, Pierre 4, 5, 7, 11, 12, 35, 63, 78, 79, 160
brands, fake 13–14, 25–7, 29–35
Brett-Smith, S. 38
Britain, *see* London
Byfield, J. 139

Calvert, Karen 100
carnival 162, 168–9, 174–5
Carsten, J. 52
celebrations 133–42
cell phones 70–4, 81
Chevalier, S. 91

children
   adoption 84, 164
   Jamaica 77
   Madrid 84
   Serbian migration and mother-child relationships 16–17, 115–25
Christian Pentecostalism 15, 69–74, 78, 79
class 5
cloth and clothing 10, 37
   bògòlan cloth 14, 37–48
   fake brands 13–14, 25–7, 29–35
   Madrid 90–1
   poverty and 69
   Yoruba women in London 131–42
communist system in Cuba 18, 145–56
computers 8
   digital networks 16, 99–110
   photography and 91–2
consumption in Cuba 148–9
copying
   bògòlan cloth 14, 37–48
   fake brands 13–14, 25–7, 29–35
creativity 91–2
Cuba
   creating order through struggle 18, 145–56
culture 3, 12–13
   bògòlan cloth 14, 37–48
   networked public culture 100–1
   space-culture isomorphism 51–2

death
   destruction of possessions of dead people 8
design and decoration 37
   bògòlan cloth 14, 37–48
destruction of possessions of dead people 8
digitization 8
   networks 16, 99–110
   photography 91–2
distinction 5

Dogbe, E. 131
Douglass, Lisa 161, 171
drinking groups 13
dualism 5
Durham, D. 135, 136
dyes 38, 41
Dzokoto, V. A. 46

education
  Cuba 150
  Islamic religious education 27
Elias, N. 95
email 8
employment
  fake brands in Istanbul bazaar 13–14,
    25–7, 29–35
  Madrid 83, 84
  markets in Trinidad 159, 161, 162–4, 174
  taxi drivers 15, 74–8, 79, 81
ethnography 11–12

Facebook 16, 99, 100, 105–7, 108
fake brands 13–14, 25–7, 29–35
families
  creating order through struggle in Cuba
    18, 145–56
  Madrid 83–96
  Serbian migration and mother-child
    relationships 16–17, 115–25
  Turkey 27
  unemployment and family life in
    Trinidad 161–6
fate 90
Ferguson, J. 51
France 5, 7
furniture in Greek house in Albania 53–6

Geertz, Clifford 5
Gell, A. 37, 52, 79, 124
gifts 141
globalization 146–7
Goffman, Erving 107, 110
Greece 51
  Albanian migration to 52–3, 60–1,
    64–5
  Greek house in Albania 14–15, 51, 52,
    53–62
Grosz-Ngaté, M. 47, 48

Gupta, A. 51
Guyer, J. I. 132

habitus 4, 35, 63
Harris, H. 132
Henare, A. 10
Hendrickson, H. 131
Hockey, J. 12
holism 5
houses
  bedrooms 100, 101–2
  Greek house in Albania 14–15, 51, 52, 53–62
  internal organization of space 4
  Madrid 84, 87–90
Hoxha, Enver 65
Hugh-Jones, S. 52

inalienability 9, 10
individualism 3
  digital networks and 99, 107–10
  Jamaica 79–80
  Madrid 83, 85–6, 92–6
innovation 40, 48
interviews 12
Islam
  religious education 27
  Trinidad 161, 166–8, 174
Istanbul bazaar, fake brands in 13–14,
  25–7, 29–35
Ito, M. 100

Jamaica 171
  individualism in 79–80
  mobile phones 70–4, 81
  Pentecostalism 15, 69–74, 78, 79
  taxi drivers 15, 74–8, 79, 81
James, D. 132
Joseph, S. 27

Kabyle people 4, 5, 7, 35, 52, 63
Kandiyoti, D. 27
Kendall, M. B. 47
Krauss, Rosalind 39, 40
Küchler, S. 37
Kula ring 10, 41

Lefebvre, H. 51
Lévi-Strauss, Claude 5

liberalism 6
Lomnitz-Adler, Claudio 155
London 4, 6–11, 80
  Serbian migration to 16–17, 115–25
  Yoruba women in 131–42

Madrid 16, 80, 83–5
  clothing 90–1
  houses/apartments 84, 87–90
  individualism 83, 85–6, 92–6
Mali
  bògòlan cloth 14, 37–48
Malinowski, B. 10, 41
manners 86–90
Maori people 10
markets
  fake brands in Istanbul bazaar 13–14, 25–7, 29–35
  fashioning individuality among Yoruba women in London 131–42
  Trinidad 159, 161, 162–4, 174
masculinity 146
  Jamaica 77
  Turkey 27, 28
microcosm 5
migration 146–7
  Albanian migration to Greece 52–3, 60–1, 64–5
  from Serbia 16–17, 115–25
military 28
Miller, Hugh 107
mobile phones 70–4, 81
money spraying 139–40
Morris, Brian 154
Myers, Fred 8
MySpace 16, 99, 100, 102–5, 108, 109

Navaro-Yashin, Yael 161, 171
networks, *see* social networks

objects 4, 123
  bògòlan cloth 14, 37–48
  destruction of possessions of dead people 8
  digital objects 8
  fake brands 13–14, 25–7, 29–35
  gifts 141
  inalienability 10
  mobile phones 70–4, 81

order
  aesthetic of 3–6
  creating order through struggle in Cuba 18, 145–56
Oyetade, A. 131, 132
Oyewumi, O. 132

Parrott, Fiona 6
participant observation 12
parties 133–42
patriarchy 27
Pentecostalism 15, 69–74, 78, 79
photography 91–2
police 162–4
post-modernism 6
poverty
  Cuba 149, 150, 156
  Jamaica 69–70
prostitution in Cuba 152–3

rebelliousness 27–9, 33, 34
relational self 46–8
religion
  Islamic, *see* Islam
  Pentecostalism 15, 69–74, 78, 79
Richmond, T. 100
routines in Madrid 87–90
Rowlands, M. 123
Russell, A. 100

self-creation 26, 33, 34–5
selfhood 21
Serbia, migration from 16–17, 115–25
sexuality 9
  clothing and 91
  prostitution in Cuba 152–3
Shaw, R. 46
smuggling 28–9
social networks
  social network sites 16, 99–110
  socialization 4, 86–90
  unemployment and family life in Trinidad 161–6
  Yoruba women in London 131–42
socialist system in Cuba 18, 145–56
society 3
space-culture isomorphism 51–2

Spain, *see* Madrid
spraying 139–40
Stafford, B. M. 37
Strathern, M. 14, 17, 124, 125
struggle, creating order through 18, 145–56

taste 5, 90–2
tattoos 9–10
taxi drivers 15, 74–8, 79, 81
theory 12
Tilley, C. 51
Tocqueville, Alexis de 85
tourism 147
transnationalism 63
    Greek house in Albania 14–15, 51, 52, 53–62
Trinidad
    aesthetic authority in public life 18–19, 159–73
Trobriand Islanders 10
Turkey
    fake brands in Istanbul bazaar 13–14, 25–7, 29–35
    military 28
    religious education in 27
Tuters, M. 100

unemployment in Trinidad 161–6, 174
United Kingdom, *see* London
United States of America
    Cuban migration to 147
    digital networks 16, 99–110

Washburn, D. 37
Weiner, Annette 10, 155
women
    creating order through struggle in Cuba 18, 145–56
    Jamaica 77
    Serbian migration and mother-child relationships 16–17, 115–25
    Trinidad 161, 162–8
    Yoruba women in London 131–42

Yan, Yunxiang 156
Yoruba women in London 131–42
Yurchak, Alexei 155